Real Bodie

Also by Mary Evans:

Missing Persons
Introducing Contemporary Feminist Thought
Jane Austen and the State

Also by Ellie Lee:

*Abortion Law and Politics Today**

*Published by Palgrave

Real Bodies

A Sociological Introduction

Edited by

Mary Evans and Ellie Lee

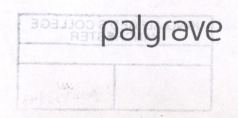

First published 2002 by
PALGRAVE
Houndmills, Basingstoke, Hampshire RG21 6XS and
175 Fifth Avenue, New York, N.Y. 10010
Companies and representatives throughout the world

PALGRAVE is the new global academic imprint of
St. Martin's Press LLC Scholarly and Reference Division and
Palgrave Publishers Ltd (formerly Macmillan Press Ltd).

ISBN 0–333–94751–7 hardcover
ISBN 0–333–94752–5 paperback

This book is printed on paper suitable for recycling and made from fully managed and sustained forest sources.

A catalogue record for this book is available from the British Library.

Library of Congress Cataloging-in-Publication Data
Real bodies : a sociological introduction / edited by Mary Evans and Ellie Lee.
     p. cm
     Includes bibliographical references and index.
     ISBN 0–333–94751–7
     1. Body, Human–Social aspects. I. Evans, Mary, 1946– II. Lee, Ellie.

GT495 .R44 2002
306.4–dc21   2002022906

10   9   8   7   6   5   4   3   2   1
11   10   09   08   07   06   05   04   03   02

Printed in China

Contents

Acknowledgements

The editors and contributors would like to offer their sincerest thanks to Catherine Gray at Palgrave for her enthusiasm, guidance and support throughout. We would also like to thank the two anonymous reviewers, for their careful and considered comments on an earlier draft of this book, which all contributors found enormously helpful.

Notes on the Contributors

Dr Sara Ahmed is Senior Lecturer in Women's Studies at Lancaster University and is currently Co-Director of the Institute for Women's Studies. Her previous publications include *Differences that Matter: Feminist Theory and Postmodernism* (2000), *Strange Encounters: Embodied Others in Post-Coloniality* (2000) and (co-edited) *Transformations: Thinking through Feminism* (2000).

Dr Hazel Biggs is Lecturer in Law at the University of Kent, Canterbury. She has published in the areas of critical, feminist and socio-legal studies, and specializes in medical law as it relates to the beginning and end of life. She is the author of *Euthanasia, Death with Dignity and the Law* (2001).

Dr Jo Bridgeman is a lecturer at the University of Sussex where she teaches healthcare law and ethics and tort. Her research interest is feminist perspectives on law, in particular concerning the health of children. Her interest in this area is enhanced by her fascination with, and enjoyment of, her children, George and Arthur.

Dr Jo Entwistle is Lecturer in Sociology at the University of Essex. Her research areas are sociology of body, gender, fashion and dress, and she is the author of *The Fashioned Body: Fashion, Dress and Modern Social Theory* (2000) and editor (with Elizabeth Wilson) of *Body Dressing* (2001).

Professor Mary Evans has taught sociology and women's studies at the University of Kent since 1971. Amongst her work are studies of Jane Austen and Simone de Beauvoir. Her book on Love will be published in 2002 and she is currently working on a book about changing perceptions of morality.

Emily Jackson is a lecturer in the law department at the London School of Economics. She is the author of *Regulating Reproduction: Law, Technology and Autonomy* (2001).

Dr Ellie Lee teaches sociology at the University of Southampton. Her research investigates the construction of social problems and social policy, especially in the area of fertility and reproduction. She has published many articles and papers about the legal and social regulation of abortion and contraception and is the editor of *Abortion Law and Politics Today* (2000).

David Morgan is a Senior Lecturer in Sociology at the University of Kent where he teaches the sociology of medicine and social theory. His current research is on the concept of 'treatability' in medical practice.

Professor Janet Sayers teaches sex, gender, and psychoanalysis in the School of Social Policy, Sociology, and Social Research at the University of Kent. Her books include *Mothering Psychoanalysis* (1991), *Freudian Tales* (1996), and *Kleinians* (2000).

Dr Sally Sheldon teaches law at Keele University. Her publications include *Beyond Control: Medical Power and Abortion Law* (1997) and numerous articles dealing with health care law and ethics, and feminist legal theory. With Michael Thomson, she is co-editor of *Feminist Perspectives on Health Care Law* (1998).

Dr Kylie Stephen gained a doctorate in feminist theory and political science from the University of Queensland (Australia). She taught women's studies at the University of Kent, worked for the Feminist Legal Research Unit at the University of Liverpool, and currently works in the Women and Equality Unit of the UK Government Cabinet Office (UK Government).

Dr Carol Thomas is a Senior Lecturer in Applied Social Science at Lancaster University. She has published widely in the field of disability studies as well as in the sociology of health and illness. She is the author of *Female Forms: Experiencing and Understanding Disability* (1999).

1

Real Bodies: An Introduction

Mary Evans

The title of this collection of essays is chosen to suggest some of the current uncertainties surrounding our understanding of the body at the beginning of the twenty-first century. For students and others with interests in this literature we hope that we have produced a series of essays that both reviews a particular aspect of the literature about the body and raises some of the problematic issues in that literature. Central to this collection is the discussion of the increasingly complex question of the status of the 'real' body: we all inhabit a specific, gendered, human body but we have also become aware that we are now able to renegotiate and change certain aspects of our lives as bodies. Feminism, for example in the work of Judith Butler and Susan Bordo, has challenged understandings of the body as biologically given and fixed, and argued that the human body is both culturally and historically specific (Bordo, 1993; Butler, 1990, 1993). Hence our title *Real Bodies* is suggestive of the ways in which the body or bodies, which we might once have regarded as fixed, is now less certainly defined. The authors in this collection of essays question the assumption of certainties about the body – the most central being the assumption that the body is 'natural' and trans-historical. With an increasing awareness of the negotiable and changeable possibilities of the body comes an increased recognition that it is impossible to speak about the 'nature' of the body or take for granted the body as a fixed category.

In these discussions about the body it would, however, be misleading to suggest that the beginning of the twenty-first century is the first time in human history that people have wished to change the nature (and quality) of the experiences of the body. Medicine is as ancient as

1

human society and no society has been willing to accept as given the realities of pain or disease or physical damage. Amelioration of the negative possibilities of the body is an ancient art, as is intervention to beautify or enhance its appearance. It is thus important to recognize that although we now frequently assume that medical technology is giving us the ability to alter our bodies in ways which are hitherto unknown, the desire to do precisely this has a long history. In terms of several of the essays in this volume this *caveat* has important implications, in that it should make us confront the fact that present renegotiations of the body do not start from a 'natural' state of the body but from a body, and a set of expectations about the body, which are already deeply socialized. As Sally Sheldon points out in the following chapter, we have only to examine the different ways in which male and female bodies have been constructed to recognize the impact of social expectations on the body. She notes too that the female body, unlike the male, has long been regarded as unstable and permeable. The male body, on the other hand, is regarded as stable and bounded.

This dichotomy between the ways in which we see the bodies of women and men could well be seen as disadvantageous to women in that it produces judgements about the instability of women and their bodies. Yet, at the same time, we could also suggest that the feminine model of the body – a body which is not absolute and which can change – allows that body to make much greater use of scientific technology and of accommodation with medical science. Advances in the technology of reproduction are one example of the way in which the apparent plasticity of the female body has allowed women to benefit from science, both in allowing them to bear children 'unnaturally' and in taking the control for reproduction out of the limitations of conventional relationships. If women are less likely than men to regard their bodies as 'fixed', then this can become, in an era of medical advance, a positive advantage rather than disadvantage.

To regard the body as a complex of attributes that can fluctuate as social norms and technological expertise change allows individuals to consider diverse possibilities about physical existence. Many readers will be familiar with the literature which suggests that the contemporary west is excessively regulatory in its attitude to the body: evidence, for example, about eating disorders in adolescent girls or social prejudices about 'fat' people both indicate vigorous normalising discourses about the appearance of the ideal modern body. Yet, at the same time, within the same culture we can point to such events as athletic meetings for people with physical disabilities, and the appearance – if only infrequently – of women amputees in *Vogue* and on the Parisian cat-walk. The old label of 'cripple' is no longer part of acceptable public culture, and there is a widespread, if not general, recognition that the human body is not perfect or imperfect but a continuum of different possibilities and different strengths.

In these shifts of thinking about the human body we might rejoice in the emancipatory possibilities of the twenty-first century, possibilities which no longer confine the sick or the injured to a forgotten social world. But before we share this rejoicing, there are two issues worth considering: the first is the obviously different material world which the sick, the disabled, the overweight and the physically frail inhabit. Their world is often, although not always, an under-privileged and disadvantaged world in ways which range from the obvious physical difficulties of mobility to more subtle questions of social prejudice and refusal of access to the conventional world. The second is that in congratulating ourselves, and our culture, on the apparent emergence of greater diversity, we lose sight of the ways in which we are becoming more rigorous and even proscriptive in our attitude to the body, and more inclined to suppose that the body should be a perfect, seamless demonstration of the virtue of efficient and perfect function. Precisely because we live, in the west, in a society which has eradicated, for the majority of the population, the major infectious and epidemic diseases of the nineteenth and early twentieth centuries, 'getting ill' has to be explained. It is then a short step to assuming that people 'get ill' because they do not achieve an efficient relationship between themselves and their body.

In this, of course, we arrive at that problem about our theorisation of the body which has beset us for hundreds of years. Medieval physicians assumed a relationship between the mind and body which was interrupted by Cartesian dualism, a duality which made possible many of the advances achieved in science about the body as both a social and an individual creation. One of the first texts to question modern attitudes to the body was Mary Shelley's *Frankenstein*, first published in 1818 (Shelley, 1998). This story, which has continued to exercise a considerable hold on the western imagination since it first appeared, was written by a woman whose mother, Mary Wollstonecraft, had vehemently protested about naturalistic connections between the female body and irrationality. Mary Wollstonecraft's *A Vindication of the Rights of Woman* was published in 1792 and it remains the definitive challenge to the gendered assumptions of Enlightenment and post-Enlightenment views about knowledge. However, the tragedy of

Mary Wollstonecraft (and hence of Mary Shelley) was that the female body which she inhabited was peculiarly vulnerable to natural processes: Mary Wollstonecraft died in giving birth to Mary Shelley.

It is scarcely surprising, therefore, that Mary Shelley became interested in the question of the creation of life, and in the relationship between science, socialization and the intelligence. The monster who emerges, fully grown as a man, from Frankenstein's creative powers, is a monster doomed to unhappiness and the destruction of others. The monster is the creation of science, the being who has known neither mother nor father. But the monster is also, we might conjecture, Mary Shelley's own imagination and her recognition of the power of the imagination. As readers of the novel will know, events take various turns for the worse in *Frankenstein* and between them Frankenstein and the monster wreak havoc on the lives of innocent people. The grandiosity of Frankenstein's project has been noted by many critics, and feminist critics (for example, Mary Jacobus, and Sandra Gilbert and Susan Gubar) have sharpened the perception of the gender relations of *Frankenstein* by arguing that the monster (the 'Creature' of Shelley's novel) is female (Gilbert and Gubar, 1970; Jacobus, 1982). Be that as it may, what the monster/Creature is not is 'natural'; as Marilyn Butler has pointed out, Mary Shelley does not introduce him, or present him to us, as a noble, natural, savage:

> The Creature's life in the woods is neither superior, nor even natural; it is not introduced as evidence of the existence of a sub-species, whether now or in the remote past, nor of man's affinity with the primates. Mary Shelley takes a more cautious view, and could even be evading or excluding the evolutionist perspective both Erasmus Darwin and Lamarck had advanced, that all forms of organic life had advanced from single cells (Butler, 1998, p. xxxviii).

Marilyn Butler goes on to point out that the Creature does demonstrate a great capacity for learning, and in particular he learns about social inequality. But – and here Marilyn Butler emphasizes the crucially important point which Mary Shelley's narrative makes – the education of the monster is stopped by human beings themselves; as Butler writes: 'The Creature cannot be part of the human family' (Butler, 1998, p. xi).

Once forced into exile, the Creature duly becomes less of a creature and more of a monster. But at the same time, so does Frankenstein himself. As the novel proceeds to its final tragedy, creator and created are locked into a deadly relationship which it is not difficult to see in terms of present relationships between science and human beings. Even though we need to recall that the monster is not human – but created by science – there remains the sense in which the monster stands for all those characteristics which are unsocialized and uncontrolled. Thus we can pity the monster, but also condemn the society from which Frankenstein emerges. The society is one which implicitly condones intellectual arrogance and the impulse to dominate and yet fails when faced with the challenge of integrating the different, or the difficult.

In *Frankenstein*, Mary Shelley avoids many of the simple dichotomies about science and nature, the natural and the created, which have plagued our thinking about the body for the past two hundred years. She recognized that societies create science and scientific rationality in ways which reflect and include their own prejudices and assumptions. That position has now been extensively argued by a long tradition of historians of science, amongst whom feminists have recently been the most vocal and the most critical. But what Mary Shelley also recognized is that there is no easy distinction between the 'created' body and the 'natural' body and *Frankenstein* demonstrates that it is untenable to speak of the 'real' body in any meaningful sense: all bodies, even those apparently created by science, are both natural and social. As Donna Haraway has written (almost two hundred years after Mary Shelley):

> Twentieth century machines have made thoroughly ambiguous the difference between natural and artificial, mind and body, self-developing and externally designed, and many other distinctions that used to apply to organisms and machines (Haraway, 1991, p. 152).

According to Haraway, we have become 'cyborgs' – not wholly machines but not wholly natural organisms either. For Haraway, 'All we touch and therefore know, including our organic and social bodies, is made possible for us through labour' (Haraway, 1991, p. 10).

In this connection the word 'labour' is interpreted in the widest sense to encompass those structures – be they institutional or ideological – which have been constructed by human action. The degree to which the products of that labour have affected our understanding of the body is the theme of this collection. In various ways, all the chapters demonstrate that it is society which 'makes' the body, in a way precisely understood by Mary Shelley. Those social structures which failed the Creature in his hour of need (most crucially the apparently benevolent bourgeois family) are still those structures which either fail (or reward) our bodies. In all these essays, however, there is a shared recognition that the body is both fixed, and 'real', and constantly changing. The body will always need the minimal requirements of food and water in order to sustain its life, and the body will always be capable of feeling pain and becoming ill. Nevertheless, we all recognize the myriad interventions in those experiences and in the fulfilment of those needs. Equally, all bodies face the same fate as Frankenstein (and his Creature): that of the ultimate mortality of the body and its inherently temporary nature. The human terror of ageing and death (which inspired Frankenstein as much as it inspires twenty-first-century subjects of cosmetic surgery) remains the fixed point at which the body is 'real'.

In the first four essays of this collection there is an explicit connection with the themes about the body raised by Mary Shelley. These themes, of the sexuality of the body, its race and its degree of perfection (or otherwise), have remained the contours within which the body (whether male or female) has been constructed. In all cases, the social world demands that the body (male or female) meets its expectations about the physical forms of human beings. Becoming male or female is the first complex negotiation for all human beings; the nature of that resolution is then located within a particular set of expectations about race and physical appearance. For example, Mary Shelley wrote at a time when debates about the abolition of slavery were at their peak; *Frankenstein* is imbued with an understanding of the body (and the relationship of ideas to the body) which is deeply engrained with perceptions of 'freedom' and 'slavery'. Indeed, as Paul Gilroy has shown in terms of the impact of slavery on western consciousness, and – more particularly – as Moira Ferguson has shown in relationship to Mary Wollstonecraft, a recognition of the meaning of slavery was central to post-Enlightenment discourses about the body (Ferguson, 1992; Gilroy, 1993). Nineteenth-century fiction and non-fiction contains endless references to 'slavery' and 'enslavement'; in many cases those references suggest a model of the body more or less literally subjected to unwelcome or uncontrollable sexual desire, or its consequences. The 'slavery of desire' is a theme which unites novelists across cultures and societies, and it contains the idea that the body must be 'freed' from the desires which can 'enslave' it.

The body is thus our means of freedom and the location of our enslavement. The west has always assumed that through the body, and the mind, we can labour in ways which will free us from the demands of an animal or subsistence existence. Marx was not alone in greeting the arrival of mechanized production as a possible precursor of human liberation and emancipation. Unfortunately, the social relations which construct the world of industrial production have not, so far, produced the life of ease and leisure which was expected. Thus although the body is no longer 'enslaved' to a life of hunting and gathering, or subsistence agriculture, the body remains the means through which we labour in capitalism. We are not 'slaves' in the technical sense of people in the eighteenth and nineteenth centuries, but the twentieth-century term 'wage slave' demonstrates how we still think in categories drawn from previous debates and discussions. Equally, it is difficult for us to emancipate ourselves from previous assumptions about slaves: slaves, to people in Britain and Europe, were black people, and black bodies were therefore those bodies most 'enslaved' to a physical existence. The association of black people with physical being rather than the intellect was similar to that of the association made between women and the body. As Mary Wollstonecraft pointed out, and as women throughout the nineteenth and twentieth centuries have continued to point out, a facet of western assumptions about the body is the view that women, unlike men, cannot emancipate themselves from the passions, desires and needs of the body. Throughout the nineteenth century, the paradoxical view of the female body was that, in its most socially appropriate model, it had no sexual desire, whilst at the same time it was assumed that women could never be free from the determining constraints of their female biology.

Women, given their limited participation in the discourses of the public world, were relatively powerless in determining medical models of their health. But male health, and the male body, were similarly constructed in terms of freeing the person from 'enslavement' to the body. Again, we meet a language about the body and its processes, which invokes perceptions of slavery and freedom, subjection and dominance. Along a continuum of freedom from, and subjection to, the body of white men stood at one extreme whilst black women stood at the other. As Sara Ahmed points out in her chapter:

> Not only is the black woman associated with her body, but that body becomes seen as hypersexual and deviant. The violence of the scientific gaze, and of the reduction of the Black female body to body parts, is made clear when we consider the 'fate' of Sarah Bartmann. Upon her death, her body was dissected and her genitalia and buttocks became items in a museum display: indeed, they remain on display in the Musée de l'Homme

in Paris. In life and in death, Black women's bodies were appropriated and dissected as sexualized 'objects' (Ahmed, in this collection).

This particular image, of the creation of the grotesque as a body, demonstrates, albeit in an extreme form, the way in which our culture can create 'monsters'. We do not, yet, create human beings (although recent successes at the cloning of mammals suggests that this is not a distant possibility) but we can create an imagined 'monster' and impose that creation of the imagination onto a 'real' body. This possibility is, indeed, precisely the process which Mary Shelley envisaged: people will create monsters out of their own fantasies and desires and impose on those 'monsters' the imaginative worlds, with all their hierarchies of race and gender, which they have access to.

In a very important sense, therefore, human debates about the body have always taken the form of attempts to retain the 'real' body against the imposition of external, created fantasies and perceptions. We may acknowledge (and since the publication of the work of Bryan Turner (1984) there is no sociological alternative) that society shapes the body, but we are increasingly aware, precisely because of the progress of science and medicine, that the body is mortal, and gendered. The essays here which deal with particular states of the body all emphasize the reality of the body, and the limits of the social model of the body. The pain which human beings feel, as David Morgan points out, is undoubtedly real, as are the forms of disablement discussed by Carol Thomas. We might acknowledge a continuum of physical ability and competence, but there remain real differences between people able, for example, to walk from and within their homes and those who cannot. Even more dramatically, the female body is either pregnant or not. Women might be anxious to be (or not be) pregnant, but the physical state of pregnancy cannot be interpreted in terms of diverse accounts of social labelling. Students of anthropology will no doubt raise the well-known literature on 'sympathetic' pregnancy by men, but even when these forms of social identification exist it is accepted that there are distinctions between the 'real' and the 'unreal' pregnancy.

The papers presented here share, therefore, an understanding of the body as both 'real' and as constructed. To quote from the conclusion to Carol Thomas's chapter:

> In my view, a sociology of impairment needs to be able to engage with the real materiality of bodies whilst at the same time understanding the ways in which bodies are simultaneously always interpreted. Though those of us

who live with marked impairments know that the body is 'real' however thoroughly it is culturally represented and positioned (Thomas, in this collection).

That comment very aptly demonstrates the limitations of all forms of social constructionism about the body, whether they belong to mainstream sociology or feminist accounts of the body such as those of Judith Butler. There is, given the diverse range of the interpretation of the human body, nevertheless a recognisable, and shared, gendered corpus to be taken account of. It might, perhaps, be more productive to suggest the following account of the body: there is both a created body of particular societies and at the same time, in the same physical space of an individual human being, a 'real' body. As already suggested, we do not actually create, in the pattern of Frankenstein, human beings. But what we do create are fantasies about the body which are often in themselves monstrous. In doing this, we can easily lose sight of the real body (as Frankenstein lost sight of the needs of his Creature) because our attention is fixed on the fantasy, and not on the real.

To illustrate this point, it is helpful to take the familiar example about what are taken to be western assumptions about the female (and particularly the youthful) female body. A commonly expressed fear about young women in the west is that they become obsessed with stereotypes about body size and because of this become 'ill' with eating disorders such as *anorexia nervosa* or *bulimia*. Discussions on this issue cite statistical information about the rise in the number of young women (and young men) affected in this way and at least part of the blame is placed on ideas about the presentable and desirable body depicted by high fashion. Editors of *Vogue* are held accountable for this phenomena and criticized for the image of the female body which they present. At the same time, however, as the pages of *Vogue* present an ideal female body which conforms to a petite dress size, we know that half the female population wears a much larger size. A glance at any high street in any town or city in the west would suggest that the models in *Vogue* do not represent normality. The 'real' bodies are, quite literally, substantially different from those in *Vogue* or on a Milan fashion cat walk. We have, therefore, in terms of actual body size, a society in which real bodies and fantasized bodies are radically dissimilar.

In this difference, the created monster is neither of the two human groups (the model and the 'ordinary' person), but the *fantasy* about appearance which is being pursued by *both* groups. Information about women's attitudes to their bodies suggests that few women are content with their body size: being 'thinner' is an endlessly pursued goal, and one supported by a huge industry of health clubs, supposedly low calorie food and technical and medical intervention. These facts of contemporary consumer culture are not in themselves 'monsters' but collectively they become monstrous as they impose upon 'real' bodies an ideal of appearance which for most people is unrealistic and unobtainable. A cocktail of needs and pressures has created, and continues to create, a fantasy body which can never be realized. This body is not just thin (and usually white and always physically perfect) but also sublimely effective. Thus, it has to be emphasized that the fantasy body created by the contemporary west is created in relationship to not only the ideals of feminine beauty and body size appropriate to *haute couture* but also the expectations and demands of capitalist society. This society has always demanded labour of the population, but the contemporary form of western capitalism in which we live, that of capitalism dominated by a service sector and the provision of consumer goods, demands a particular form of labour: a labour force which is educated but also efficient, effective and in itself an advertisement for the products of its labour. The 'ideal' employee of late capitalism is, therefore, not just a hard-working individual, but a person who possesses the public characteristics, of being an acceptable shape, size and 'well dressed', and who, therefore, confirms the desirability of the products of a service-sector economy.

The visual policing of the body within late capitalism has produced, inevitably, its reactions in the form of street fashions such as body piercing, the code of dressing known as 'grunge' and the determined abandonment of those previous boundaries about the appropriate clothes for the appropriate occasion. When Madonna appeared in public in what appeared to be her underwear she took this form of sartorial displacement to a wide audience. Aided by the skills of Jean Paul Gaultier she deliberately set out to challenge assumptions about what can be worn when. Inevitably, her appearance gained the attention it sought and was interpreted as a challenging act rather than as a choice in a long history of choices about dress in which the unconventional has threatened the conventional. Debate about dress, and the refusal of appropriate dress, is less an issue here than the context in which such refusals occur: a context which demands bodily conformity at a time when knowledge about diversity (and its manufacture) is more available than at any other period in the planet's history.

We live in an epoch of global cultures. Within this global culture, the relationship between the body and society has become part of a complex relationship between nature and culture. As Sarah Franklin has pointed out, for certain writers, notably Ann Tsing and Donna Haraway, nature exists inseparably from its function as a zone of appropriation for culture (Franklin, 2000). For both Tsing and Haraway, the extent to which nature persists as more than the sum of its appropriations is the source of its majesty and awesomeness. Franklin writes:

> Both accounts locate the capacity of nature to operate as a magical sign by appealing to its movement, its trafficking capacity, and its border-function as a kind of conversion device. The materiality of nature is dually signified: as an inscription device or coding system, capable of shaping objects and subjects, such as bodies and landscapes; and as an agentic domain independent of culture that is unpredictable, beyond reach of domestication and unknowable (Franklin, 2000, p. 50).

What this account importantly contains is the understanding of the body, which we wish to communicate here. At the same time as affirming the thesis that the form of the body is a social construction, we wish to suggest the nature of the body is beyond the social: that the physical world which we individually, rather than socially, inhabit is 'real'. Moreover, we wish to propose that the social which constructs our bodies, and our individual understanding and experience of them, is not a 'real' other body; not, in fact, the monster created by Frankenstein, but the fantasies which led Frankenstein to attempt to replace the 'natural' body with the unnatural. The collectively produced fantasies, needs and desires of late capitalism are, as far as the body is concerned, genuinely monstrous, in that they deform, manage and direct the body in ways geared to the needs of the social system rather than human needs. This is not, then, an argument for the 'natural' body, in the sense of a pre-social or a-social body. Rather, it is an argument for the acknowledgement of the needs of the 'real' body, needs for social and individual affirmation which are just as real for us today as for the creature produced by Frankenstein. Unless we are, collectively, to become the creatures of Mary Shelley's novel, we need to re-affirm the 'real' body against the claims of the social.

In the following chapters the authors in this collection discuss the 'real' body in a number of contexts and situations. Although the themes and the contexts discussed vary considerably there are two ideas which appear in all the essays: the centrality of the recognition of Cartesian dualism to all debates about the body and the way in which ideas can be both discourse and institution. All students of the body (a process in which all living human beings are by definition professional participants) need to recognize these aspects of 'body thinking'. Equally, it is one of the main aims of this collection to emphasize that thinking about the body begins (although it certainly does not end) with a 'real' body.

The 'real bodies' discussed in this collection vary in their condition and their situation. But they share the characteristic of being living human beings rather than the creatures of fantasy. Some of these bodies (and some of the experiences of these bodies) may well be the stuff both of our wildest nightmares as well as our most optimistic dreams, but they are all 'real' in the sense that they generally available for study and discussion.

One of the themes of late twentieth- and early twenty-first-century writing about the body is the view that we increasingly 'organize' our bodies and expect them to behave in orderly ways. In this collection we have followed the first of these expectations and organized the bodies discussed here into groups (we have not, however, expected authors to conform to particular ideas of 'order'). The groupings do not follow the chronology which confronts all human bodies (we have not, therefore, started with pregnancy and moved to old age) but we have invoked distinctions between nature, culture and society.

The first three chapters in the collection (by Sally Sheldon, Kylie Stephen and Sara Ahmed) deal with generally recognizable differences between bodies, of gender and race. The second section – containing contributions by David Morgan and Carol Thomas – discusses states which the body may experience but are not inevitable parts of human existence. The third section takes us to those states – of dependence and pregnancy – which are temporary parts of the human condition. Here Jo Bridgeman, and Ellie Lee and Emily Jackson discuss the ways in which these phases of our lives are constructed by the legal frameworks surrounding them. Finally, the chapters by Janet Sayers, Joanne Entwistle and Hazel Biggs consider aspects of the social world where it is arguably the case that the intervention of culture on, and with, the body is most immediately apparent.

The various papers in this collection cover, as readers will discover, a considerable range of material, from a diverse range of perspectives. That academic point also serves to emphasize a theme which unites our concerns here: the idea that the body itself is multi-perspectival and impossible to categorize as either 'natural' or 'social'.

Our bodies serve many purposes and the ambiguity which we as human beings experience as we live in our bodies (as children, mothers, fathers, employees, patients, and so on) has to be recognized in the ideas which we use to understand our experience. Recognizing – and allowing – ambiguity, and the absence of answers, is not necessarily a position which is socially welcome. We would argue, however, that an appreciation of ambiguity is central to any understanding of our 'real' bodies.

Further reading

Lykke, Nina and Braidotti, Rosi (eds), *Between Monsters, Goddesses and Cyborgs: Feminist Confrontations with Science, Medicine and Cyberspace* (London: Zed Books, 1996).

Essays which suggest ways in which ideas about nature (and the body) inform social and feminist theory: an important statement about the way in which we think not just about our bodies, but through them.

Haraway, Donna, *Simians, Cyborgs and Women: The Reinvention of Nature* (London: Free Association Books, 1991).

A collection of ten essays which develop the author's argument that nature is constructed, not discovered.

Ortner, Sherry, 'Is Female to Male as Nature is to Culture?', in (eds) M. Rosaldo and L. Lamphere, *Women, Culture and Society* (Stanford: Stanford University Press, 1974).

The now classic statement about the association of men with culture and women with nature: an idea which underpins much subsequent work.

2

The Masculine Body

Sally Sheldon

> Ironically, men's bodies tend to be absent from much of contemporary
> feminist scholarship on the body. The attempt to develop explicitly femi-
> nist analyses of the body have – somewhat paradoxically – shored up the
> dualism which links bodies and bodily matters to women and femininity
> (Davis, 1997, p. 19).

When I was asked to contribute to this volume, I was particularly
struck by the novelty of writing a chapter dealing with the masculine
body.[1] This focus on *masculine* specificity is an interesting reversal
of the more usual state of affairs which is to treat female difference in
relation to an unstated male norm. Of course, in the context of the
sociology of the body, this apparent reversal becomes much less surprising. Whilst the body may have had only a 'submerged history'
(Turner, 1984, p. 34) or existed as an 'absent presence' (Shilling,
1993, p. 9) in mainstream sociological scholarship, the exploration
and problematization of received understandings of the female body
has been far more central to feminist thinking.

The importance of the body for feminist writers can be explained
in large part by reference to the obvious role which bodily factors
have played in women's subordination. Women have often been perceived as more intimately connected to their bodies, with men enjoying a more cerebral existence (Davis, 1997). First, women have often
been reduced to little more than bodies, understood as controlled by
biochemical processes (such as hormonal flows) and mysterious
female mental disorders (such as hysteria) with the possibility of truly
autonomous female action thus marginalized or denied. Secondly,
beliefs that the female body is weak, fragile and easily damaged have

14

historically served to support policies excluding women from a variety of social goods including, for a long time, access to higher education. Thirdly, the female body's capacity to contain a fetal body during pregnancy and birth has thrown up particular problems for women, given legal and social orders accustomed to assuming bounded, individuated subjects (see Lee and Jackson, this volume). Finally, women have often been more conscious of having/being bodies in the sense that these bodies can function as a locus of discrimination. This last claim is well illustrated by a conversation between two women reported by American scholar, Michael Kimmel. One of the women, who was white, was arguing for a common bond which united all women regardless of racial difference. The other woman, who was black, disagreed:

> 'When you wake up in the morning and look in the mirror, what do you see?' [the black woman] asked. 'I see a woman', replied the white woman. 'That's precisely the problem,' responded the black woman. 'I see a *black* woman'. To me, race is visible every day, because race is how I am *not* privileged in our culture. Race is invisible to you, because it's how you are privileged. It's a luxury, a privilege, not to see race all the time. It's why there will always be differences in our experience (Kimmel, 1996, p. 4).

These women express themselves as aware of their bodies only in so far as those bodies represent a cause of disadvantage or discrimination. Kimmel relates that this exchange was revelatory to him in problematizing, for the first time, the fact that when he looked in the mirror, he saw a human being. As a middle-class white man, he had 'no class, no race, no gender [he was] the generic person' (1996, p. 4). If Kimmel is right, then there is an important psychological sense in which women are more aware of their bodies. In this sense, embodiment becomes noteworthy when it impinges on us in some way – through bodily changes, physical discomfort or when particularities in one's form of embodiment – such as race, gender or physical abnormality – act as a disability in the context of particular social settings.

Kimmel notes that he sometimes thinks on that day he *became* a middle-class, white man; obviously not in the sense that he did not belong to these groups before, but rather in that it was only at this point that he became aware of his membership of them. Along with Kimmel, mainstream sociology is now increasingly waking up to the fact that men have bodies too and that the dense grid of social meanings investing them has still to be explored. For example, all of the explanations given above for why feminists have been interested in the body have an interesting masculine flipside: men have been understood as rational, autonomous, less connected to and controlled by their bodies; masculine bodies have been constructed as stronger, less liable to dysfunction; they are bounded and individual; and embodiment is seen to have impinged less on men. Whilst feminist scholarship can offer some insights in understanding this masculine flipside, such help may be limited. Whilst work on the female body has often contrasted it against a male norm, this norm has often remained largely idealized and unscrutinized in itself. Further, even such scholarship as does exist on the male body reveals a relative neglect of a particularly interesting and important aspect of it: male reproductivity. It is this which will form the focus for this chapter.

It is not just such neglect which makes the male reproductive body an interesting study for this collection, however. It also seems to me that such an analysis can provide a useful heuristic device for addressing a broader issue in the sociology of the body: to what extent are there 'real' sexed differences between the bodies of men and women? Or, to put the question the other way around: what does it mean to argue that sexual difference between men and women is actually socially constructed, that it is a product of our understanding of male and female gender roles? The issue of reproduction poses a particularly interesting and challenging case for the strongly constructivist view, for surely if any 'real' difference exists between male and female bodies, then this is in reproductive capacity. What can it mean to talk of sexual difference as socially constructed in this context? In attempting to respond, I hope to show that the way in which we choose to answer is not just of academic interest but has important social and political consequences. In order to reinforce this last point and to ground the subsequent, more theoretical, discussion, I want first to introduce a case study which will highlight these issues.

A case study: Johnson Controls Inc. and 'fetal protectionism'

> Men's bodies may be appropriated as well as women's, but appropriation is not gender neutral either. Women's bodies are appropriated more often and more completely. The appropriation of women's bodies may be equally violent, but these are differences we are only beginning to observe and can hardly articulate (Frank, 1991, p. 95).

Some years ago, Johnson Controls Inc., an American manufacturer of batteries, was sued in the United States courts following its introduction of what is known as a 'fetal protection policy'. The policy had sought to exclude 'women who are pregnant or capable of bearing children' from jobs involving exposure to lead on the basis that such exposure could harm their reproductive capacity and result in children being born with congenital defects. Thus excluded were 'all women except those whose inability to bear children is medically documented.' Some women chose to become sterilized in order to avoid losing their jobs, others accepted transfers to other positions with lower pay. Some of the company's employees responded by taking their employers to court to challenge the policy and eventually the United States Supreme Court held that the company's policy constituted sex discrimination and was therefore unlawful under Title VII of the Civil Rights Act 1964 (*International Union, United Automobile Workers* v. *Johnson Controls Inc*, 499 US 187, 1991).

Not surprisingly, the company's actions provoked a storm of critical comment, which tended to focus on the dreadful dilemma facing those women forced to choose between their jobs and their reproductive capacity (Blank, 1993; Daniels, 1993, 1997; Roth, 2000; Thomson, 1996, 1998). Less widely noted was the fact that one of the plaintiffs was a man. Donald Penney had complained that he was denied a request for leave of absence for the purpose of lowering his lead level because he intended to become a father. Whilst the dangers to male reproductivity resulting from lead exposure were already well known at this time, Penney too found himself subject to discrimination, being refused the possibility of taking advantage of the very health measures which were being imposed on his female colleagues.

Fetal protection policies on both sides of the Atlantic have been roundly criticized for making the assumption that all women are potential child bearers unless they are medically incapable of conceiving. This, it has been argued, denies female agency and reduces women to nothing more than reproductive bodies, positing maternity as women's natural and inevitable function. What is also implicit in the Johnson Controls case, however, is the refusal to see men in this same way. This is meant not merely in a weak, negative sense (that there is an *omission* to reduce men to nothing more than reproductive bodies) but in a stronger, more positive sense: that this aspect of the male body is *explicitly denied* or trivialized, deemed unimportant relative to the male imperative of paid work. Donald Penney's agency is also denied. He is refused the possibility of prioritizing his body's reproductive capacity over and above its ability to labour, as surely this prioritization is forced on his female colleagues.

How should we understand the actions of Johnson Controls? Are they those of a responsible employer concerned about its employees' reproductive health; a litigation-conscious employer worried about being sued for toxic exposure leading to damaged children; a paternalistic employer assuming that reproduction is most important for its female employees and imposing this choice on them; or a manipulative and sexist employer using reproductive capacity as a justification to shore up existing industrial segregation by excluding women from certain (traditionally male-dominated) sectors? And what about the science of 'fetal protectionism' on which Johnson Controls based their actions? Was this simply 'bad' science reflecting the gender role assumptions of sexist researchers? Or was it 'good', objective science producing uncomfortable truths with regrettable social and political conclusions?

It is my contention that an understanding of how the sexed body is produced is essential to answering these questions, and it is to this which we will now turn. As is clear from the story of Donald Penney, such understandings of reproductive bodies can have profound consequences for men (and, indeed, their offspring) as well as for women. It will be seen that, whilst women have been harmed by a reduction to nothing more than (reproductive) bodies, the failure to recognize men's (reproductive) bodies is likewise not without consequences. First, however, I need to lay some theoretical groundwork regarding the relationship between sex and gender in relation to our understandings of the body.

The sex/gender binary

One of the great achievements of early feminist scholarship was the distilling of sex and gender into two distinct analytical categories, with sex understood as anatomical difference and gender as the social construction of masculinity and feminity on the basis of these biological facts. In an early and influential text, US feminist, Kate Millett, cites the work of Robert J. Stoller to explain this distinction:

> the word *sex* ... [refers] to the male or female sex and the component biological parts that determine whether one is a male or a female; the word *sexual* [has] connotations of anatomy and physiology. This obviously leaves tremendous areas of behaviour, feelings, thoughts and fantasies that are related to the sexes and yet do not have primarily biological connotations. It is for some of these psychological phenomena that the term gender will be used: one can speak of the male sex or the female sex, but one can also

talk about masculinity and feminity [sic] and not necessarily be implying anything about anatomy or physiology. Thus, while *sex* and *gender* seem to common sense inextricably bound together ... the two realms ... are not inevitably bound in anything like a one-to-one relationship, but each may go into [sic] quite independent ways (Stoller, 1968 cited in Millett, 1970, p. 29, emphasis in original).

Such early work was of tremendous political importance. It under-pinned challenges to the traditional gendered order of society, allow-ing feminists to argue with clarity and force that the simple biological facts that women gave birth and could breastfeed (sexual difference) did not *per se* explain the division of labour within the nuclear family with women primarily responsible for child care and men being the primary breadwinners (gender difference). A distinction between sex and gender was central to Millett's own important exploration of patriarchy as a political institution, allowing her to argue that 'many of the generally understood distinctions between the sexes in the more significant areas of role and temperament, not to mention status, have in fact, essentially cultural, rather than biological bases' (Millett, 1970, p. 28).

However, more recent work has problematized the sex/gender binary, with some writers reversing it in order to argue that sex is a product of gender rather than vice versa. For these commentators, the body with all its attributes including sex and race is produced within social discourse rather than existing outside of it. For example, in *The Making of Sex*, Thomas Laqueur (1990) has tracked scientific under-standings of sex in order to demonstrate what he describes as a move-ment from a 'one sex' to a 'two sex' model. Drawing on early medical illustrations of male and female genitals in support of his claim, he documents how, for thousands of years, it was common to think that women had the same genitals as men but inside, rather than outside, the body. The vagina was conceived as an interior penis, the labia as the foreskin, the uterus as the scrotum, and the ovaries as the testicles. In or about the late eighteenth century all of this changed and the sexes came to be seen as opposites:

> the old model, in which men and women were arrayed according to their degree of metaphysical perfection, their vital heat, along an axis whose telos was male, gave way by the late eighteenth century to a new model of radical dimorphism, or biological divergence. An anatomy and physiol-ogy of incommensurability replaced a metaphysics of hierarchy in the representation of woman in relation to man (Laqueur, 1990, pp. 4–5).

Whilst Laqueur is not claiming that there are no biological differences between the bodies of women and men, he does show that our understandings of these differences are profoundly influenced by our broader social understandings. Current understandings of men and women as biological 'opposites' are revealed as historically contingent. As Laqueur puts it, 'sex ... is situational; it is explicable only within the context of battles over gender and power' (1990, p. 11).

How should we understand this claim? Is it pointing out socially constructed gender roles to note say that (most) women of a certain age will menstruate and that men will not, or that (most) women of a certain age are capable of conceiving a pregnancy and men are not? On one hand, the answer to this question must clearly be 'no': differences between men and women surely exist outside the realm of discourse. However, in another way it does make sense to answer this question in the affirmative. The way in which we are forced to phrase this question already reveals some tensions with the insertion of the 'most' and the imprecision of 'a certain age' revealing that the biological 'facts' are, in themselves, not straightforward. Although not all women menstruate and not all can conceive, we do not want to exclude them from the category of 'woman'. And even the examples given here are not so clear cut. In other times, and in various places, it was believed perfectly natural and even healthy for men to menstruate. To bleed from various orifices was seen as fulfilling the same physiological function as menstruation: allowing a body which had too much blood in it to release some of it (Pomata, unpublished). More generally, consider the response of gender theorist, Judith Butler, who asks herself how one should respond to the idea that there are at least certain minimal sexually differentiated parts, activities, capacities, hormonal and chromosomal differences which could be conceded without reference to construction:

> Although at this moment I want to offer an absolute reassurance [that such biological differences exist] some anxiety prevails. To concede the undeniability of 'sex' or its 'materiality' is always to concede some version of 'sex', some formation of 'materiality' ... To claim that discourse is formative is not to claim that it originates, causes, or exhaustively composes that which it concedes: rather, it is to claim that there is no reference to a pure body which is not at the same time a further formation of that body (Butler, 1993, p. 10).

In other words, Butler does not deny that we are/have material bodies which differ from each other in a variety of ways. However, as Sara Ahmed illustrates in Chapter 4, through her discussion of 'racialization', in seeking to map and catalogue these differences, to order them along certain axes, to describe the objective 'reality' of bodies, the descriptor will inevitably impose particular understandings and values to construct a particular version of what is described.

The elaboration of objective truth is a laudable scientific aspiration, but sociologically speaking it remains an impossibility: there is no possibility of unmediated access to a pre-social unconstructed 'reality' of the body. In this light, the issue becomes less one of whether 'real bodies' exist and more one of how particular materializations or understandings of bodies function to sustain or to challenge received cultural norms and established social orders. As Butler explains:

> the regulatory norms of 'sex' work in a performative fashion to constitute the materiality of bodies and, more specifically, to materialize the body's sex, to materialize sexual difference in the service of the consolidation of the heterosexual imperative ... Once 'sex' itself is understood in its normativity, the materiality of the body will not be thinkable apart from the materialization of that regulatory norm (1993, p. 2).

The challenge which Butler and Laqueur present to us, then, is in the reversal of the sex/gender binary: to think of sex not as a description of natural, biological difference, but rather as a normative concept, as a 'regulatory ideal', imposing certain values in the service (as Butler has it) of maintaining the 'heterosexual imperative'. It is thus only through understandings of the world which are profoundly influenced by gender that we can grasp what we perceive to be the 'reality' of the material, sexed body.

Writing on the development of medical science, Valerie Hartouni has noted the belief of scientists in their own neutrality in uncovering the 'real', objectively knowable body. They believed 'that the body could and did simply speak for itself' and they trusted to 'their own objectivity and, thus, their authority to see, hear, and transcribe the body's permanently silent directives – its conditions as well as its constitution' (1997, p. 22). For Hartouni, the task now facing social scientists is to unpick the cultural narratives concealed in this scientific work:

> The question is how this transcription, this text of difference or narrative of justification, was achieved, and the task, then, is to decipher its plot – to decipher, on one hand, the cultural work this text performed, while, on the other, tracking the particular constellation of assumptions and

presuppositions ... about the meaning of socially marked differences and their basis that framed, mediated, circumscribed, and were already implicated in what was regarded as 'natural,' what counted as 'evidence', what was observed and, in the end, could appear within the visual field (Hartouni, 1997, p. 22).

A well known example of this kind of work is Emily Martin's description of the way in which research into human reproductive biology reproduces stereotypes of appropriate gender behaviour. Martin (1991) presents two different biological accounts of human conception, both equally clearly displaying evidence of gendered imagery. On the one hand, scientists described conquering, active 'macho' sperm which would race and fight with each other in their attempts to be the first to penetrate the waiting egg. This presents a clearly gendered model which parallels a particular understanding of appropriate male and female roles during sexual relationships – whilst men chase, conquer and penetrate, women are passive, waiting for the male advance and submitting to penetration. A second strand of scientific writing has challenged this model, putting forward the idea of the 'seductive egg' which selects an appropriate sperm. Again this draws on a particular, if different, understanding of a sexual encounter where it is the woman who initiates the sex, enticing a man into her bed. Note the imagery deployed in the following citation from a scientific report influenced by the latter model:

> A human egg cell does not idle languidly in the female reproductive tract, like some Sleeping Beauty waiting for a sperm Prince Charming to come along and waken it for fertilization. Instead, new research indicates that most eggs actively beckon to would-be partners, releasing an as-yet-unidentified chemical to lure sperm cells (*Science News* cited in Daniels, 1997, p. 592).

Important here is not just the language which is used in presenting these 'findings', but the extent to which gendered understandings influence what the scientists actually see. The 'seductive egg' model would seem to have at least as much to do with the presentation of a different understanding of gender relationships (where women enjoy a less passive role), as it has to do with a different account of the biological 'facts' of human reproduction. What Martin's work achieves is not an attack on individual scientists who have, in some way, failed to do their work properly. Rather it is a clear example of the constraints on scientific understanding: in seeking to see, describe or understand the world, scientists – like all of us – will inevitably rely on ideas and conceptual frameworks which are already available to them. Any study will thus inevitably be informed by existing beliefs.

Fetal protectionism and the sexed body

> Debates over fetal risk are not so much about the prevention of fetal harm as they are about the *social production of truth* about the nature of men's and women's relation to reproduction (Daniels, 1997, p. 579, emphasis in original).

To recap: I have argued that whilst 'real bodies' and 'real' differences between bodies do exist, it is impossible ever to have unmediated access to this 'reality'. Any account of sexual difference will always and inevitably be informed by existing gendered understandings. With this in mind, now let us return to our case study of Johnson Controls Inc. and the cultural understandings at play in the science of fetal protectionism. Here the research of American political scientist, Cynthia Daniels, is particularly useful. Daniels notes that, for a long time, scientists assumed only female transmission of mutagens (toxins which effect the fetus or the sperm/ova which create it) was possible. Indeed, men were believed either to be invulnerable to harm from the toxicity of drugs, alcohol, environmental or occupational hazards, or to be rendered completely infertile by any vulnerability to risk. In particular, sperm which crossed the line from virile to vulnerable by being damaged by reproductive toxins were assumed to be incapable of fertilisation. The converse was also true: men not rendered infertile by their toxic exposures were assumed to be immune from any other reproductive risk (Daniels, 1997, p. 582).

Daniels provides the example of Gladys Friedler, a scientist working at Boston University in the 1970s. Friedler was the first to document a link in mice between paternal exposure to morphine and birth defects in their offspring. At that time, cultural constructions of male reproduction made Friedler's work simply unbelievable and, as such, its scientific validity was challenged (Daniels, 1997, p. 591). Unlike the scientists described in Emily Martin's work, Friedler was swimming against the tide, contradicting deeply embedded assumptions about male and female reproductive bodies.

Today, however, Friedler's work has become far more credible and further studies have supported her findings. Male reproductive exposures are now proven or suspected of causing a whole range of fertility problems and fetal abnormalities. Further, as Daniels notes, scientists are now noting particular cause for concern regarding male mediated harm: as men's reproductive organs are on the outside of the body, they are more susceptible to heat and caustic exposures, and sperm are some of the smallest and most vulnerable cells in the body. As sperm is continuously produced throughout a man's life time, the germ cells from which they originate are continuously dividing and developing. During this developmental process, sperm may be particularly susceptible to damage from toxins since cells that are dividing are more vulnerable to toxicity than cells that are fully developed and at rest, as are eggs in the female reproductive system. She comments: 'a different interpretation of the available data might be that men are *more* susceptible to harm than women ... In a different social order, the existing medical evidence could be used to exclude *men* from toxic workplaces' (Daniels, 1993, p. 78, emphasis in original).

What socially produced 'truth' can we find within the discourse of fetal protectionism on which these policies rely and how can the idea of the sexed body help our understanding? I would argue that the logic of fetal protectionism reflects radically different images of the male and female reproductive bodies – images which I believe can also be discerned in other contexts (see Sheldon, 1999). The female body is here understood as frail and susceptible to injury and thus an appropriate object of protection. It is constructed as permeable and penetrable – open to the invasion of foreign substances – and thus volatile, dangerous to itself and to others (particularly the fetus within), and as such in need of (medical) surveillance and supervision (Bridgeman and Millns, 1995; Grosz, 1994; Sheldon, 1997; Smart, 1995; Thomson, 1998). This understanding of the woman's body is implicitly contrasted against an idealized male norm. The 'normal' idealized male body is seen as stable, safe, bounded and impermeable. It is not liable to dysfunction, and hence is not in need of constant medical control. It is strong and invulnerable, not liable to succumb to penetration by foreign bodies such as toxins. It is self-contained, bounded, isolated and inviolate, not connected to other bodies.

Its relationship to reproduction is one of bodily distance being, as it is, physically disengaged from pregnancy. These understandings of men's and women's bodies resonate in obvious ways with contemporary gender wisdom about male and female social roles: men are seen as stronger, harder, not connected to reproduction, their bodies are more stable, less likely to dysfunction; women are understood as weaker, softer, intimately connected to reproduction, their bodies are less stable, more likely to dysfunction.

Fetal protectionism and the 'heterosexual imperative'

Whilst recognising the contingency of understandings of male and female bodies is valuable in itself, the work of theorists like Foucault, Butler and Laqueur invites us to go further and to examine how these particular materializations of the body function to sustain or challenge particular social orderings. As was seen above, Butler expresses this in questioning how particular materializations of the body function to consolidate the 'heterosexual imperative'. This parallels Foucault's focus on how bodies are constructed and deployed to support and legitimate different regimes of domination. More specifically, he contends that it is only by a management of individual bodies that the life of populations can be managed and this involves a growing concern with welfare, with power over the life of people (Foucault, 1978, p. 139). For Foucault, 'the disciplines of the body and the regulations of the population constituted the two poles around which the organization of power over life was deployed' (Foucault, 1978, p. 139) (see Chapter 8 for further discussion of this idea).

How might we understand the science of fetal protectionism and the images of male and female reproductivity on which it is predicated as functioning within and supporting a specific socioeconomic system? Whilst it is beyond the scope of this chapter to endeavour to present any causal explanation for the failure to recognize men as reproductive bodies liable to be damaged by toxic exposure, it is worth noticing a strikingly close fit between these representations and a particular form of social order. Fetal protection policies have typically been used to exclude women from particular traditionally male industries – normally chemical and heavy manufacturing – whilst retaining men within them (see Thomson, 1996, 1998; Sheldon, 1999). Moreover, the policies assume that where a woman chooses to act 'irresponsibly', that is in contradiction to what the legislature or her employers see as the best interests of her fetus, such 'responsible' behaviour can be forced on her. In other words, a woman's reproductive destiny 'trumps' any other choices which she may wish to make. In this sense, Michael Thomson has written that:

> the indiscriminate nature of the policies constructs all women as potentially pregnant, as primarily bearers and rearers of children, first and foremost 'biological actors'. A woman's reproductive role is seen as considerably more important than her economic role, regardless of the impact of unemployment on herself, her pregnancy or her existing children. In defining women by their generative organs, as primarily breeders, women become

homogenized. Foetal protection policies ignore individuality and the existence of autonomous interests beyond the traditional family group. The possibility that women may choose not to have children, or may plan when to have them, is not recognized. Women may only participate in the public/economic sphere within the terms of heterosexuality and traditional views of womanhood (Thomson, 1996, p. 259).

As we have seen, the same assumption of reproductive intent is not made regarding men. Procreation is not their only available choice, but when men do choose to have children, it is expected that they will work in order to provide for their families (see Collier, 1995; Sheldon, 1999). Fetal protection policies appear to be inherently predicated upon the norm of the nuclear family with a male breadwinner.

Within such a model, where continued employment may result in harm to reproductive capacity, this makes it an inappropriate choice for a woman. Exclusion from the workplace, or being forced to take another, less lucrative, job is for the woman's own good as it will allow her to fulfil her primary purpose as a mother of healthy children. On the other hand, as our opening example of Donald Penney and Johnson Controls Inc. demonstrates, male reproductive capacity is largely ignored and men are thus excluded from the regime of protection offered by the fetal protection policies. A man is expected to continue in employment in order to provide for his family with other considerations marginalized. As such, the understandings of male and female reproductive biology on which the science of fetal protectionism is predicated might be usefully located within the terms of Butler's 'heterosexual imperative'.

Conclusions

'Sex' is an ideal construct which is forcibly materialized through time. It is not a simple fact or static condition of a body, but a process whereby regulatory norms materialize 'sex' and achieve this materialization through a forcible reiteration of those norms. That this reiteration is necessary is a sign that materialization is never quite complete, that bodies never quite comply with the norms by which their materialization is impelled (Butler, 1993, p. 2).

In this chapter, I have argued that we make important assumptions about men's bodies which have both been influenced by, and in turn influenced, biomedical research. The case of the fetal protection policy described above shows that the negation of male reproductive capacity has been harmful to individual men in the same way as women's reduction to nothing more than reproductive capacity has been harmful to women (note that I make no claim that it has been *as* harmful).

However, whilst fetal protection policies continue to focus on female bodies, the science underpinning them is not static. An ever-growing body of scientific research now implicates male reproductive exposures in the causation not only of fertility problems, but also of miscarriage, low birth weight, congenital abnormalities, cancer, neurological problems and other childhood health problems (see Daniels, 1993, 1997; Sheldon, 1999; and Thomson, 1996, 1998 for references to a large number of scientific studies in this area). Media reports and articles in men's magazines have begun to warn of the reproductive dangers of smoking, alcohol and other drug use and even coffee drinking and toiletries. One newspaper recently reported: 'Warning: shaving foam can damage your manhood' (Merritt and Macdonald, 1997). Further, in other contexts, men are advancing scientific evidence in order to establish the fragility of their reproductive bodies which are liable to be harmed by exposure to certain toxins. The most obvious example is that of the litigation involving 'Gulf War Syndrome' where men in both the USA and the UK are alleging that they have suffered harm to their reproductive capacity as a result of exposure to certain chemical mixes used during the conflict.

What should we make of this shift? Is 'good' science triumphing over 'bad'? Is this development towards understanding men as reproductive bodies with correlative responsibilities towards the health of their future offspring in some way linked with changing broader social understandings about men's role in reproduction? Is it coincidental that these trends in the scientific discourses arrive at a time when fathering roles seem to be undergoing a noticeable shift with men exhorted to be more actively involved in hands-on childcare rather than assuming an exclusively 'bread winner' role in the family (see Lupton and Barclay, 1997)? Whilst attempting to answer these questions is well beyond the scope of this short chapter, raising them is in itself an important political task. Asking these kinds of questions implies a recognition that whilst physical, material bodies exist, any scientific or other understanding of them is inevitably mediated and partial. The social scientist must always be alive to the contingency of the natural sciences' claims to unmask the objective truth of the 'real body'. When the stories of science are at their most convincing and compelling it may be because they speak most clearly to our own cultural understandings and values and this, I would suggest, is when they are at their most pernicious.

Further reading

Butler, Judith, *Bodies that Matter: On the Discursive Limits of 'Sex'* (New York and London: Routledge, 1993).

An extremely interesting book which offers particularly useful insights on the relationship between sex and gender.

Daniels, Cynthia, 'Between Fathers and Fetuses: The Social Construction of Male Reproduction and the Politics of Fetal Harm', *Signs: Journal of Women in Culture and Society* 22 (3) (1997) 579–616.

A very insightful and accessible paper dealing with antenatal harm and the differences in the ways in which male and female genitors are treated and represented in legal and broader cultural discourses.

Davis, Kathy (ed.), *Embodied Practices: Feminist Perspectives on the Body* (London: Sage, 1997).

A useful collection with an introduction which provides a very valuable overview of feminist work on the body.

Notes

1. I would like to thank Ellie Lee for inviting me to contribute this chapter and for her comments on an earlier draft of it. I also acknowledge with gratitude the research award from Keele University and the Jean Monnet Fellowship at the European University Institute in Florence, which gave me the opportunity to write this chapter.

3

Sexualized Bodies

Kylie Stephen

There are many ways in which we can conceive of bodies as being 'sexualized'. Bodies are considered 'sexed' in the biological sense that they are either male or female. Thus bodies can be sexualized in terms of their anatomy. Secondly, these sexed bodies may in turn be seen to display certain gendered behaviour. Thus bodies can be sexualized in terms of their masculinity and femininity. Finally, bodies can be seen as sexualized because they engage in certain sexual practices, for example, heterosexual or homosexual sex. Thus bodies can be sexualized in terms of their sexuality. The usual assumption is that the terms sex, gender and sexuality are definable and universal experiences; however there are many cultural norms associated with these terms and how they are developed and adopted. Upon closer examination, it soon becomes apparent that what we understand by the concept of sexualized bodies is not unproblematic and a natural given.

There are essentially two schools of thought when it comes to explaining and defining sexuality. The first school takes the 'naturalist approach', exemplified in the work of Havelock Ellis and by psychoanalytic thinkers, in particular Sigmund Freud. The work of Ellis is essentially a chronicle of sexual behaviour and beliefs and is mainly descriptive in form. In the work of Freud, on the other hand, theoretical constructs take precedence over empirical evidence. Both these views, however, represent an essentialist view of sexuality; sex is conceptualized as an overpowering yet functionalist force in the individual that shapes not only personal but social life as well. All sexuality is derived from or developed in relation to a male heterosexual drive that can be explained in terms of a hydraulic understanding of

29

sexual desire: men are active sexual agents with 'natural' sexual urges that cannot be ignored; women are passive recipients of men's sexual desires. This approach generally shapes our everyday notions of sexuality, and is often evident in the legal and social understandings of rape law (illustrated later in this chapter).

The second school of thought is characterized by newer approaches, which forcibly challenge these essentialist notions of sexuality. This second school of thought includes neo-psychoanalytic approaches which see sexuality and sexual desire as constituted in language (the work of Freud reinterpreted via Jacques Lacan; a position that has been taken up by feminists such as Juliet Mitchell). It also includes discursive or poststructuralist approaches which take as a starting point the work of Michel Foucault who argues that sexuality is an historical apparatus and sex is a complex idea that was formed with the deployment of sexuality.

What links this second group of theorists is the recognition of social and historical sources of sexual definitions and a belief that bodies are only *unified* through ideological constructs such as sex and sexuality. That is; sex and sexuality are, and have been, shaped and determined by a multiplicity of forces (such as race, class and religion) and have undergone complex historical transformations. We therefore give the notions of sex, gender and sexuality different meanings at different times and for different people. These notions combine to create understandings of 'sexualized bodies' which are subsequently expressed and reinforced through a variety of mechanisms; for example through marriage laws, the regulations of deviance, the judiciary, the police, as well as, more generally, the education system, and the welfare system (Weeks, 1989, p. 9). This view of sexuality as 'constructed' is in agreement with the view of sex as 'given' on the basis that sex and sexuality define us socially and morally. However, this second view suggests that sexuality could be a potentiality for choice, change and diversity, but instead we see it as destiny – and depending on whether you are male, female, homosexual, heterosexual, young, old, black or white, for example, your destiny is set in certain ways. As Weeks explains:

> The sexual potentialities of the body have been integrated into a vast range of different social contexts ... some cultures have seen no connection between sexual intercourse and conception; others have seen only justification for sex in reproduction. Some cultures have made little distinction between heterosexual and homosexual forms, concentrating rather on age or class of the partner; our culture [white Anglo-Saxon] has

made the distinction of prime social significance. In some societies, sex is a simple source of pleasure, a key to the glorification of the erotic arts; in others it is a source of danger and taboo, of mortification of the flesh (Weeks, 1989, p. 11).

This chapter will set out the discursive or poststructuralist position that explores the specificities of the way male and female bodies and sexualities are constructed and understood. Foucault, in particular, offers us an alternative view of seeing the relationship between sexuality and wider social forces in contrast with the functionalism of many traditional interpretations (for example that of hydraulic male sexuality). Using the work of Foucault, I seek to explore similar questions to those posed by Sally Sheldon in Chapter 2 of this text. I will illustrate what it means to point to the contingency of our understandings of sexuality – to show how our knowledge of sexuality is in fact profoundly influenced by our cultural belief systems (specifically around biological sex and race). Further, in order to examine the place of 'sexualized bodies' in contemporary consciousness, I will examine the ways in which sex and race combined to create sexualized bodies in two examples – the Hill/Thomas Senate hearings and the Mike Tyson rape trial. These case studies will help to explain the theoretical issue posed by poststructuralist thinking: what it means to talk about sexuality as being socially constructed or discursively produced.

Poststructuralism and sexuality

The term poststructuralism has been understood, and functioned variously, as an historical characterization, a theoretical position and a type of social theory. Yet, poststructuralism is widely understood to abandon the universal Cartesian subject as having a mind which controls the body (this idea is discussed further in Chapter 6), in favour of a socially and linguistically decentred subject/individual (Best and Kellner, 1991, p. 5). For poststructuralists, such as Derrida, all social phenomena are structured semiotically by codes and rules of discourse; therefore all social phenomena are amenable to linguistic analysis. Meaning is not simply given, but discursively constructed across a variety of sites and practices. What is significant about poststructural discourse theory is that it exposes the subject positions from which people speak, and the power relations that inform these positions. Discourse becomes a site and object of struggle where different groups strive to control the production of meaning (Butler, 1995). Thus, where the notion of sexuality is seen to presuppose sex as a functionalist force stemming from the predominance of white male heterosexuality, this construction can be said to be historically and linguistically specific.

Poststructuralists argue that there is no such thing as a value-free theory or science. The concepts we use are popular because they are socially and politically useful. In the case of sexuality, the poststructuralist argues that the modern idea of sexuality was constructed in a particular social and historical context. Hence Foucault argues that, contrary to popular belief, sexuality was not repressed in Victorian times and reawakened in the twentieth century, because there is no essential human sexuality that can be repressed at one point in history and liberated at another. Instead he argues that there are sexualities that are constantly produced and modified by social forces (Foucault, 1978).

The distinguishing mark of human sexuality, therefore, is the unique role of language, consciousness and symbolism in its construction. Human beings produce and give order and meaning to an ever-changing human world. The content of sexuality is ultimately that provided by human social relations, activities and consciousness: 'The history of sexuality is therefore the history of a subject whose meaning and contents are in continual process of change. It is the history of social relations' (Padgug, 1999, p. 20). Sexuality is relational. It consists of active social relations and not simply 'sexual acts'. The particular interrelations and activities that exist at any moment in a specific society create categories of sexuality which determine the broad range of modes of behaviour available to individuals within that society. Sexual categories do not represent sexual essences implicit within individuals; rather they are the expression of the active relationships of the members of that society.

The poststructuralist critique of the subject/individual is particularly instructive for feminists and other emancipationists alike. Poststructuralist critiques of the way in which the individual is constructed are concerned with issues of power and perspective. A critical examination of the 'subject as constituted in and through power/discourse formations' (Fraser, 1991, p. 171) might lead to an analysis and understanding of how society perpetuates and naturalizes subordinating images of women or people from different ethnic groups in ways that reflect the views and serve the interests of those in dominant positions relative to them. This kind of critique can destabilize accepted understandings of men, women, sex and gender by exposing their social constructedness and allowing the radical reconstruction of the subject and its sexuality so that it does not represent a sexist and racist ideal. Understanding the subject as something that is politically constructed means understanding sexuality as also being politically constructed.

Indeed feminists have drawn extensively on the poststructuralist argument that sexuality is constructed through language and is therefore a culturally specific mixture of various subject positions. Foucault is a major contributor to this argument. Specifically, his theory of power and its relation to the body has been used by feminists to explain aspects of women's oppression (Butler, 1995; Diamond and Quinby, 1988; McNay, 1992). Foucault's idea that sexuality is not a natural quality of the body, but rather the effect of historically specific power relations, has provided feminists with a powerful analytical framework by which to explain how women's experience is controlled by culturally determined images of feminine sexuality (Marcus, 1992).

It is tempting to assume that one's birth sex automatically endows one with cultural ways to 'live' that biological sex. It is generally thought that one's gender and sexuality are supposed to correspond to one's biological sex. Subsequently, male bodies should display masculine characteristics and female bodies should display feminine characteristics. But the assumptions that biological sex and gender are the same and natural and that therefore everyone's sex and gender should and will conform are essentialist positions. Foucault's theory of the body has given feminist thought a way of conceiving of the body as something that is 'real' but without aligning its biology with a fixed gendered essence. Sex roles and gender are not inborn and automatic depending on your sex. Male and female bodies display masculine and feminine traits in varying degrees. Male and female bodies have different social value and significance that, in turn, have a marked effect on our consciousness and the way we perceive and make sense of our bodies (Gatens, 1983). Differently sexed bodies determine different experiences of what it means to be an individual and how bodies can actively work to produce themselves and either confirm or deny the various social inscriptions they are given.

Critics such as Benhabib (1991) argue that poststructuralism prevents the possibility of committed political action, specifically action that is guided by the goal of emancipation. They argue that rejecting the universality and uniformity of concepts such as 'equality', 'women' and 'black' subverts the project of organizing women and others to fight modes of oppression. That is to say, if we cannot define 'women', for example, as an homogenous group identifiable

by specific characteristics, how can they experience collective oppression or discrimination and how can we claim to act on their behalf?

However, the critique offered by poststructuralism does not prevent appeals to general norms; 'it only requires that these too be
regarded as situated' (Fraser, 1991, p. 170). Thus, it is possible to talk
about groups as if they are homogenous so long as we recognize the
context and culture that shapes them. They may be heterogeneous in
composition but they share common experiences mediated by that
heterogeneity. Part of the problem with articulating such a position is
the language. While criticizing an entrenched political vocabulary, it
appears necessary to make tacit use of the same rhetoric one claims to
be rejecting (Fraser, 1989, p. 57). That is to say, in emphasizing the
construction of the term 'sexuality' it would seem that we in turn are
developing a new meta-theory of sexuality; one where subjects and
sexualities are always constructed or mapped onto people, where
there is no agency of the individual to develop their own sexuality. This
position becomes the new 'essentialist' theory of sexuality. However,
theories which attack universalism, essentialism and foundationalism
are useful for those seeking equality because they highlight differences
between individuals, groups and subject positions and encourage us
to be critical of the assumptions we may unwittingly bring to whatever
subject we investigate (Fraser and Nicholson, 1988).

There is nothing, in principle, that prevents the subject from being
both culturally constructed and capable of critique (Fraser, 1991,
p. 172). The poststructuralist project is not about negating or dis-
pensing with a notion of the subject altogether. Subjects are products
of discourse, but they should not be considered passive. Rather, we
should think of the subject as being in process, as something that is
constituted differently by different forms of discourse, and individuals have an active role in structuring their reality. Poststructuralism
therefore provides us with a useful tool to think about sexuality as a
conception that is in process, something that is constructed and
which also constructs, rather than as a universal and unified identity,
depending on an individual's sex, ethnicity, class and so on.

The construction and reproduction of essentialist
notions of sexuality

We give supreme importance to sex in our individual and social lives
today as the history of modern western society has assigned a central
significance to everything sexual. The apparatus of sexuality is of central

importance in the modern play of power. But what are the concrete mechanisms and practices through which power operates? Foucault suggests that power operates through the construction of particular knowledges. And it is through the constructed knowledge of sexuality that control over individuals is exercized. Thus his work directs us to investigate the role of certain knowledges in shaping our conceived notions of sexuality and sexualized bodies.

Law is one such concrete mechanism and body of knowledge that is particularly effective in the reproduction and construction of essential notions of sexuality (the place of law in constructing the body is also discussed in later chapters in this volume). Assumptions about men's and women's sexuality are constructed and reinforced by law because law is situated within the context of, and actively engaged in, the projection of sexist visions of male and female sexuality. That is, law attributes specific sexualized meanings to the specific bodies of men and women. Consequently, law, in its statutory framing, recognizes the current political and cultural structures of society. Rape law and the law relating to sexual harassment represent particularly relevant examples whereby women and men's sexualities are framed by sexist legal language.

Foucault suggests that law is a powerful discourse because it claims scientificity, and that to define a field of knowledge as science is to claim that it speaks a truth (Foucault, 1980). Law has its own method (of ostensibly impartial and objective decision-making), its own testing ground (the courts), its own specialized language (terms like 'standards of evidence', 'criteria of relevance', 'corroboration' and '*mens rea*') and system of results (arrived at through the use of juries and judges) (Smart, 1990, p. 197). This has a significant effect on how law is perceived in society and what kind of authority it wields. Because law is seen as scientific truth, it is perceived as authoritative. Law is then thought to be always or invariably right or correct. MacKinnon argues, however, that 'truth is produced in the interest of those with power to shape reality' (MacKinnon, 1983, p. 640). Law legitimizes itself by reflecting a view of existing society that it helped to make and thus reinforces that view by defining it as reality (MacKinnon, 1983, p. 644).

Legal discourse is situated within the social and political context of a masculine culture. Masculinity is prioritized and culture and power are structured to meet the needs of the masculine imperative. While the state must try and accommodate pressures for law reform, it cannot ignore the privileged status of law within our society and its essentially conservative role (Thornton, 1991). As part of a larger masculine cultural system, law participates in the construction and reproduction of masculine thinking, knowledge, meanings and sub-jectivities. Law constructs and reconstructs masculinity and feminin-ity, race and class and contributes regularly to common perceptions of sexual difference, which sustain the masculine culture that femi-nists and others attempt to challenge (Smart, 1990). Legal represen-tations are therefore part of a complex socialization process that influences how we think about gender roles and identities. These representations are themselves drawn from popular culture, but once they are set out in legal discourse they gain authority and appear to be truth – the product of objectivity and principle.

For example, in relation to rape law, it is observed that the action rape, and associated terms, has the ability to label some sexual acts negatively, and by implication condone others:

> How these terms are defined [and by whom] affects how people label, experience, evaluate, and assimilate their own sexually coercive incidents. In addition, the definitions of these terms convey numerous assumptions about power and coercion, sexuality and gender (Muehlenhard and Muehlenhard, 1992, p. 24).

In other words, the representation of rape is understood to be the physical reality of the event though it is a product of power and perspective.

If white heterosexual men determine the 'truth' of rape, then the law of rape will reflect society as experienced by white heterosexual men. Women's sexual experiences will only be understood in terms of this masculine reality and law may, consequently, work against women's interests. Representations of rape thus often naturalize female passivity and legitimize male sexual aggression, treat only cer-tain classes or types of people as rapable and have a disciplinary effect on men and women's social behaviours. Such representations typi-cally depend on stereotyped notions of men and women's sexuality and limit the range of identities that each can safely occupy when they present themselves in such legal cases. This is illustrated more fully in the case examples set out later in this chapter.

The social world is traversed by relations of power (class, gender, race and so on) but these can only signify and hence be understood by individual subjects through available discourses. These aspects of power inequalities, shifting meanings and the ways in which ideas give shape to, and are shaped by, prevailing power and knowledge structures, suggest that the idea of discursive configurations provides a helpful theoretical framework for understanding what we mean by sexuality.

In taking this approach, we start to question the eternal validity of social roles, and recognise that the way in which we define masculinity and femininity, motherhood and fatherhood, are culturally specific and not simple products of biology (Weeks, 1989, p. 11). The examples of the Hill/Thomas Senate hearings and the Mike Tyson rape trial highlight these points and illustrate how the social mechanism of law exercizes power to construct and reinforce sexist and racist understandings of sex, gender and sexuality. These cases illustrate the manner in which bodies are sexualized in contemporary society through language and discourse and how these differ according to certain social, political and economic factors that can be attributed to the key players. It is to these two case studies that I will now turn.

Sexualized bodies: the complex relationship between sex and race in the Anita Hill/Clarence Thomas hearings and the Mike Tyson rape trial

Both the Hill/Thomas Senate hearings and the Tyson rape trial can be read as constructions of specifically black male and female sexuality, informed by representations of gender, race and class. It is plausible to argue that these cases should be viewed in the narrow context of their very specific facts as they each differ in terms of locations, legal precedents, witnesses and so on, which go a long way to explaining their respective outcomes. But any analysis that does not address the portrayal of gender and race stereotypes will fail to appreciate how the discourses used in, and generated by, the two cases work to socially construct our common understandings of sexualized bodies and teach us to 'perform' as men and women in society.

On 6 October 1991, National Public Radio's reporter, Nina Totenberg disclosed that some information had been passed on to her that suggested that there were charges of sexual harassment against Clarence Thomas, a black man who had been nominated to become a Judge for the Supreme Court in the United States. As a result of her reporting this information, the United States Senate decided to hold a public hearing from 11–13 October 1991, as the nomination was within days of being confirmed by the Senate. The allegations came from Anita Hill, a black Professor of Commercial Law at Oklahoma State University.

What the hearings proceeded to do was to force the public to debate the meaning of sexual practices so widespread as to seem to many as 'natural'. That is the 'natural' way in which men and women related. What they also proceeded to do was to highlight the dynamics of sex and race in constructing individual sexualities and sexualized bodies. They were of symbolic significance for the transformation of the position of women and blacks in American society. Most significantly, for the purposes of this chapter, the hearings participated in the construction and reproduction of stereotyping about male and female black sexuality.

Hill testified that Thomas kept asking her to go out, would not accept 'no' as an answer, and made constant sexual references. Both inside and outside the hearings, many charges were made against Hill. For example, it was argued that if she had really disliked what Thomas was doing so much, she would have quit her job; that her not quitting showed that she welcomed his attentions; that a 'reasonable person' would not have been disturbed by these attentions. The reasonable person being based on what a man would, or be expected to, do in the same circumstances. In Hill's case, argument over what 'the reasonable person' would have done was further distorted by race; most viciously in an attack by a Harvard African-American sociologist named Orlando Patterson who charged in the *New York Times* on 21 October 1991, that black women *understood* the kind of banter Thomas was engaging in with Hill and that Hill was simply pretending to be offended.

This attack on Hill explicitly asserts that this kind of sexual behaviour by men is reasonable and in fact 'normal'. It reasserts the idea of active male sexuality and passive female sexuality. But it also highlights the influence that race has on the construction of sexuality, because not only are women to be passively accepting of this 'normal' behaviour (although they should also be embarrassed because of their delicate nature and morality) but that black women in particular understand this behaviour because their sexual nature is different (this is understood to be in relation to white women's sexual nature) – they are highly sexed themselves and therefore should not be offended.

Hill was portrayed variously as a lesbian who hated men and a vamp that could both ensnare and be painfully rejected by them. Hill became both the oversexed Jezebel anxious for sex and the rejected vindictive woman who trumps up a charge of sexual harassment. This was in keeping with historical assumptions about black female sexuality. As Sara Ahmed discusses in the following chapter, prevalent images of black women derive almost exclusively from slavery. These images work duplicitously to attach essentialist qualities of sexuality to black women and continue to justify their oppression. As Patricia Hill Collins warns:

> From the mammies, Jezebels, and breeder women of slavery to the smiling Aunt Jemimas on pancake mix boxes, ubiquitous Black prostitutes, and ever-present welfare mothers of contemporary popular culture, the nexus of negative stereotypical images applied to African-American women has been fundamental to Black women's oppression (cited in Holmberg, 1998, p. 69).

Despite the fact that, on the one hand, Thomas' actions were portrayed as being within the bounds of normal male sexuality (and Hill's response unreasonable in this context of normality) he also came to represent the sexualized figure of the black man as the date raper and sexual assaulter (Morrison, 1993, p. xvi). His actions were thought to be typical not only of male sexuality in general, but particularly of black male sexuality which has traditionally been characterized as aggressive and rapacious. Similar portrayals of black male and female sexuality were evident in the Mike Tyson rape case.

On 10 February 1992, Mike Tyson, the world's most famous boxer, was convicted of one charge of rape and two charges of 'criminal deviate conduct' (Jefferson, 1997, p. 281). He was sentenced to ten years' imprisonment on each count, to run concurrently, with four of these suspended. His victim was a young beauty queen by the name of Desiree Washington.

The prosecution portrayed Tyson as all predator and Washington as all victim. Tyson was said to be a loud-mouthed, sexually predatory, crass young man. He was a 'wolf in sheep's clothing'; grossly explicit in the nature of his sexual advances. Desiree Washington was seen as a wholesome, religious, small-town innocent abroad. The defence, interestingly enough, used a slightly modified version of this discourse of male sexuality which rests on essentialist notions of a natural male sex drive that women inflame at their peril. It was deemed acceptable on one level for Tyson to identify with the super-stud position – a hypermasculine subject position in which the number of sexual conquests is paramount, a position certainly more available to men who are rich and famous. This was congruent with the construction of black male sexuality already described.

On the other hand Washington's identity was constructed out of contradictions. The prosecution portrayed her as small-town provincial, narrow-minded, static, traditional, religious, deferential and sexually repressive. The defence portrayed her as a vindictive liar, fantasizer, scorned neurotic and mentally unbalanced. A sophisticated, cynical little gold-digger who was going to date Tyson simply because he was rich and potentially manipulable.

Upon examination of the permissive discourse of male sexuality, it should be pointed out that the current state of gender–power relations still effectively denies a positive subject position for women within it. There is, in other words, no positive female discursive equivalent to the promiscuous male 'stud', only the highly derogatory labels of 'slag', 'whore' 'tart' and the like, despite the so-called 'sexual revolution' of the 1960s (Jefferson, 1997, p. 286). This was the discursive position used by the defence, which effectively argued that Washington should have known better. The gendered nature of her sexuality does not allow her to occupy the same sexual space as Tyson – which would constitute deviant sexuality on her part. She inflamed his natural male sexual desire at her peril and was now crying 'wolf'.

But clearly race relations complicate the picture further by multiplying the number of subject positions and because the power relations these positions signify can be contradictory. As indicated above, for African-American men for example, the discourse of 'male sexual drive' includes a unique subject position of 'super-sexuality'. In relation to gender, the subject position of 'super-sexuality' renders every black man a potential stud 'plus' – a positive connotation. But the state of race relations which positions black men as inferior to white men ensures that super-sexuality has negative connotations too, as a sign of animality (Jefferson, 1997, p. 287). This was the discursive position used effectively by the prosecution. But what is most apparent from the characterizations of sexuality in both these cases is that sex is the main theme associated with blackness.

The history of black women as victims of rape has not yet entered the collective, international (specifically American) mind. That is to say, black women's reputed hypersexuality has not yet been reappraised: the stereotype of black women as sexually available has yet to be revised. The sexually promiscuous black woman has always stood as the mirror image of the virginal white woman on the pedestal. Thus, in both cases (and despite the fact that Tyson was found guilty), race was used to cast doubt on the 'sanctity' of both Hill and Washington's gender.

Out of the basic assumption that slaves lack humanity, come a series of racist beliefs regarding black people's sexuality that are still with us today. However, as these examples illustrate, the imagery of sex in race has not and does not work in identical ways for black women and men.

Stereotypes of black women remain fairly securely in place, and the public discussion that would examine and dislodge them has only begun to occur around the 'mammy' image. The oversexed-black-Jezebel is more likely than not still taken at face value. This stereotypical black woman not only connotes sex, like the working-class white woman, but unlike the latter, is assumed to be the instigator of sex (Painter, 1993).

The disciplinary function of representations about women's sexuality varies with race. Black women must allay the view that they want sex under any circumstances, or that they are able to take sexual harassment or assaults 'in their stride' due to their presumed promiscuity. Subsequently, black women bear a large burden of establishing their sexual innocence. This status is much more readily granted to white women, unless issues of class enter the equation. The range of available identities is narrow for black women who are victims of sexual harassment or assault, although differently narrow than it is for white women.

Overdetermined cultural discourses such as these constrain black men as well. Mike Tyson's defence team was forced to confront ingrained stereotypes about the sexual aggressiveness of black men. It is arguable whether the lawyers of any white defendant would have adopted the strategy his defence team did (although again this might depend on issues such as class and professional background). Tyson's defence disastrously exploited this stereotype of black male sexuality and in effect reinforced it as 'truth'.

As highlighted in earlier sections of this chapter, insofar as the law is a product of historical and political power struggles its function is not to transcend but to reproduce and reinforce existing social discourses. Specifically in relation to the Tyson case, it is evident how:

> The law forces both sides to construct a particular narrative of the participants sexualities to fit prevailing legal interpretations (of consent etc) and in the process simplifies (and hence distorts) accounts in order that one truth may be chosen (albeit one which is as historically and politically specific as the legal categories through which it is necessarily constructed) (Jefferson, 1997, p. 286).

In both cases the interplay between sex and race in the construction of sexuality drew out many of the major power conflicts in

American (and indeed broader) society. As Lamont (1994) has argued, these two cases symbolized how:

- white people pit black people against one another to serve their own purposes;
- white people use black women to undermine black men;
- white feminists subordinate blacks to feminist causes;
- white males dehumanize all women;
- light-skinned black people marginalize dark-skinned black people;
- black accommodationists sell out their own to benefit their personal careers;
- black men force black women to subordinate their interests to those of race, even if it means protecting the black men who subjugate them.

African-American men were faced with a particular dilemma: in the face of pervasive ideology that bestializes African-Americans and stereotypes black males as oversexed and potential rapists by nature, many felt that to support the accusers in the Thomas/Hill and Tyson/Washington cases was to lend support to racist mythologies. Subsequently, Anita Hill and Desiree Washington were viewed by some African-American men and women as betrayers of the black community and its struggle against racism.

But as Bordo points out, the problem with the 'betrayers-of-the-black-community' argument is not its attentiveness to racism, but its sexist reduction of the struggle against racism to the struggles of black *males*. The female accusers in these cases, after all, were also members of 'the black community'. And as has been illustrated, African-American women have also been bestialized by racist ideology: portrayed as amoral Jezebels who can never truly be raped/sexually harassed because both terms imply an invasion of *personal* space or modesty and reserve that the black woman has not been imagined as having (Bordo, 1992, p. 199).

Clarence Thomas was able to bring stereotypes of black male sexuality to the attention of the Senate hearings and make an issue of them. He was implicitly daring the senators to treat him with anything less than the utmost respect, lest they be seen as racists. Anita Hill was not afforded the same luxury as she was interrogated about penises and pornography, with barely a thought for her moral and religious upbringing. Similarly when the 'National Committee for

Mercy for Mike' spoke of Tyson as an 'African-American hero' and 'role model for black youth', they offered a map of reality on which the experience of African-American women who identified with Desiree Washington's ordeal did not appear.

When Clarence Thomas described his hearings as a 'high-tech lynching', he cynically exploited the analogy in two ways. First Thomas not only presented himself as a racialized victim but as a sexual victim too. As Bhavnani and Collins explain:

> this is because lynching connotes 'race' and sex simultaneously, for black men in the United States were often castrated when they were lynched by white people. Also, lynchings were presented as an appropriate sanction when there were allegations that black men had slept with white women (1993, p. 500).

Clarence Thomas used race as his main means for rebutting the charge of sexual harassment – but his accuser was a black woman.

Secondly, as Bordo points out, he exploited an analogy that, in the context of Anita Hill's accusations, submerged the historical realities of African-American women's lives; black men were never lynched for abusing or raping black women. This is not to claim that the nomination and confirmation of Thomas was free of racism. Certainly William Kennedy Smith (acquitted of raping Patricia Bowman) was never publicly characterized – even by the prosecution – as an instinctual animal (unlike Mike Tyson who was portrayed in this way by both prosecution and defence alike) (Bordo, 1992, p. 200).

By failing to acknowledge the operations of racism at a variety of levels in both these cases, and by suggesting instead that racial justice could simply and only be served by the exoneration of the African-American male 'accused', both Anita Hill and Desiree Washington were constructed as being 'outside' the net of racism (Bordo, 1992, pp. 199–200). Therefore, in drawing on racism, Thomas is able to draw on a key tension within prevailing feminisms, and thus imply that any woman who accuses a black man, whether she is black or white, will be 'buying into' racism' (Bhavnani and Collins, 1993, p. 501). The commitment of black women to dealing with racism is then used to control and silence black women on sexism – which is what happened to Anita Hill. Setting up an opposition between sexism and racism suggests that claims of sexism are a means of perpetuating racism against black men when in fact sex and race are deeply interconnected. Both cases reveal a dynamic between the discourses of gender and race that depend on and reinforce stereotypes about female sexual passivity, aggressive male sexuality and the vulnerability that accompanies social inferiority.

Conclusion

Through the use of poststructural analysis, the sexist and racist constructions of sexuality can be subverted and subjectivity can be reconceptualized to incorporate the existence of sexed bodies. Internal contradictions in seemingly coherent systems of thought can be uncovered. Definitions that masquerade as universal, such as that of natural sexuality, can be seen as premised on sexist and racist norms of embodied existence. By focusing on the textuality of such terms as sex, gender and sexuality, the ways in which racialized discourses intercut with discourses about sexual oppression to produce a particular conception of culturally acceptable sexuality become apparent.

Poststructuralists, such as Foucault, stress the importance of differences over unities, encouraging the dispersion of meaning in opposition to universalizing theories. Significantly, poststructuralism is able to demonstrate how the very establishment of theories and systems, for example those about sexuality, imply the existence of theories and systems beyond themselves, precisely by virtue of what they exclude (Cornell, 1992). Stereotypes around black sexuality have no empirical reality apart from mainstream white sexuality. They are mutually reinforcing of each other. To talk about the construction of black sexuality is therefore to implicitly discuss the construction of white sexuality, as the two are caught in a binary dynamic. If the distorted images of black men and women disappeared tomorrow, black male and female sexuality would still be considered qualitatively distinct from white male and female sexuality. For the two to be the same, both groups would have to have had the same cultural conditioning and social circumstances.

Importantly then, conceptions of sexuality that may have once been historically necessary are not logically necessary. Sexuality is varied and socially defined. We need to be alert to which symbolic representations are invoked, how, and in what contexts, in order to better understand the ways in which sex and race combine to create understandings of sexuality in contemporary society. It is possible to stand against dominant sexual stereotypes because they have been used to reinforce social hierarchies without knowing what the alternative depictions of sexuality might be. The problem lies in the fact that stereotypes are deployed by some to keep others in a position of social inferiority. While it might actually be impossible to escape such depictions and discourses of gender, race and sexuality altogether, poststructural analysis allows us to at least recognize when they are present, analyze their impact and take greater responsibility for the manner in which they are used.

Further reading

Best, Steven and Douglas Kellner, *Postmodern Theory: Critical Interrogations* (London: Macmillan Press – now Palgrave, 1991).
   A comprehensive introductory text to postmodern and poststructural theory. It cites and explains the work of many of the key authors in this school of thought and provides contemporary critiques of the same.
Foucault, Michel, *The History of Sexuality. Volume One* (London: Penguin Books, 1978).
   The first in a series of three volumes on this topic by Foucault, but acknowledged as his seminal work on the construction of sex and sexuality.
Morrison, Toni (ed.), *Race-ing Justice, En-Gendering Power: Essays on Anita Hill, Clarence Thomas, and the Construction of Social Reality* (London: Chatto and Windus, 1993).
   A large collection of brief essays, which examine the Hill/Thomas Senate hearings: they discuss how contemporary understandings of sex, race and class are constructed and the overall impact of the hearings on American society.
Nicholson, Linda J. (ed.) *Feminism/Postmodernism* (New York: Routledge, 1990).
   A collection of essays which examine the interaction between feminist theory and postmodern theory: they specifically examine the degree to which feminists can utilize postmodern thinking for the purpose of promoting gender equality.

4

Racialized Bodies

Sara Ahmed

What does it mean to describe bodies as 'racialized'? The term 'racialized bodies' invites us to think of the multiple processes whereby bodies come to be seen as 'having' a racial identity. One's 'racial identity' is not simply determined, for example, by the 'fact' of one's skin colour. Racialization is a process that takes place in time and space: 'race' is an effect of this process, rather than its origin or cause. So, in the case of skin colour, racialization involves a process of *investing* skin colour with meaning, such that 'black' and 'white' come to function, not as descriptions of skin colour, but as racial identities. The term 'racialized bodies' has another implication, of course. It suggests that that we cannot understand the production of race without reference to embodiment: if racialization involves multiple processes, then these processes involve the marking out of bodies as the *site* of racialization itself.

In my discussion of the racialized body, I will question any presumed opposition between essentialism and constructionism (Fuss, 1990). One approach would be to challenge the race/ethnicity distinction, in a similar way that Judith Butler (1990) challenged the sex/gender distinction (see the earlier chapters by Sally Sheldon and Kylie Stephen for further discussion of this idea). It could be argued that race, which is ordinarily assumed to be the intrinsic property of bodies does not come before ethnicity, which is ordinarily assumed to be the cultural inscription of group identity. Race as bodily difference is a consequence rather than the origin of ethnicity. The response to this argument should not simply be the replacement of 'race' with the term 'ethnicity'. For the term 'race' allows us to signal the history of the construction of the racial body. To replace 'race' with 'ethnicity' would be to erase too many traces of this history. In my discussion of colonial and scientific discourses below, it will become clear that this history is a history of appropriation and violence. It is important that we keep explicit the link between this history and the racialization of bodies, and the shift from 'race' to 'ethnicity' in official discourses of multiculturalism often means the forgetting of these histories of violence, and hence a de-politizing or neutralization of the terrain (Ahmed, 2000, Chapter 5).

Here I will use the term 'race', but will argue similarly, that 'race' is an *effect* of racialization, not its cause, and that 'the racial body' is a product of the process of racialization. Racialization involves the production of 'the racial body' through knowledge, as well as the constitution of both social and bodily space in the everyday encounters we have with others. Although I will argue that the racial body is discursively constructed, I will also suggest that 'essence' does not disappear. Rather, 'essence' is an effect of construction. So, although we might say there is no such thing as race as the intrinsic property of bodies, this does not mean that race does not exist, as an effect of the very way in which we think, know and inhabit the world. In some sense, what we need to examine is the production of 'essence' itself, by asking the question: *how is it that bodies come to be lived as having essential characteristics?*

Thinking of racialization as a process whereby bodies come to be seen, known and lived as 'having' a racial identity means attending to the multiple histories of the *production* of racialized bodies. In this chapter, I cannot do justice to the multiplicity of such histories. Rather, I will attend to particular moments in the 'evolution' of the concept of race in modern British imperial history, before thinking through how bodies become racialized in everyday encounters with bodily others. By framing the chapter in this way, I will demonstrate that we cannot trace the production of racial bodies without reference to the history of European colonialism. In other words, the invention of race as something that belongs to bodies, and belongs to different bodies differently, was a means of justifying and legitimating the period of imperial expansion in the nineteenth century. At the same time, I will show how we cannot isolate the production of racial bodies from the gendering and sexualizing of bodies. This chapter will be informed by Black feminist arguments that race and gender are mutually constitutive forms of oppression (hooks, 1992), as well as post-colonial feminist arguments that colonial discourses are gendered in contradictory and unstable ways (McClintock, 1995).

In examining the production of racialized bodies, I will also exer-
cize different theoretical frameworks: a Foucaldian approach to
discourse, a psychoanalytical model of desire, fantasy and ambivalence and a phenomenological emphasis on lived experiences of
embodiment.

The production of racial bodies

Clearly, European colonialism involved the direct and violent control
of the bodies of others in histories of slavery, as well as in the power
seized over the bodies of natives in settler colonies. Indeed, one way of
thinking of how colonialism involved power over the bodies of others
is to think of the history of museums. Not only were sacred objects
from the colonized countries removed and appropriated as items in
museum displays, but also skulls and other parts of dead bodies were
taken (Pearce, 1994, p. 7). The violence of such appropriation of dead
bodies in museums existed alongside the violent appropriation of living bodies in slavery and other forms of direct exploitation of the lives
and labour of indigenous peoples.

However, colonialism also operated to produce the bodies of the
colonized as already raced, by constituting them as objects of knowledge. What does it mean to think of racial bodies as *produced*? We can
evoke here Foucault's (1978) notion of power as *productive*. Rather
than seeing power as repressive, that is, as constraining, delimiting
or prohibiting what bodies can do (which is not to say that some power
does not operate in this way), Foucault argues that power produces
certain effects; it is both generative and enabling (1978, pp. 11–12). If
power is productive, then power also produces bodies. Foucault's
analysis in *The History of Sexuality* challenges the model of sexuality as
repressed that has been inherited, in part, from Freudian psychoanalysis. He argues that sex cannot be understood as the thing that is
not talked about, which is censored and forbidden in the Victorian
era. Rather, he suggests that everybody was talking about sex – whether
in scientific or expert knowledges, in religious confessions or in popular manuals, journals and magazines. Foucault describes this process
of constituting that which is ostensibly forbidden as an object of
knowledge as 'an incitement to discourse' (1978, pp. 17–35). Another
way of thinking of this incitement to discourse is the incitement to
constitute 'bodies' themselves as objects available in a discursive field.
That is, 'bodies' themselves were produced as objects, as things to be
known, seen and regulated.

While Foucault's emphasis here is on sex and sexuality in the nineteenth century, we can consider how 'race' was also produced or *incited into discourse*. This incitement to discourse operated precisely through the desire to know the 'truth' about the bodies of others who were marked as different to the white masculine subject of knowledge (the white body is here unmarked). Rather than talk of racial others being forbidden as dangerous, it was the very perception of the danger posed by others that justified the incitement to know more about those others. Indeed, we can understand the colonial enterprise, the violent acquisition of control of other lands and peoples as involving an incitement to discourse. Through producing knowledges about those other people and places (both of which become transformed into the category of nature/native), the colonizers sought to bring the others into its field of knowledge. In other words, what was produced was 'an imperial archive' (Richards, 1993), but an archive built out of the dissection of the bodies of the colonized, an archive made out of skin and bone. This *proliferation or multiplication of discourses* attempted to account for the truth of the 'colonized' by the formation of scientific classifications and typologies.

Clearly, scientific knowledges were crucial in the construction of the racialized body. As Sandra Harding suggests, science involves 'a racial economy': it involves 'those institutions, assumptions, and practices that are responsible for disproportionally distributing, along 'racial' lines the benefits of Western sciences' (1993, p. 2). While western science legitimated itself as objective, disinterested and value-free, it was interested, situated and value-laden. It sought to legitimate itself by defining its object ('race') as 'the nature' that must be understood in order to be controlled. In the early to mid nineteenth century, one of the major debates in science was whether or not the different races constituted one species (monogenists) or different species (polygenists) (Young, 1995, p. 10). In a debate that pre-dated the contribution of Charles Darwin, scientists examined the bodies of men and women from colonized countries to 'look' for evidence of difference and similarity, that is, to look for evidence to support monogenetic and polygenetic arguments. They would seek to establish the 'truth' of human variation using the bodies of indigenous men and women from the colonies, in particular, from Africa and Australia.

The bodies of others hence became the means by which scientists attempted to mark out the difference and superiority of 'the white race'. Or, more precisely, by defining what was other (perverse, abnormal, unnatural and so on), scientific discourse sought to constitute what was normal and ideal. Rather than *finding* evidence of racial difference, science was actually *constructing* or even inventing the very idea of race itself as bodily difference and bodily hierarchy. Indeed, one of the main scientific theories of the early nineteenth century – phrenology and craniology – assumed that racial difference and hierarchy was a result of difference in the size of skulls. As Nancy Stephan argued, 'The importance of the skull to students of human difference lay in the fact that it housed the brain, differences in whose shape and size were presumed to correlate with equally presumed difference in intelligence and social behaviour' (1993, p. 363). The size and shape of the skulls of Negroes were seen to be closer to apes than they were to the white man's: through 'seeing' the black race as closer to apes, the scientific discourses of the time were able to construct Blackness as more primitive, or less evolved (Haraway, 1989).

With Darwinism, the search for the 'truth' about the human body proceeded through the invention of racial difference as *racial type* (Young, 1995, p. 13). Following from the work of scientists before him, such as Knox, Nott and Gliddon and Agassiz, Darwin differentiated between racial types, which were seen as different stages in human evolution. Conceiving human history as 'the survival of the fittest', Darwinism saw the advancement of the white races as a consequence of their fitness: 'When civilized nations come into contact with barbarians the struggle is short' (Darwin 1871, p. 178). Through observing 'the natives' on imperial expeditions, Darwin saw the degeneration or decline of native populations as a sign of their inherent lack of fitness. Indeed, rather than seeing their low tolerance of the diseases that were imported from Europe and elsewhere as a consequence of the colonizing process, he saw such low tolerance as a confirmation of primitiveness and the inevitability of the extinction of indigenous peoples through the natural process of selection. Darwin suggests that even when 'the natives were well treated', they suffered greatly in health (Darwin, 1871, p. 179). In this way, the consequences of the violence of colonialism become readable as the consequences of nature, while nature is represented through the differentiation between bodily types. Not only is racial difference seen as the product of a difference in bodily type, but 'bodily type' becomes a means of establishing 'race' itself as 'group', in which the different groups are separated by time (evolution) as well as space. In other words, humans become 'grouped' together, and apart from other humans, through the invention of race itself.

Scientific thinking throughout the nineteenth century involved the setting up of deviations from the white male body, which is taken as the somatic ideal and norm. Given this, scientific discourses operated through a set of analogies between different others (Stephan, 1993). Women and 'the lower races' were seen to be alike in their bodily difference from white men: an analogy which allowed women as a group to be racialized, and 'the lower races' as a group to be feminized. By the 1850s, the measurement of women's skulls was also becoming an established part of craniology. For example, the data in Vogt's *Lectures on Man* attempted to show how women's smaller brains were analogous to 'the lower races' (Stephan, 1993, p. 367). As Nancy Stephan has argued, the reliance on analogies shows how scientific discourses *constructed* race and gender, by seeking to establish similarities between the bodies of those who were seen as other to, and less than, the white male body. In such a narrative, the black woman would be seen as having the most primitive of bodily forms.

We can examine the role of gender in the construction of an opposition and hierarchy between white and black bodies in the following image (Figure 1). Here, we have a representation of a white male scientist examining the body of a Black woman through a telescope. The black female body is the object of a gaze. Her body is scrutinized, and becomes the means by which science accumulates knowledge. The image works through a series of binary oppositions. He comes to 'stand for' whiteness, masculinity and rationality by being defined in opposition to her: she comes to 'stand for' Blackness, nature and the body. Indeed, the image positions a dog alongside the white male subject. The implication of this astonishing juxtaposition is that even the dog can be domesticated and brought into the realm of culture. The dog shares the white male subject's gaze and, in so doing, the black woman comes to embody *that which cannot be brought into the realm of culture.*

Importantly, the white male subject sees the black woman's body through the telescope: it is available to him as an image. It is technology that *mediates* what he can see, allowing him to see her more closely without getting physically closer to her. The relationship of knowledge and looking in the image make the black female body into an object of his gaze, but it does so in a way which frames that object, making it appear *as body part.* We can note the violence of this 'dissecting' gaze by contextualizing the image. The image is a German caricature of Sarah Bartmann, otherwise known as 'the Hottentot Venus'. Sarah Bartmann was exhibited around Europe in 1810. Scientists were

Figure 1 'The Hottentot Venus', popular engraving c. 1850

fascinated by what they saw as her primitive genitalia, although the public display emphasized her buttocks (Gilman, 1986, p. 235). In the image, we see the white scientist looking at the black woman: we see that all he can see is her buttocks. As Sander Gilman has argued, there is a long history of 'seeing' the buttocks as the site of sexuality and sexual deviance (1986, p. 238). Not only is the black woman associated with her body, but that body becomes seen as hypersexual and deviant. The violence of the scientific gaze, and of the reduction of the Black female body to body parts, is made clear when we consider the 'fate' of Sarah Bartmann. Upon her death, her body was dissected and her genitalia and buttocks became items in a museum display: indeed, they remain on display in the Musée de l'homme in Paris (Gilman, 1986, p. 235). In life and in death, Black women's bodies were appropriated and dissected as sexualized 'objects'.

This images demonstrates how the other – in this case, the black woman – becomes associated with the body, but a body that is 'grotesque', to use Bakhtin's (1984) term. As Stallybrass and White argue, the grotesque body is:

> multiple, bulging, over- or undersized and incomplete. The openings and closures of this carnival body are emphasized, not its closure and finish. It is an image of impure corporeal bulk with its orifices (mouth, flared nostrils, anus) yawning wide and its lower regions (belly, legs, feet, buttocks and genitals) given priority over its upper regions (head, 'spirit' reason) (1986, p. 9).

The grotesque body is an open body, which is excessive, and which leaks from its orifices. A grotesque body can be seen as both sexualized and primitive. By the projection of sexuality onto her body in this image, the white masculine body becomes elevated; it is closed or classical (Bakhtin, 1984, p. 320). In other words, through the reduction of the black woman to body, the white male body becomes a somatic norm only insofar as he ceases to be body, becoming instead simply the place from which he thinks and knows *through* her. It is not simply that the Black woman's body becomes an object of knowledge: rather, she becomes seen *as body*, and as a body that is excessive, sexualized and primitive.

We can also consider how the sexualizing of black women's bodies takes place in relation to the construction of white women's bodies. As I have already argued, in nineteenth-century scientific discourses, white women were considered less evolved than white men, and evolution was traced in their bodily difference to white men, and similarity to 'the lower races'. However, as Diane Roberts has argued, white women, although they were also associated with bodies in this way, were seen as having a very different relationship to their bodies than Black women in the Victorian era: 'White women were not so much physically brutalized as hemmed in by rules of "virtue", "chastity" and "modesty"' (1994, p. 11). The absence of the white woman's body from this image is hence symptomatic. Although she is, as woman, associated with her bodily limits, she is also, as member of 'the higher race', considered to be able to transcend the bestiality and sexuality of the body (if she is 'hemmed in' or protected from others). In this way, the projection of sexuality onto the figure of the black woman allows white women's bodies to be represented, in their absence, as pure, as well as policed or 'protected' from the sexuality of others.

The scientific knowledges of the mid to late nineteenth century – although they were diverse and often in conflict – were based around the normalization of the white male body and the pathologizing of difference (McClintock, 1995). Difference from this body was not only consigned to pre-history, but was also seen as linked to disease, dirt and indeed to all that threatened the moral survival of empire and nation. The association of black bodies with disease was crucial in the policing of the boundaries of white bodies as well as white spaces. Indeed, other bodies including Irish bodies, and the bodies of prostitutes, lesbians and the working classes were also seen to be diseased and a potential source of contamination (Gilman, 1986). A link was established between disease and sexuality (a link which has a contemporary manifestation in discourses around AIDS), and bodies that were marked as other were seen as both diseased and sexualized. As Lola Young points out, 'through this link of the pathological and the sexual, black African women in particular, came to stand for both excessive sexuality and corruption and agents of racial decay' (1996, p. 51).

It is not enough to argue that race is constructed in the nineteenth century through the association of whiteness with cleanliness, purity, advancement, reason and Blackness with dirt, disease, primitiveness and bodies. We also need to investigate how these discursive constructions *legitimated* the colonial project (for example, in Darwinism, which argued that the 'lower races' were already dying out). Indeed, one of the ways in which they legitimated colonialism was by re-defining the colonial project as a mission, as a moral project of 'cleaning' or 'civilizing' the (dirty/impure) other who becomes, in the colonial imaginary, almost the same/white, but not quite (Bhabha, 1994). The construction of white and black bodies was crucial to the discursive transformation of the imperial project from one of violent appropriation, to a natural process, and then to a moral imperative. So while the White and Black bodies were constructed through 'the incitement to discourse', these constructions had material effects, and the effects were violent.

Lived experiences of racism

In the previous section, I argued that 'racial bodies' are discursively constructed: race is an effect of a process of racialization rather than its origin or cause. However, while it is important to trace such a history, it is also important to think of how that history impacts on bodies that are lived, and that themselves, materialize through 'assuming' racial categories or norms. So, for example, if Blackness is pathologized, what does it mean to inhabit a body that is seen as black? How does the pathologizing of difference and sexuality affect the way different bodies inhabit the nation? In posing such questions, I am trying to bring together a Foucauldian emphasis on 'the incitement to discourse' with a phenomenological emphasis on lived experiences of dwelling with other bodies, and a psychoanalytical concern with intra- and inter-psychic economies of desire and repulsion. To this extent, my argument is informed by the approach to inter-embodiment or inter-corporeality advanced by Maurice Merleau-Ponty (1968) (see Weiss, 1999), although my work provides an implicit critique of the anonymity and undifferentiated approach to 'our body' offered by this writer (see Ahmed, 2000, chapter 2). My work is in explicit dialogue with the work of an Algerian psychoanalyst, Frantz Fanon. Although I do not have space here to investigate fully the problems with employing psychoanalysis to discuss racism and racialization, one key problem is the very use of a theory of sexuality and sexual differentiation to frame an analysis of race, since such an approach tends to position race as secondary and derivative of the process of sexualization itself (McClintock, 1995). At the same time, psychoanalysis is useful because of its very emphasis on sexuality, the unconscious and the body as the site of pleasures and pains that are tied up with the 'future' of the subject (see Ahmed, 1998 and Young, 1996 for a further discussion of the relationship between psychoanalysis and race).

It is not sufficient to argue that everyday encounters between others are determined by the categories that are already in place in the dissemination of both scientific and commodity racism. The 'incitement to discourse' and the materialization of bodies in the world are both processes: they hence involve the negotiation, and re-negotiation of categories and norms that are never fully fixed in place, though at times it may feel as if they are (and the fact that it may feel this way is important, and the conditions of possibility for this need to be investigated). While 'knowledges' of race are clearly always contested, and while the ways in which we encounter others as raced are never fully determined, our task is also to see the relationship between knowledge, and ways of inhabiting bodies and spaces, as *a failed translation*: there is always a gap, to be filled as it were, between how we construct the racial body, and how it is lived.

I want to begin here with an encounter described by Frantz Fanon, whose work is informed by both existential phenomenology and psychoanalysis:

> Look, a Negro! ... Where shall I hide? 'Look at the nigger! ... Mama, a Negro! ... Hell he's getting mad ... Take no notice, sir, he does not know that you are as civilized as we. ... My body was given back to me sprawled out, distorted, recolored, clad in mourning in that white winter day. The Negro is an animal, the Negro is bad, the Negro is mean, the Negro is ugly; look, a nigger, it's cold, the nigger is shivering because he is cold, the little boy is trembling because he is afraid of the nigger, the nigger is shivering with cold, that cold that goes through your bones, the handsome little boy is trembling because he thinks that the nigger is quivering with rage, the little boy throws himself into his mother's arms: Mama, the nigger's going to eat me up (Fanon, 1986, pp. 113–14).

Fanon's work emphasizes how various racist stereotypes are exercized in the everyday encounters of public life. Erving Goffman describes 'public life' as the realm of activity generated by face-to-face interactions that are organized by norms of co-mingling (1972, p. ix). For Fanon, it is in such face-to-face encounters that bodies become racialized. In this encounter, the little white boy 'knows' about the black man: these knowledges are repeated in the very physicality of his response to the black body (or he constructs that body as black in the physicality of his response). I will investigate later the significance of such encounters for the reorganization of social and bodily space. What I want to emphasize here is the importance of the visual in the encounter. The black body is 'seen' in a 'hate stare'; it is caught by the gaze. It is the seeing of the body that transforms it into both an object and other: 'and already I am being dissected under white eyes, the only real eyes. I am *fixed*' (Fanon, 1986, p. 116). We can recall the caricature of Sarah Bartmann discussed in the previous section. Here, the black female body is dissected under the scientific gaze. The relationship between knowing and looking is crucial: it is by 'seeing' bodily others, that they are 'known', and this knowledge serves to constitute the subject (in this case the white subject) as *the one who knows*.

As Fanon's example shows, the 'knowledges' that are established in the violence of the white gaze – 'The Negro is an animal, the Negro is bad, the Negro is mean' (1986, p. 113) – affect how both white and black bodies are inhabited. The life of such racial categories is in this way a *bodily life*. So the little white boy in seeing a black male body (and in recognizing that body as a black body) is afraid. His response to the black body is both physical (he recoils) and emotional. But it is not just the white body that is, if you like, reorganized by the encounter. The black body is shivering; it is afraid. The fear that is expressed in the shivering of the body is misrecognized by the white child as a sign of its rage. The failure to see the black subject in the seeing of the black body is important: the white can only reorganize itself, move away from the black body, through such a failure. In other words, in seeing the bodies of others, we are always engaged in practices of both recognition and *reading* that fail to grasp the other. The perception of others as 'the black other' involves wrapping the bodies of others in fantasy. Indeed, the monstrous black body is represented here precisely as a white fantasy, or as a fantasy that works to constitute whiteness in the first place.

Importantly, Fanon allows us not only to think of how racial stereotypes both affect and are affected by the everyday encounters we have with others, but also how racialization involves both intra- and interpsychic processes: others become racialized through economies of desire and repulsion. The relation to others is one of ambivalence: precisely because 'the other' is required in the constitution of the subject in the first place. So the little white boy is both fascinated by the black body – he can't help but see it, to talk of it – and yet he is also repelled by the body. Similarly, in the caricature of Sarah Bartmann, the scientist is fascinated by the Black female body, at the same time as her body is represented as grotesque (as repulsive). The sexualization of the racial other is crucial to this ambivalence.

It is the construction of the apartness of the white body that seems to be at stake in both encounters: the black body needs to be seen as other, in order for the white body to define itself as 'apart' from the world of other bodies. We could read such encounters between the white and black body using a psychoanalytic model of projection. Laplanche and Pontalis provide a useful definition of projection:

> Projection emerges ... as the primal means of defence against those endogenous excitations whose intensity makes them too unpleasurable: the subject projects these outside so as to be able to flee from them (e.g. phobic avoidance) and protect himself from them ... the subject now finds himself obliged to believe completely in something that is henceforth subject to the laws of external reality (1988, p. 352).

In other words, projection becomes a means of establishing a boundary line between inside and outside, through pushing out all that is undesirable from the self, and transforming the outside into an other or an object. One way of reading everyday encounters of racism, would be to see that the black body is such a fantastic projection: all that is undesirable (including sexuality) is projected onto the black body (or the 'objectness' of that body is itself an effect of projection) in order for white subjecthood to be granted. Returning to the image of Sarah Bartmann, the white masculine subject's self-representation as culture/reason/mind requires the Black woman to become all that he is not: to stand as other before him. In other words, it is by projecting all that is dangerous onto her figure that he can come to inhabit the body that he does.

It is certainly important to think of racialization as a process that involve bodies, and with it, the sensual, emotional registers that we often describe as belonging to 'the psyche'. My analysis suggests an intimate relationship between the psychic and bodily dimensions of racialization and the organization of social life and relationships of power. One of the problems with using psychoanalysis to discuss lived experiences of racism is its tendency to take the psychic dimension for granted as an object of study. To discuss forms of racialization, the psychic dimension must be seen as contingent on specific histories of othering. We need to understand how it is, for example, that some bodies are seen as more dangerous and threatening than other bodies.

Bodily space and social space

In order to investigate further how racialization involves 'seeing' and 'feeling' of black bodies as more dangerous than others, and how this perception is a mechanism for reordering both bodily and social space, I will discuss an encounter from Audre Lorde's *Sister Outsider*:

> The AA subway train to Harlem. I clutch my mother's sleeve, her arms full of shopping bags, christmas-heavy. The wet smell of winter clothes, the train's lurching. My mother spots an almost seat, pushes my little snow-suited body down. On one side of me a man reading a paper. On the other, a woman in a fur hat staring at me. Her mouth twitches as she stares and then her gaze drops down, pulling mine with it. Her leather-gloved hand plucks at the line where my new blue snowpants and her sleek fur coat meet. She jerks her coat close to her. I look. I do not see whatever terrible thing she is seeing on the seat between us – probably a roach. But she has communicated her horror to me. It must be something very bad from the way she's looking, so I pull my snowsuit closer to me away from it, too. When I look up the woman is still staring at me, her nose holes and eyes huge. And suddenly I realize there is nothing crawling up the seat between us; it is me she doesn't want her coat to touch. The fur brushes past my

face as she stands with a shudder and holds on to a strap in the speeding train. Born and bred a New York City child, I quickly slide over to make room for my mother to sit down. No word has been spoken. I'm afraid to say anything to my mother because I don't know what I have done. I look at the side of my snow pants, secretly. Is there something on them? Something's going on here I do not understand, but I will never forget it. Her eyes. The flared nostrils. The hate (Lorde, 1984, pp. 147–8).

In the above encounter, recalled as memory, Audre Lorde ends with 'the hate'. It is an encounter in which something has passed, but something she fails to understand. The sense that some-thing is wrong is communicated, not through words, but through the body of another, 'her nose holes and eyes huge'. What is the woman's body saying? How do we read her body? The woman's bodily gestures express her hate, her fear, her disgust. The encounter is played out *on* the body, and is played out *with* the emotions.

The encounter, while ending with 'the hate', also ends with the reconstitution of bodily space. The bodies that come together, that almost touch and co-mingle, slide away from each other, becoming relived in their apartness. The particular bodies which move apart allow the redefinition of social as well as bodily integrity: black bodies are expelled from the white social body despite the threat of further discomfort (the woman now must stand in order that she can keep her place, that is, in order to keep Audre at a distance). The emotion of 'hate' aligns the particular white body with the bodily form of the white community – such an emotion functions to substantiate the threat of invasion and contamination in the black body. The gestures that allow the white body to withdraw from the black body hence reduce that body to dirt, to 'matter out of place' (Douglas, 1996, p. 36), such that the black body becomes recognized *as the body out of place*. What is interesting here is how the encounter involves, not just reading the black body, but defining the contours or boundaries of the white body. The white body becomes the body-at-home, through the very gestures that enable a withdrawal from the black body's co-presence in a given social space.

Does Audre's narrative of the encounter involve her self-designation as the body out of place? Certainly, her perception of the cause of the woman's bodily gestures is a misperception that creates an object. The object – the roach – comes to stand for, or stand in for, the cause of 'the hate'. The roach crawls up between them; the roach, as the carrier of dirt, is that which divides the two bodies, forcing them to move apart. Hence, Audre pulls her snowsuit, 'away from it too'. But the 'it' that divides them is not the roach; Audre comes to realize that 'it is me she doesn't want her coat to touch'. What the woman's clothes must not touch, is not a roach that crawls between them, but Audre herself. Audre becomes the 'it' that stands between the possibility of their clothes touching; she becomes the roach – the impossible and phobic object – that threatens to crawl from one to the other: 'I don't know what I have done. I look at the side of my snow pants secretly. Is there something on them?' Here, the lived experience of inhabiting the black body hesitates on the question, 'am I the roach?' or, 'am I the dirt which forces me away?'

An analysis of lived experiences of racism suggests that the marking out of the boundary lines between bodies involves social practices and techniques of differentiation. That is, bodies become differentiated not only *from each other* or *the other*, but also through differentiating *between* others, who have a different function in establishing the permeability of bodily space. Crucially, in such bodily encounters, others are differentiated as familiar (safe, touchable) or strange (dangerous, untouchable). In the encounters discussed in this chapter, the white body does constitute itself (as apart) through differentiating itself *from* the black body – a differentiation which is spatially organized (the white body moves away from the black body). However, the process of othering is more complex than this. In racist encounters, the white subject also aligns itself with other white bodies, as closer to them, and against other black bodies, as further away from them. Indeed, different bodies come to be lived through the very habits and gestures of marking out bodily space, that is, through the differentiation of 'others' into familiar (assimilable, touchable) and strange (unassimilable, untouchable).

Returning to the encounter offered in *Sister Outsider*, we can consider how the white woman's refusal to touch the Black child does not simply stand for the expulsion of Blackness from white social space, but actually *reconstitutes social space through the reconstitution of the apartness of the white body*. The reconstitution of bodily and social space involves a process of making the skin crawl; the threat posed by black bodies to bodily and social integrity is registered on white skin. But the black body cannot be reified as the untouchable. Although the white woman refuses to touch Audre's clothes, she is still touched by Audre; her bodily gestures express precisely the horror of being touched. In other words, to withdraw from a relation of physical proximity to black bodies is still to be touched by those bodies, in such a way that the white subject is moved from its place.

As bodies move towards and away from each other, in relationships of proximity and distance, both bodily space (the shape of the skin) and social space (the skin of the community) expand and contract. The bodily encounters we have with others who are assimilable (close) and unassimilable (distant) involve the re-forming of both bodily and social space. One could argue that racialization takes place through spatial and tactile negotiations; through different ways of touching and being touched by others, and different ways of inhabiting space with others, boundaries are established between bodies. Crucially, as my reading of the encounter in *Sister Outsider* suggests, such boundaries also work to align some bodies with the body of the nation, or the body of the community. What is at stake in the racialization of bodies, then, is not simply the reading of the black body as dirt and filth, but the re-forming of the contours of the white body, through the very affective gestures that enable withdrawal from the black body's cohabitation in a given social space.

Conclusion

I have, in this chapter, attempted to think through how the 'knowledges' of race that legitimated colonialism, through re-imagining the violence of appropriation as a moral imperative, served to produce white and black bodies in relationship to each other. Such a relationship crucially involves differentiation, although it is not a matter of finding difference *on* the body. Rather, differences are established in the very marking out of boundaries between bodies, by the very ways in which bodies inhabit the world differently, or are touched by some others differently than other others. In making this claim, I have examined a few encounters, which we can describe as racist encounters, as represented in the work of Frantz Fanon and Audre Lorde. It is important to register that my argument has moved from such 'local' instances, and indeed local instances that are also textual, which are available only in the mediated form of writing, to more general claims.

Given this, we must register also that racialization does not always take the form discussed in this chapter. While racialization is always about differentiating between bodies that inhabit the world together, it does not only operate through the production of the black body as the body that must be kept at a distance. Other bodily encounters might involve the desire to get closer to black others, who have also been seen, throughout the history of empire, as exotic and desirable and not just grotesque. For example, bell hooks (1992) has examined the desire to 'eat the other' partly by having relationships of intimacy with racial others. Crucially, then, racialization does not have one

spatial logic, or indeed, one body, although it is always both spatial-
ized and embodied. Returning to my analysis in section two, the
relationship between white and black bodies (bodies, that is, that are
constructed and lived *as* white and black bodies) has always been one
of ambivalence. So, for example, it is not just about whether black
bodies are represented as desirable or repulsive: what is at issue is
how black bodies become 'seen' as other, as marked by their difference from the white subject.

Reflecting on the spatiality of bodies, on bodies that are involved
in networks of 'here' and 'there', and in relationships of proximity
and distance, is crucial to any investigation of differences that matter
such as race. It is through *how* some bodies dwell with others, in acts
of getting closer to, or moving apart from other others, that bodies
are lived as racial bodies. In each moment of recognition, when we
see others as *having* a racial identity (although it is always possible that
we cannot tell the difference), we are opening up a history of racialization, and becoming part of that history. Whether we move away or
get closer, our little acts of reading the bodies of others as racialized
have a debt to this history, even if we don't wish to be indebted. The
history of racialization is precisely a history of different bodies who
inhabit the world differently and who, whether or not they say 'yes' or
'no' to racism, cannot forget its violence. Our bodies remember this
history for us, even when we are unaware of it. Our bodies remember,
as we shiver, as we tremble, as we shake. My body, given back to me
(Fanon, 1986, p. 113), is never alone in its fright.

Further reading

Ahmed, Sara, *Strange Encounters: Embodied Others in Post-Coloniality* (London:
    Routledge, 2000).
        This book uses feminist and post-colonial theory to argue that the racial-
    ization of bodies takes place through differentiating between bodily others
    on the grounds of familiarity and strangeness.
Fanon, Frantz, *Black Skin, White Masks* (London: Pluto Press, 1986).
        A classic psychoanalytical account of how racism operates through fixing
    the Black body as an object of the gaze.
McClintock, Anne, *Imperial Leather: Race, Gender and Sexuality in the Colonial
    Context* (London: Routledge, 1995).
        Using both Marxist and psychoanalytic approaches, this is an excellent
    historical account of the way in which the gendering and sexualizing of
    white and black bodies was crucial to the colonial project.

Mohanram, Radhika, *Black Body: Women, Colonialism, Space* (St Leonards, NSW: Allen and Unwin, 1999).

A clear and introductory account of racial embodiment, which both theorizes Black embodiment in relationship to landscape and space, and offers close readings of particular texts from Australia and New Zealand.

Roberts, Diane, *The Myth of Aunt Jemina: Representations of Race and Religion* (London: Routledge, 1994).

This book specifically examines the relationship between white and black embodiment in an American context, using Bakhtin's distinction between the classical and grotesque body.

5

The 'Disabled' Body

Carol Thomas

The wheelchair, the white cane and the crutch signal bodies that do not work in 'normal' ways, bodies that we commonly refer to as being 'disabled'. If we have missing limbs, debilitating chronic diseases, or cannot see or hear, then we can expect to be grouped with others whose bodies and bodily behaviours are seen to vary from the usual in problematic ways – then we belong to the ranks of 'the disabled'. Cultural reactions to bodies that have something permanently 'wrong' with them range from disgust and abhorrence to heartfelt pity – 'what a tragedy'. Medical responses are to try to 'fix' the bodily deviation, to create or restore normality, and to prevent the births of 'deformed' or otherwise 'defective' fetuses (J. Morris, 1991; Shakespeare, 1999). This medical agenda has been hugely boosted by recent developments in genetic science which, at least in popular media representation, promises to rid human beings of much the burden of disease and disfigurement (Shakespeare, 1999). Thus, disability seems to be all about real bodies that are physically, sensory or intellectually different in undesirable ways. What could remind us more forcibly of the 'real' nature of bodies if not a missing leg or the inability to make the sounds that we call speech? In dialogue with these apparent certainties, this chapter sets out to show that this is terrain where the fixities about bodies, and the meanings invested in bodily differences, can be as thoroughly questioned and found wanting as they can in discussions about gender or 'race', as outlined in previous chapters. However, in exploring this I resist the contemporary pull to dismiss the material reality of bodies and bodily differences.

The chapter is structured as follows. First, it reviews the iconoclastic ideas about disability that have been generated by the politicization of disabled people themselves in the last three decades. Second, some of the current debates about disability and impairment within the disabled people's movement and its academic wing, Disability Studies, will be discussed. Finally, linkages will be made between this domain of debate and some of the themes in the wider sociological literature on the body.

Separating the body from disability

In the 1970s, in Britain and elsewhere, there were signs that disabled people were no longer willing to accept their lot as supposedly helpless objects of pity who should be provided for mainly through institutionalized residential care and segregated 'special' schools (Campbell and Oliver, 1996; Thomas, 1999). Groups of disabled people in residential settings began to organize their resistance to what they named their *social oppression*. The idea began to take hold that people with impairments were subject to socially oppressive practices and exclusions in every domain of social life. The disabled people's movement thus emerged in Britain, in parallel with developments in other countries. The history of this movement is too rich to summarize here (see Campbell, and Oliver, 1996), but its central idea – known as the *social model of disability* – needs to be discussed.

The social model of disability proposes that the relatively non-impaired majority socially oppress people with marked physical, sensory or intellectual impairments. This oppression manifests itself as *disablism*, most sharply expressed in the form of material and attitudinal 'social barriers' that prevent impaired people from playing a full role in society. There are social barriers preventing people with impairments from entering employment, travelling about freely, obtaining suitable housing, having a decent standard of living and education, or being able to access dimensions of cultural and political life (Thomas, 1999; Zarb, 1995). For example, buildings (shops, workplaces, entertainment venues) and transport systems are often inaccessible to wheelchair users and people with other types of impairment. Employers often actively discriminate against impaired people, effectively excluding them from employment or failing to consider them for promotion if they do have a paid job (Barnes, 1991). In the face of a myriad of social exclusions, disabled people have to find in themselves and in their allies the powers to resist this disablism.

Consider Lisa's personal account; her narrative is among those
discussed in my book *Female Forms: Experiencing and Understanding
Disability* (Thomas, 1999) (a full account of the methodology used to
obtain these personal narratives can be found in the book):

> *Lisa, a wheelchair user in her mid 20s.* (Extracts from her written account).
> When I first left the spinal [injury] unit at 19 years of age I had to rely very
> heavily on my family. At my parents' home there were no facilities for me
> (bathroom and toilet). So for several months I had a commode and bed
> baths in my Mum's front room. My Mum gave up work to look after me. It
> was hard on everyone. A year later I had a shower/toilet room built and
> the through lounge/dining room was finally blocked off to give me my
> privacy. I went to college for 2 years which helped me come to terms with
> my disability. The college I went to as a day student was for people with dis-
> abilities. A lot of the other students had more severe disabilities, which
> made me feel that I was lucky to be able to do as much as I could. When
> I first started college I needed help to go to the loo. When I left I was
> fiercely independent. The worst thing about those first few months at
> home was having to rely on everyone to drive me from A to B. Now seven
> years down the road, I have my own one bedroom adapted flat, about one
> and a half miles from my mother's house, handy for dropping off the
> washing. I work full-time at the [organisation of disabled people] … and
> I drive my own hand-controlled car. It's been a struggle to get completely
> independent but it's worth it, and I wouldn't give it up for anyone. Unless
> I meet the right partner, but he will have to be pretty special.
>   Having gone to college, when I left, I was well geared up for work.
> However finding a job was very difficult, access to the work place was the
> biggest problem. I remember being asked to go for an interview in an
> office that was two flights of stairs up and there was no lift. I telephoned to
> tell them that I used a wheelchair and could not manage any steps. They
> told me it would not be a problem, as they would arrange for someone to
> carry me up and down. Were they going to do this twice a day and when I
> went out for lunch? I think not! They got a nasty letter from me. As getting
> a job was so difficult I did voluntary work for about a year and through this
> I got offered a paid job. Unfortunately this lasted only about six months as
> the company went bankrupt. So I went back to voluntary work. Then I got
> a job selling wheelchairs. Now I've just got a new job for [an organisation
> of disabled people], which has a pretty good salary. It's hard to find work
> with a decent salary, as a disabled woman you're put at a disadvantage even
> before the interview. The answer is not to put disabled on the application
> form, unless you know being disabled is an advantage.

In this account we can see that Lisa's difficulties stem not from her
impairment per se but from the social reactions to her impairment.
Her parents' 'normal' house, built for 'normal' people, made life very

difficult for Lisa. A potential employer did not understand her needs as a wheelchair user, and was located in an inaccessible building. This illustrates the central idea of the social model of disability: it is not the body's impairment that causes the social exclusions and difficulties encountered. Rather, the disadvantaged position of the person with impairment is caused by the social response to the impaired body. Hence disability is seen to be a social product instead of an inevitable consequence of having an impairment. Impairment is causally unhooked from disability (Barton and Oliver, 1997; Oliver, 1996a; Thomas, 1999). This idea was most famously first expressed in the 1970s by an organization of disabled people, the Union of the Physically Impaired Against Segregation (UPIAS):

> *Impairment*: 'lacking all or part of a limb, or having a defective limb, organ or mechanism of the body'.
> *Disability*: 'the disadvantage or restriction of activity caused by a contemporary social organisation which takes no or little account of people who have physical impairments and thus excludes them from the mainstream of social activities' (UPIAS, adapted from Oliver 1996a, p. 22).

The UPIAS reference to the physically impaired in this statement was later revised by disabled people's organizations so that all types of impairment were included (Barnes, 1991).

This conceptual severing of impairment, of features of the body, from disability – now seen as a socially created phenomenon – directly challenges the pervasive medical view of disability. The medical model defines 'disability' as the social restrictions of activity that inevitably *result from* being impaired. This is codified in the World Health Organization's *International Classification of Impairments, Disabilities and Handicaps* (ICIDH, Wood, 1980; United Nations, 1983; see the discussion in Thomas, 1999). The ICIDH defines disability as follows: a disability is any restriction or lack, *resulting from impairment*, of ability to perform an activity in the manner or within the range considered normal for a human being. The social modellist stance also challenges the commonplace lay idea that someone's impairment *is* their disability ('her disability is that she can't hear'), and it undermines the 'personal tragedy' view of disability that was so often portrayed by charitable organizations in the past (and, to a lesser extent, still is).

These challenges have been of great personal and political significance for disabled people (Campbell and Oliver, 1996; J. Morris, 1991; Oliver, 1996a). Once introduced to the social model perspective, they find themselves able to throw off the idea that their impairments are the cause of the difficulties and disadvantages that they experience in social life: they can see the source of the problem as lying outside their bodies. The dominant individualized personal tragedy view of disability can be replaced with one that identifies the social barriers 'out there' that work to exclude and oppress. This is tremendously liberating for individual disabled people, as this author can personally testify. Collective political action to demand the removal of these barriers becomes a possibility, and became a reality from the 1970s. Not least, the organized pressure represented by the disabled people's movement in Britain has played a key role in bringing about the belated formal political recognition that disabled people are indeed a socially disadvantaged and discriminated against segment of society – in the shape of the *Disability Discrimination Act* (1995). It should be noted, however, that this Act is viewed as grossly inadequate by organizations of disabled people such as the British Council of Disabled People (Drake, 1999). The United States has long had more comprehensive anti-discrimination disability legislation.

Debates within Disability Studies: what about the body?

Given its political and personal significance, the social model of disability is fervently defended by Disability Studies writers against attack by outsiders such as medical sociologists (see the debates in Barnes and Mercer, 1996). However, in the last decade there has been heated discussion *within* Disability Studies and the disabled people's movement about some difficulties that the social model conceptualization and its practical application give rise to (Thomas, 1999). Some of these difficulties revolve around the dimensions of disability professedly excluded by a focus on the material, or structural, social barriers that prevent disabled people acting freely in the world (barriers in employment, transport systems and so forth). This focus is said to downplay the cultural and representational dimensions of disablism, that is, the ways in which language, discourses and cultural forms (like cinema and painting) work to construct negative meanings about people with impairment, undermining their status as fully human beings (Corker, 1998; Shakespeare, 1996, 1997). Another criticism made particularly by disabled feminists is that the writings of leading male social modellists like Mike Oliver (1990, 1996a) and Colin Barnes (1991) pay insufficient attention to *differences* among disabled people – differences associated with gender, 'race', sexuality, and so forth. The recognition that disablism is experienced differentially has led to calls for the interaction between different dimensions of social oppression to be more fully acknowledged and understood.

A third dimension of this critical engagement with the social model, and one that is of greatest relevance to the discussion here, relates to the severing of the medical model's causal link between impairment and disability: the conceptual move at the heart of the social model. In expressing this move, Oliver says 'disability is wholly and exclusively social ... disablement is nothing to do with the body' (1996b, pp. 41–2). The criticism that has been made by some disabled people, most notably by feminists such as Jenny Morris (1991, 1996), is that social modellists like Oliver have problematically ignored the significance of impairment – both conceptually and in terms of its impact on day-to-day life (see also French, 1993; Corker and French, 1999). Morris expressed the criticism as follows:

> there is a tendency within the social model of disability to deny the experience of our own bodies, insisting that our physical differences and restrictions are entirely socially created. While environmental barriers and social attitudes are a crucial part of our experience of disability – and do indeed disable us – to suggest that this is all there is is to deny the personal experience of physical or intellectual restrictions, of illness, of the fear of dying. A feminist perspective can redress this, and in doing so give a voice to the experience of both disabled men and disabled women (J. Morris, 1991, p. 10).

Morris and others have thus drawn attention back to 'real bodies', bodies that frequently experience real pain, nausea, fatigue and weakness. While staunch advocates of the social model for political purposes, feminists like Morris note that *some* of the restrictions of activity experienced by disabled people *are* directly attributable to the body and would not disappear with the removal of all disablist social barriers. They note that the lived experience of disability involves struggling with both social barriers and the effects of illness and other features of impairment. In the feminist tradition, they insist on the importance of personal experience as a starting point for theorizing and politics. The ensuing debate has been a markedly gendered one. Oliver (1996) and other male social modellists have replied that by giving prominence to features of bodily impairment and to personal experience, Morris and others give succour to the medical model approach – the approach that has played a key role in the oppression of disabled people in capitalist societies. Oliver argues that it is politically dangerous to divert attention away from the main goal: challenging the socio-structural social barriers 'out there' (Thomas, 1999).

These differences of opinion about the significance of the body and of bodily impairment continue to occupy writers in Disability Studies: the 'body question' will not easily go away. The political dangers of giving sustenance to oppressive medical model ideas, and thus to medical practices, are very real. And yet people with different forms of impairment often do face difficulties associated with what I have termed immediate 'impairment effects' (Thomas, 1999). Oliver (1996b) has conceded that perhaps there should be 'a social model of impairment' as well as, but separate from, the social model of disability. He suggests, though, that the efforts of Disability Studies researchers should be redirected away from any focus on impairment.

If we accept that the issue of impairment should be addressed, how can impairment and 'impaired bodies' be theorized? So far in this discussion I have made a distinction between 'impaired bodies' and 'normal' bodies, though taking care to make use of qualifying inverted commas. But what is the nature of this distinction? Can it be sustained? Postmodernist writers tell us that any categories distinguishing social types or groups are social constructions. They assert that these categories (for example, men/women, black/white) do not map onto fixed, essential, biological types of bodies but rather, through discursive representations, *constitute* these bodily types. Applied to the question of impairment, this suggests there is no biologically essential 'normal' or 'abnormal' body: these are actually social constructions.

Social constructionist perspectives have become increasingly influential within Disability Studies in recent years, and those drawing on them have challenged the Marxian/materialist perspectives of leading social modellists like Oliver. Oliver is accused not only of ignoring impairment and bodily experiences but also of buying into the modernist idea that bodies can be unproblematically divided into normal and impaired types. It is argued that while Oliver sees disability as socially created, impairment remains for him an essentially biological phenomenon. Hughes and Paterson express it as follows:

> there is a powerful convergence between biomedicine and the social model of disability with respect to the body. Both treat it as a pre-social, inert, physical object, as discrete, palpable and separate from the self. The definitional separation of impairment and disability which is now a semantic convention for the social model follows the traditional, Cartesian, western meta-narrative of human constitution (1997, p. 329).

A number of feminist writers have made similar points, drawing on postmodernist and poststructuralist perspectives to question the fixity of body types. For example, influenced by the work of Judith Butler (1993) in the deconstruction of 'sex' categories discussed in earlier chapters, Janet Price and Margrit Shildrick say:

> The postmodernist claim that there is no essential biologically given corpus upon which meaning is inscribed, and no unmediated access to a body prior to discourse, remains contentious. It is not that the materiality of the body is in doubt, but that materiality is a process negotiated through the discursive exercise of what Foucault (1980) calls power/knowledge. To both the biomedical profession with its fantasy of descriptive objectivity, and to the [disability rights movement] with its investment in the notion that impairment can be separated off from disability, the claim is anathema. While both may subscribe to the view that health care practices are both normative and normalizing, there is little recognition that those practices are also constitutive of the body. As Judith Butler puts it … 'there is no reference to a pure body which is not at the same time a further formation of that body' (1993, p. 10). What that means is that the physical impairments of the body, and the socially constructed disability are equally constructs held in place by regulatory practices that produce and govern all bodies (Price and Shildrick, 1998, p. 234).

So, for Price and Shildrick, powerful discourses in medicine and other regulatory domains invested with power work to represent, construct and position some people as 'impaired' or 'disabled' and others as 'normal'. In this view, there is nothing inherent, or pre-social, in individuals' bodily states that can sustain the idea of 'real' bodily differences (see also the work of Mairian Corker, 1998; Corker and French, 1999).

These social constructionist challenges show that 'the impaired body' is terrain where fixities and certainties about bodies can be strongly questioned. The point being made moves far beyond the more obvious observation that, because there are *degrees* of impairment among people, there is a grey area between 'normal' and 'impaired' bodily states inhabited by people with 'mild' impairments (for example, by those who wear glasses to correct a relatively minor visual impairment). Nor are fixities being questioned simply on the grounds that people move between these bodily categories (for example, from being 'normal' when they are young to being impaired in old age). A much stronger claim is involved. The suggestion is that people with an impairment are culturally constituted as such and do not have bodies that in some real sense are 'essentially' different. Their bodily differences are representations.

However, such full-blown social constructionist views do not sit easily with some writers in the disability field, including myself (Thomas, 1999). I have argued that the materiality of the body must be kept in view, and that in theorizing impairment there must be a place for the biological (Thomas, 1999). In analyzing her own experiences of living with the chronic fatigue syndrome, ME, the Canadian feminist philosopher, Susan Wendell thinks similarly:

> I want to distinguish [my] view from approaches to cultural construction of 'the body' that seem to confuse the lived reality of bodies with cultural discourse about and representations of bodies, or that deny or ignore bodily experience in favour of fascination with bodily representations ... I do not think my body is a cultural representation, although I recognize that my experience of it is both highly interpreted and very influenced by cultural (including medical) representations. Moreover, I think it would be cruel, as well as a distortion of people's lives, to erase or ignore the everyday, practical, experienced limitations of people's [impairments] simply because we recognize that human bodies and their varied conditions are both changeable and highly interpreted (Wendell, 1996, p. 44).

Thus Wendell's experience of her own body tells her that it has 'real' physical features that really do set it apart from other, usual, bodies. So, in an important sense there are essential, biologically based, differences between bodies. Nevertheless, she acknowledges that these essential differences are always overlaid by, and mediated through, meanings and cultural interpretations. Jenny Morris is more adamant about her 'difference' as a disabled woman:

> we are often physically different from what is considered the norm, the average person ... Our bodies generally look and behave differently from most other people's (even if we have an invisible physical [impairment] there is usually something about the way our bodies behave which gives our difference away). It is not normal to have difficulty walking or to be unable to walk; it is not normal to be unable to see, to hear; it is not normal to be incontinent, to have fits, to experience extreme tiredness, to be in constant pain; it is not normal to have a limb or limbs missing. If we have a learning disability the way we interact with others usually reveals our difference.
>
> These are the types of intellectual and physical characteristics which distinguish our experience from that of the majority of the population. They are all part of the human experience but they are not the norm: that is, most people at any point in time do not experience them, although many may experience them (J. Morris, 1991, p. 17).

In this way, Morris sees bodily differences as both 'real' and as something that should be celebrated rather than lamented: they are all part of human experience.

These differences in perspective among feminist writers in Disability Studies are important, not least because they are tied up with questions of self-identity and thus with the possibility of a collective identity for the purposes of political struggle. That is, the possibility of an identity politics – a disabled people's movement. The issue here is: are identities derived from having 'real' bodily differences associated with being impaired and being (socially) disabled, or, as postmodernists would have it, are identities always unstable and insecure because, lacking any real foundation, they have to be continuously reconstituted by being 'performed' (Thomas, 1999)? To put it another way, do I identify as a white disabled woman because I have an impairment, experience disablism, and am a woman (both in terms of biological sex and socially constructed gender) and was born with a white skin, *or* is my identity something that I internalize and 'perform' because powerful cultural discourses constitute and position me as a 'white disabled woman'? The first position suggests that identity is *categorical* – determined by categories with which people identify such as gender, 'race', sexuality, class, age, and bodily impairment/normality. In this view, expressed by Morris as follows, a collective identity (a sense of 'we') based on shared characteristics is possible:

> But we are different. We reject the meanings that the non-disabled world attaches to disability but we do not reject the differences that are such an important part of our identities.
> We can assert the importance of our experience for the whole of society, and insist on our rights to be integrated within our communities. However, it is important that we are explicit about the ways in which we are not like the non-disabled world. By claiming our own definitions of disability we can also take pride in our abnormality, our difference (J. Morris, 1991, pp. 16–17).

The second, postmodernist, formulation suggests that identity is a shifting phenomenon, something continuously reconstructed and 'performed', and that a collective identity is not a lasting possibility:

> If our self-identity is provisional and unstable, identity politics breaks down, for it is not possible to identify a fixed unifying factor, whether material or discursive, that brings such an apparently disparate group together within, for example, the disabled people's or the women's health movement (Price, 1996, p. 44).

These positions on the nature of impairment thus have contrasting implications for disabled people who self-identify as such and who want to struggle with people 'like them' against their oppression.

This debate about whether impairment concerns essential, biologically based differences between bodies *or* whether it should be seen
in terms of culturally constructed differences without any real biological foundation will no doubt go on. It can be referred to as the
'essentialist versus constructionist' debate about the impaired body
(Fuss, 1990), and I will return to it in the next section. Before doing
so, however, it is useful to introduce a different and important way of
thinking about the social construction of impairment. This relates to
the work of Paul Abberley (1987, 1996), a Disability Studies writer
who has also taken issue with the tendency among leading social
modellists to ignore the subject of impairment, effectively leaving it
in the realm of 'naturally occurring biological phenomena'. Unlike
postmodernist or poststructuralist social constructionists, however,
Abberley has drawn attention to the material *social production* of
impairment in society, and his position is illustrative of a materialist
approach to impairment.

Abberley points out that *social* processes and practices either directly
create impairment by damaging the body, or produce higher levels of
impairment in society by enabling people with previously unsustain-
able impairments to stay alive for longer. For example: wars and ter-
rorist activities across the globe produce millions of impaired bodies;
individual acts of violence such as rape can cause lasting physical damage to bodies; hazardous workplaces can generate diseases amongst
exposed workers; the social activity of smoking tobacco produces lung
and circulatory diseases; advances in medical science – a social phenomenon – enables growing numbers of people with impairments to
have a greater life expectancy. These few examples suggest that impairment is created at the biological-social interface in particular historical
contexts, and is, in an important sense, socially produced. Abberley's
perspective rests on the idea that bodies are real material phenomena
that are literally moulded by the interaction of biological and social
processes.

Interestingly, a similar perspective on the social determinants of
disease and impairment is found in the sociological and social epi-
demiological literature on inequalities in health (Bartley et al., 1998;
Blane et al., 1996; Graham, 2000). However, this literature exists on a
parallel track – few have made connections between the debates
about the social production of impairment in Disability Studies and
debates about the social determination of health in the health
inequalities field (Thomas, 1999). In both fields, our attention is
drawn to the ways in which our flesh, bone, and embodied emotions

are subject to innumerable social forces operating in spatial and environmental contexts, some of which produce the effects that we know as impairment.

The sociology of the body: can it help us to understand the impaired body?

This book engages with the literatures in sociology and feminism on the nature of the body and embodiment. Can these wider literatures assist Disability Studies writers in their own debate about the impaired body? In my view the answer is, unfortunately, 'not much' because of the dominant social constructionist character of much of this work. In the 'essentialist versus constructionist' debate, the constructionists dominate and the 'reality' of bodies is generally denied. However, there are signs that real bodies are making something of a comeback. Of particular note is the work of Simon Williams and Gillian Bendelow in their book *The Lived Body* (1998). In their review and critique of the work on the sociology of the body, these authors reject the 'shifting sands' social constructionist project of reducing the body to a series of representations. At the same time they wish to retain some of the valuable insights that a constructionist perspective offers:

> In theorising the body, it is not, therefore, a question of choosing between order and control, materialism or constructionism, experience or representation, but of exploring their dialectical relationship to each other and the emergent properties contained therein (Williams and Bendelow, 1998, p. 8).

Among other things, what I find useful in Williams and Bendelow's approach is their recognition that the body is a bio-social material entity and that this has to be central to its theorization, without, however, lapsing into biological reductionism and naturalistic essentialism. Whilst they barely touch on matters of disability and impairment per se, these authors do attempt to bring 'real' biological bodies back into the sociological frame. As they put it: 'a certain bodily 'realism' is retained, thus puncturing the over-inflated claims of constructionists and their privileging of the 'social' (Williams and Bendelow, 1998, p. 208). They talk a great deal about the necessity of breaking down the dualisms that plague social theorizing in this area: biology/society, nature/culture, mind/body. They also argue that sociologists, as embodied subjects themselves, need to move from

the theorization 'of' the body (in which the body is objectified) to
an embodied sociology:

> theorising not so much *about* bodies (in a largely disembodied male way)
> but *from* bodies as *lived* entities, including those of its practitioners as well as
> its subjects. Social institutions and discursive practices cannot be under-
> stood apart from the real lived experiences and actions of embodied human
> beings across time and space. Social theory must therefore be rooted in the
> problems of human embodiment (Williams and Bendelow, 1998, p. 209).

It seems to me that disabled feminists are way ahead on this particular
point, as witnessed by the earlier quotation from Susan Wendell (1996,
p. 44) where she said: 'I do not think my body is a cultural representation'. As disabled feminists we are always aware of our materially
embodied status, although we may theorize this differently. It seems
that it is the academics who are not (yet) troubled with the realities of
living with significant impairment who have to remind themselves
about their own 'real' bodies and reflect, with curiosity, upon its
absence from their day-to-day consciousness.

In the difficult task of developing a sociology of impairment within
Disability Studies the work of Williams and Bendelow and of others
who seek to engage with the reality of biological bodies in socio-
cultural contexts will certainly to be of assistance. Impairment can be
seen to involve marked biological or physical differences, or variations,
between bodies. Somehow, bodies need to be theorized as, at the same
time, bio-socially produced and culturally constructed entities. Both
biological reductionism and cultural reductionism need to be avoided.
Significant impairments need to be seen as real differences from the
'usual' body whilst simultaneously understood to be invested with
meanings or representations that construct these differences in the
socio-medical language of 'impairment', 'disfigurement', and so forth.
In addition, we need to work on an understanding of the way in which
the biological reality of bodies is shaped by, and impacts back upon,
social and environmental processes and practices: that is, on the ways
in which bodies are the effects of bio-social interaction. These are just
some possible pathways for theorizing the relative states of impaired
and non-impaired bodies.

Conclusion

This chapter has looked at the nature of the 'disabled' body. In the
first section we saw that the very idea of 'the disabled body' has been
rejected by the disabled people's movement with its social model

of disability. From a social model perspective the body itself is not disabled but impaired. The concept 'disability' is invested with an altogether different meaning: disability is the socially oppressive response of the non-impaired to the impaired in society. Disability becomes a form of social oppression and is a social relational phenomenon. The medical model view that impairment causes disability is thrown out.

I have noted the tremendous political and personal significance that this social modellist stance represents for disabled people; we are able to challenge the idea that the problems we face are the inevitable, 'tragic', consequences of having impaired bodies. On the other hand, this stance also appears to mean that we should ignore the sometimes difficult realities of living with impairment. In the chapter's second section I explored the debates that have emerged about this eclipsing of impairment. We have seen that disabled feminists have been at the forefront of bringing the body back in by drawing attention to impairment, so challenging the social modellist view that such matters can be analytically left aside. However, we have also seen that disabled feminists use contrasting theoretical perspectives in their analyses of impairment. An apparently 'essentialist versus constructionist' debate about the nature of impaired bodies is evident. My own difficulties with a fully socially constructionist position on the impaired body (or on any kind of body) have been stated.

In the final section of the chapter, attention was turned to the wider sociological literature on the sociology of the body. Does it help us develop a sociology of impairment? On the whole, the answer has to be 'not much' because of its largely social constructionist character denying the reality of bodies and bodily differences. However, the work of Simon Williams and Gillian Bendelow (1998) was cited approvingly because it challenges some of the problems with a constructionist analysis and attempts to bring in the biological without falling foul of biological reductionism. In my view, a sociology of impairment needs to be able to engage with the real materiality of bodies whilst at the same time understanding the ways in which bodies are simultaneously always interpreted. Those of us who live with marked impairments know that the body is 'real' however thoroughly it is culturally represented and positioned.

Further reading

Corker, Mairian, and Sally French (eds), *Disability Discourse* (Buckingham: Open University Press, 1999).

A valuable collection of essays on the theorization and lived experience of disability.

Morris, Jenny (ed.), *Encounters with Strangers: Feminism and Disability* (London: The Women's Press, 1996).

An important collection of papers on the need for a feminist engagement with disability questions.

Thomas, Carol, *Female Forms: Experiencing and Understanding Disability* (Buckingham: Open University Press, 1999).

This book examines key debates about disability and impairment from a feminist perspective, making use of disabled women's narrative accounts.

Susan, Wendell, *The Rejected Body, Feminist Philosophical Reflections on Disability* (London: Routledge, 1996).

This author explores key dimensions of knowledge about disability and disability experience.

6

The Body in Pain

David Morgan

Pain is an ubiquitous human experience. It is one of the most common reasons for seeking medical attention, accounting for approximately one quarter of general practice consultations and half of all outpatient attendances and hospital admissions in the UK (Royal College of Physicians, 1996). For some people, persistent pain is an unrelieved condition of daily life. Yet despite the prevalence of chronic and debilitating conditions, indices of social well-being seldom include pain as a factor affecting the quality of life. Pain is commonly seen as a symptom of other complaints rather than an adversity in itself. Although injury and disease can be detected by observation and clinical tests, pain is a peculiarly private experience that cannot be reduced to anything else; it cannot be x-rayed, or calibrated like blood pressure on a standardized scale, nor can we feel another's pain. Unlike most other states of consciousness, pain has no object or referential content: it is not of anything or for anything, nor can it be easily defined. We commonly resort to suggestive metaphors to describe what we feel in terms of something else – as a 'shooting', 'burning', 'throbbing', 'gnawing' sensation. Sometimes the sheer intensity of what we feel seems to defy language and we can only speak of 'excruciating', 'unbearable' or 'indescribable' pain. As David Morris remarks in his engaging study *The Culture of Pain*, 'Pain not only hurts but more often than not frustrates, baffles, and resists us. Yet it seems we cannot simply suffer pain but almost always are compelled to make sense of it' (Morris, 1991, p. 18).

The problem of making sense of pain has become a specialized domain of medical science. The tendency within medicine to treat pain, and more generally the body, as an objective, ordered, mappable process, contrasts with the chaotic subjective experience of pain which confounds coherent thought. However, medical interest in pain as an object of scientific inquiry is relatively recent. For a long time, pain was recognized simply as an indication of illness or injury; concern with the patient's experience of pain was at best secondary to medicine's more pressing engagement with disorders and disease. Although relief from pain and suffering was foremost for the patient, the doctor's gaze focused narrowly upon lesions and disease, often with little consideration for the patient's discomfort or well-being. Rey (1995) suggests this is indicative of a physician–patient relationship that has persisted over time. It arises, she believes, from medicine's overly optimistic faith in its technical achievements and an increasingly specialized approach to human dysfunctions. The downside has been a virtual neglect of human suffering, pointing, she says, to 'the absence of the patient as an independent subject' and 'the generalised negation of his opinion and his will' (Rey, 1995, p. 6).

But if the patient's experience of pain has been a minor consideration in the development of clinical medicine, advances in experimental physiology and biochemistry have made significant contributions to understanding the transmission and symptomatic control of pain (Wall, 1999). By focusing upon pain as a specific sensation, a complex circuitry of sensory nerve fibres, pain receptors, way stations and gate control mechanisms has gradually been unravelled to reveal an anatomical model of how we feel pain. This model, which is continually being refined and modified with advances in experimental and clinical research, provides the basis for modern aetiological theories and therapeutic strategies for the relief and clinical management of pain (Cambier, 1995; Wall, 1999). The intellectual significance of these achievements should not be underestimated, yet they point to a recurrent tension in the analytic study of pain between two limiting and divergent perspectives.

On the one hand, by treating pain as a specific physical sensation, experimental research has dissected the physiology of pain. Yet these complex processes arguably tell us little about the conscious experience of pain. To feel pain is not simply to be aware of a noxious sensation. We need to distinguish between having a body which reacts to painful stimuli, and being a body which responds to the significance of what is felt. This dynamic between the body's experience and our experience of the body suggests an interpretation of pain which goes beyond the perception of pain as a sensory event. Especially in the case of severe or persistent pain, anxiety, fear, anger, resentment affect the intensity of pain, relations with others and our perception of self. In Elaine Scarry's apt phrase, the 'sheer aversiveness' of pain can 'unmake our world' (Scarry, 1985, p. 52). From this point of view, pain can no more be reduced to a biological substrate of tissue pathology than the body can be constructed in language alone. We cannot be aware of pain without having a body, but to be unconscious of pain is a contradiction in terms.

The following discussion will consider the implications of these different perspectives both for the explanation and management of pain. I shall begin by briefly considering the assumptions underlying the prevailing biomedical model before turning to the medically anomalous experience of chronic pain. In the remainder of the chapter, I shall draw upon a number of studies which illustrate how the lived experience of pain calls for an understanding that brings together the biological, cultural and psychosocial dimensions of human affliction in our attempt both to manage and make sense of pain.

The legacy of Cartesian dualisms

As the introductory chapter pointed out, Cartesian dualism is a key theme in the sociology of the body, and is of central importance in relation to discussion of the body in pain. The premises of medico-scientific research into pain follow from Descarte's distinction between perceptions which 'relate to our body' and those which 'relate to our soul'. Of the former, Descartes wrote, 'the cognizings we refer to our body...are those we have of hunger, thirst and other natural appetites – to which may be added pain' (Descartes, 1953, p. 290). This categorical distinction between body and mind has continued to exercise a seminal influence on medical thinking (Kirmayer, 1988). Pain has been investigated as a specific bodily sensation, autonomous from the psyche and what Descartes described as 'objects external to us', including our relations with the social world. Within this closed and dualistic system, pain functions like a warning signal to tell us something is wrong. The problem that has exercised philosophers and medical scientists to this day is how this neural alarm system triggers the conscious and emotionally disturbing reactions we experience as pain.

Posing the problem in this way has led to a search for connecting links between physical processes and mental events. The idea that physical stimuli in some sense cause our experience of pain was aptly pictured by Descartes' 'delicate threads' that activate a conscious reaction like the pull of a rope on a bell. Nowadays, Descartes' imagery has been updated by a more intricate model of sensory signalling, but the structure of this explanation remains much the same. Accordingly, it is now widely held that when tissue is damaged – possibly by a cut or a sprain or a burn – a sensory stimulus is transmitted by peripheral nerve fibres through the spinal cord to the brain stem and to the higher centres of the brain where it is assumed signals are scanned, collated and amplified to give us the perception, recognition and reaction to pain. Experimental research into the finer mechanisms of these sensory processes has gradually led to a more sophisticated understanding of both the neurophysiology and biochemistry of pain which has recently begun to yield fascinating clues to the analgesic action of the brain itself (Wall, 1999, p. 55).

However, whilst the premises of this model continue to inform research and clinical practice, they reduce the experience of pain to what Vrancken (1989) describes as 'somatico-technical' processes which take little or no account of the affective and psychosocial dimensions of being in pain. Pain is not just a sensory signal – or even a reliable sensory signal – but a complex perception that is liable to vary with an individual's cognitive and emotional state. Melzack and Wall (1988) note that the conventional paradigm does not adequately account for the common observation that pain is not a single sensation but has many dimensions; moreover, the site of a pain is often removed from the location of the injury; its intensity may vary without apparent cause, and sometimes persistent pain may be experienced without evidence of tissue damage or other cause. Melzack and Wall argue these anatomical and psychological anomalies 'defy explanation in terms of a rigid, straight-through specific pain system' (1988, p. 156); rather it would appear transmission is modulated by the complex interaction of sensory, psychological and affective responses which influences the perception of pain. Melzack and Wall postulated a neural mechanism in the dorsal area of the spinal cord that 'acts like a gate which can increase or decrease the flow of nerve impulses into the central nervous system' (1988, p. 165). Moreover, they found that the operation of this control system is responsive to the descending influences of the brain: thus, cognitive, motivational and emotional states, such as, attention, anxiety, fear, anticipation or memory of past experiences, appear to modify sensory perceptions and hence the subject's reaction to pain.

One implication of the gate-control model seems to be that individuals exposed to the same painful stimulus are liable to perceive the experience in different ways, depending upon the personal, medical and cultural significance they attribute to the pain. For instance, Melzack and Wall observed that patients who believe abdominal pains are an early indication of stomach cancer are likely to report persistent and worsening discomfort, yet the pain may suddenly vanish when tests prove negative and their fears are allayed (1988, p. 21). In this way, the experience of pain appears to be affected by the meaning that individuals associate with it, including their present thoughts, fears and future hopes (1988, p. 32). Whilst Melzack and Wall's investigations are still firmly rooted within a neurophysiological model of pain, their observation of the interactions between sensory, affective and psychological processes challenge orthodox assumptions of a rigorous split between body and mind. Yet, ironically, it is consistent with Descartes' original – though less commonly cited axiom – that 'the soul is linked with every part of the body' and thus exerts a general influence over our perception of bodily states (Rey, 1995, pp. 73–80; Starobinski, 1989).

Chronic pain

The need for a perspective that brings together biological, psychological and social dimensions of pain is nowhere more evident than in the analysis and management of chronic pain. Unlike acute pain, chronic or persistent pain, though far from infrequent, is medically anomalous. Whilst acute pain is relatively short lived and can be effectively suppressed, chronic pain just doesn't go away. These persistent and seemingly intractable syndromes frequently lack a clearly identifiable physical cause. In the absence of a specific etiology, they are commonly attributed by default to a psychological origin and are thus likely to be treated as clinically 'insignificant' – if they are treated at all. What unites these chronic conditions is not the absence of 'genuine' illness but their resistance to medical intervention. Health practitioners and patients struggle with the pain, but more often than not the patient never seems to get well.

The prevalence of chronic pain in post-industrial societies appears to have reached epidemic proportions. It is estimated that nine per cent of the adult population in the United States suffers from 'moderate to very severe' persistent non-malignant pain. Over half (56 per cent) have reportedly suffered for more than five years, most commonly from headaches, pains in the neck and lower back, abdominal pains and painful joints (American Pain Society 1999). The estimated cost of treating lower back pain alone is believed to exceed $25 billion each year. Similar findings have been reported from Australia and Sweden (Blyth et al., 2001; Linton and Ryberg, 2000). The risks are not confined to those in manual occupations: repetitive strain injuries, migraine, backache, sports injuries and unremitting muscular pains afflict office workers, teachers and sales personnel as well. As David Morris remarks, 'chronic pain, mysterious, dull and nonfatal, might be called the defining illness of our low-profile, private, safe-sexed, self-absorbed era' (D. Morris, 1991, p. 66).

Yet chronic pain is widely acknowledged to be one of the most difficult and frustrating problems encountered in medical practice, not least because the pain may persist without a specific and agreed cause. This unequal challenge is frequently recognized by patients themselves, many of whom become resigned to the inability of modern medicine to diagnose and effectively treat their complaints (Bendelow, 1996). The American Pain Society survey revealed that 40 per cent of respondents reporting 'moderate to severe pain' had given up seeking medical advice within a year. Others shuttle from specialist to specialist in a continual round of hospital referrals. Most are dependent upon painkillers and suffer physical impairments, social isolation, anxieties and sleepless nights. For such patients, the persistence of unexplained pain, the reality of which is neither validated nor effectively alleviated by medical attention, constitutes a massive threat to self-esteem and the legitimacy of the everyday world. However, whilst patients are certain of their pain, its unyielding persistence is often for others a source of doubts.

The attribution of 'psychogenic' pain questions the physical nature of the patient's complaint. In the absence of an identifiable cause, it implies that the affliction is 'all in the mind', and further suggests that for some reason the patient wants or 'needs' to be in pain (Engel, 1959; Morris, 1998, p. 124). These assumptions are based upon the distinction between pain as a sensory process and the patient's emotional and behavioural response. Accordingly, therapy aims to change 'pain behaviours' – such as, taking painkillers and time off work – by removing the emotional and social gains which 'reward' the persistence of chronic pain (Tyrer, 1986). For example, a controversial International Association for the Study of Pain report recommends that workers with unexplained lower back pain who do not return to work within six weeks should cease to receive disability benefits and be made unemployed (Fordyce, 1995). There is no doubt that people learn to adjust to the experience of enduring pain, yet the distinction between 'physical' and 'psychogenic' pain can have unintentionally distressing consequences and can easily confound what needs to be explained (see Lewis, 1972).

Numerous studies have found that chronic pain sufferers are likely to be more anxious, more depressed and have lower self-esteem than pain-free controls, suggesting that those afflicted may have an emotional predisposition to remain in pain. However, it would be more consistent to recognize that all episodes of pain – whatever their origin or duration – have emotional and cognitive dimensions (Elton et al., 1983). In a detailed study of people afflicted by rheumatoid arthritis, Locker (1983) found that coping with this painful and unpredictable disease is as emotionally debilitating as it is physically disabling. A similar conclusion is reached by Williams (1995) who describes the moral struggle between not 'giving in' to the illness and the anxiety and dread of progressive pain. These studies of rheumatoid arthritis suggest that anxiety, depression and seeking 'secondary gains' can be understood as situational responses to the daily reality of coping with disabling pain. Anxieties, coping strategies and continual pain merge into an ongoing affliction which cannot easily be reduced to a specific psychological or physical state. Indeed, the evidence in favour of psychogenic pain could just as easily be interpreted in the other direction. For instance, it has been found that relief from persistent pain significantly reduces signs of depression, anxiety and hypochrondriasis and raises the patient's self-esteem (Wall and Jones, 1998). Whether an organic basis can be determined or not, the evidence suggests that neither the physical nor emotional reality of pain can be lightly ignored if we are to understand the hold it can have over people's lives (see Melzack and Wall, 1988, p. 32).

Pain as a lived experience

The uncertain status of chronic pain challenges the common idea that illnesses have a specific pathology and that 'real pain' is symptomatic of something that is 'seriously wrong' – an idea no less firmly adhered to amongst patients as medical practitioners. Patients understandably feel frustrated or angry when repeatedly reassured that there is 'nothing to worry about' or that their pain is 'all in the mind'. There is, of course, a profound yet obvious sense in which only those afflicted can bear authentic testimony to the intensity of their pain. However, on one thing pain sufferers agree: you do not get used to persistent pain. It assaults physical integrity and totally dominates conscious life. As one patient wrote, 'Pain slips into my vision, my sensations, my judgments: I am being infiltrated ... the more one is in pain the more one is afraid of pain ... there is a kind of panic, the fear of pain becomes worse, and the more the body is made to suffer, the more it objects' (cited in Herlich and Pierret, 1987, p. 88). Severe pain overwhelms the body: we are not merely threatened but consumed by pain. The standard medical definition of pain as 'an unpleasant sensory and emotional experience' conveys little of the anguish and desperation that accompanies the unrelenting immediacy of 'total' pain (Autton, 1986; Saunders, 1970). As Melzack and Wall observe, it is the kind of 'unpleasantness' that makes people scream, fight, undergo crippling, disfiguring operations, or commit suicide (1988, p. 45). Pain of this intensity radiates a spectrum of disturbing emotions and meanings. It is a category of experiences that evokes a deeper and more invasive level of suffering than a 'meaningless' sensory event. The emerging contribution of the social sciences lies in clarifying how this 'category of experiences' is shaped by sentiments and the discursive practices of everyday life. But here we have to widen our perspective and go beyond the parameters of biomedical research to consider how minds and cultures, emotions and beliefs shape the meaning and experience of pain, as well as the consequences of seeking medical help.

Dys-embodied pain

If we think about the experience of being in pain, in relation to our perception of the body, two relevant considerations emerge. The first touches upon the intimate sense in which the body is normally experienced as an integral part of ourselves. Our perception of reality and our ability to accomplish everyday tasks depends upon an embodied self. Usually we pay little attention to the complex bodily systems and functions that are required to perform even the most elementary tasks, such as picking up a pen or walking across the room. In performing these activities, the body is not experienced as an alien object or machine, but as a spontaneous agency that realizes our intentions and actions in the world. However, this sense of acting within the body is radically altered when something goes wrong. In a dramatic instance, Oliver Sacks describes the case of a young woman afflicted by the onset of a rare type of polyneuritis which left her unable to feel the ground beneath her feet and with little dexterity in her hands (Sacks, 1986, p. 42). As the illness progressed, she lost most of her 'sixth sense' (proprioception) which automatically monitors and adjusts the muscles, tendons and joints which articulate the body's movable parts. Although not in pain, she felt strangely disorientated: 'Something awful's happened', she said, 'I can't feel my body. I feel weird – disembodied'. Here, the normally seamless relation between body and self is strangely disrupted. In order to undertake ordinary movements – holding a pen without dropping it, standing up without falling down – the body had to become the consuming object of this patient's attention.

Pain has a similar potential to shatter our sense of embodiment. Its sheer aversiveness threatens our conception of self. The usually compliant, docile body now aggressively opposes the unquestioned certainty of what it is like to be ourselves. Here, the experience of pain cannot be reduced simply to sensory responses or organic dysfunctions: severe or persistent pain dislocates our way of being-in-the-world, constricts the parameters of space and time, restructures our priorities and changes our relationship with others and ourselves. In short, the psychosocial significance of pain disrupts the relationship between agency and intention and the usually unhesitating sense we have of our bodies in relation to ourselves.

This draws attention to a second consideration. Human beings are not like organisms which are directly subjected to nature; our relationship to natural phenomena, including sensations and bodily states, is mediated by an elaborated culture of meanings and unquestioned beliefs. To say, 'I am in pain' is not an involuntary reaction to an unpleasant sensation, it is an evaluative description of a change in my conscious awareness of self. In ordinary language we distinguish between the sensory experience of pain and our relationship to that experience as an observing self. Accordingly, we have at least some notion of what Oliver Sack's patient means when she says 'I feel my body has no sense of itself' (Sacks, 1986, p. 49). Similarly, Scarry remarks that people in pain tend to perceive their body as an alien presence, provoking such thoughts as, 'I must get rid of this! This not me!' (Scarry, 1985, p. 44). These statements only make sense if we recognize that the body is perceived phenomenologically as having two dimensions: as an objective, sensory, physical existence, and as an animated, reflexive agency that is conscious of itself (see Turner, 1992). The relationship between the two is mediated symbolically by language, or rather, by discursive practices which convey a system of meanings and significations that structure our perception of bodily states. Accordingly, to be aware of pain is not simply to be conscious of a sensation; our perception is loaded with meaning and intention, alerting us to the implications of how we feel in relation to present, past and future activities. In this way, perception is always framed by an implicit sense of what Freud described as the 'body-ego'; an active, subjective, communicative agency that is altogether different from the silent, detached object of scientific analysis and the clinical gaze.

The social context of pain

These considerations draw attention to those discursive practices which inform both the personal significance and social responses to being in pain. Although the sensation of pain is entirely subjective, how it is perceived, configured, communicated, explained, relieved or amplified, and its affect upon a person's relationship to others and themselves, are shaped inter-subjectively by cultural beliefs and social practices, including, not least, by prevailing medical categories and beliefs. The language, expectations and sentiments of health professionals, benefit agencies, employers, colleagues, family and friends, shape the world of those afflicted and the significance attributed to their pain. In this way, the experience of pain can be seen as the intersection or 'embodiment' of bio-psychosocial processes which link the body and self to the social world.

For the most part, biomedical approaches to treatment have largely ignored, if not scorned, these psychosocial dimensions in a singular quest for physical causes and solutions to the symptomatic reduction of pain. Thus, if acute chest pain is traced to an occluded coronary artery and subsequently relieved by surgical intervention or drugs, this is usually regarded as a medical success. However, the discursive practices that pragmatically constitute this 'success' – including the knowledge and skill required in diagnosis and treatment – assume that the body has an autonomous reality which can be investigated, modified and managed independently of the web of psychosocial processes that enmesh an individual within everyday life (Gordon, 1988). Yet the limitations of this tenacious assumption circumscribe its success: although pain may be alleviated by arresting a cardiovascular disease, the experience of pain is liable to embody multiple meanings and tensions in the patient's personal life. Fractious family relationships, or over-demanding commitments at work may be felt not just as burning, stabbing, cramping sensations in the chest but as emotional anguish and spiritual exhaustion, transforming a painful way of life into a clinically recognizable disease. What tends to be lost in medical discourse is the dynamic between these biophysical and psychosocial processes which affect both the aetiology and experience of pain.

This limitation is all the more apparent in the case of persistent pain for which no organic disorder or effective remedy can be found. These medically anomalous conditions challenge the dualities of mind and body, biology and culture and bring into closer perspective the shifting discourses and relationships which shape the experience of enduring pain.

Kotarba (1983) identifies three phases in the careers of people who seek treatment for chronic pain which are useful here in drawing upon the actual experiences of patients presenting with medically unexplained pain, all of whom were eventually referred for psychiatric assessment and advice (Morgan, 1989). In the early stages, the onset of pain is perceived to be both transitory and indicative of a 'real' and treatable illness. Painful symptoms are a threat to habitus, and give rise to a quest for explanation and meaning: What is happening to me? And what does it mean? A medical diagnosis both validates and makes sense of the patient's experience, temporarily restoring meaning and order to the patient's life. Treatment holds the promise of effective relief and a return to normal health. At this early stage, the patient's sense of estrangement towards the body aligns with medical practice in a collusive campaign against a 'real' objectified disorder that is causing pain.

The second phase begins with the emergence of doubt. When initial tests prove negative and treatment apparently offers little relief, the patient – and also perhaps the physician – begins to suspect the condition might have been misdiagnosed. Specialist advice is sought on diagnosis and treatment. Inconclusive reports begin to raise doubts about the organic basis of the patient's complaints. Further referrals to hospital specialists may follow with inconclusive results. Without a clear clinical picture, the physician tends to 'wait and see'. In the lives of most patients and their families this is commonly a period of anxiety and stress in which routine activities are disrupted and the patient's self-confidence is shaken by persistent and painful symptoms which neither they nor their doctor can adequately explain. These tensions tend to amplify symptoms and renew demands for medical attention. The episode that follows is typically frustrating for doctor and patient alike: unsure whether the cause of the pain is predominantly somatic or psychogenic, the physician is likely to prescribe for both. As Vrancken observed:

> The patient is yo-yoed between two views while his confusion grows. Initially his pain was dealt with, as if it were 'organic' but subsequently he

is persuaded that it is 'psychic' pain. While his confusion and frustration adds to his suffering, the physician will say that he is somatized, and the psychologist calls him alexithymic [unable to recognize or verbalize emotional experiences] (Vrancken, 1989, p. 440).

Painful symptoms are liable spill over into painful doctor–patient relations as doubts are expressed about the authenticity of the complaint. After a number of fraught exchanges with her GP, one patient (who described her pain 'like steel rods' behind her eyes) remarked: 'He must think I'm a fool or a liar. He puts it all down to nerves ... Of course I nervous. I'm in such pain. I worry all the time – about losing my sight!' (Morgan, 1989, p. 750).

Often by now the patient's confidence in the efficacy of medicine (or at least the competence of their own doctor) is in doubt and the patient enters the last phase of becoming what Kotarba calls a chronic pain-afflicted person. The patient's concern 'to get to the bottom of the problem' is typically frustrated by repeated reassurances that 'there is nothing serious to worry about' and palliative advice. Eventually, such patients are likely to become part of a rolling case load of 'difficult' patients for whom it appears little further can be done (O'Brian, 1998; Smith, 1985). However, Kotarba notes that it is almost never the case that chronic pain patients are prepared to accept that all they can do is 'learn to live with the pain' (1983, p. 16). They react to the variable intensity and uncertain nature of their pain by reaching out to medical or alternative explanations of their affliction in a continuing search for interpretation and effective relief.

The careers of pain-afflicted patients provide evidence of the authenticity of their pain and the frustration they and their families experience in negotiating medical help. These transactions channel the perception of pain through an inconclusive and, at times, opposing dialogue between existential certainty and clinical doubts, mounting distress and reassuring advice. These confusing inflections between body and mind – sometimes heightened by a sudden intensity of symptoms, or a hiatus in doctor–patient relations, or tensions elsewhere in the patient's life – are like the twisting inversion of a figure eight in which the inside and outside continuously merge (Grosz, 1994; Morgan, 1989). This indeterminate process, which takes up disproportionate resources and time, contributes to the patient's anxieties and failing self-esteem. The only constants in this process tend to be the patients' distress and the doctor's frustration in the face of unremitting complaints.

Cultures of pain

This uneasy dialogue between clinical categories and subjective experience has been a recurring theme in the sociology of medicine, particularly in relation to unexplained pain (Bendelow, 1996; Mishler, 1989; D. Morris, 1991; Strauss, 1973). It draws attention to the limitations of medical conceptions of human disorder as well as to medicine's dominance over both therapeutic resources and cultural representations of illness and pain.

Medicine accords the highest value to knowledge that can be objectively verified. What the patient reports (symptoms and feelings) is perceived as subjective and unreliable. As a result, the patient's experience does not count for much. Diseases, over which doctors claim authoritative expertise, are regarded as objective and factual. Consequently, transactions between doctors and patients are tellingly one-sided: as David Morris remarks, 'one knows, the other feels; one prescribes, the other complies' (Morris, 1998, p. 38). This basic conceptual distinction in medical thinking between 'illness' and 'disease' leads patients and doctors to view disorders from different perspectives. Patients narrate their personal experience; the doctor deconstructs this into symptoms, diagnostic indications and clinical tests. However, as we have seen in the case of 'unexplained' pain, failure to find objective and verifiable causes leaves a penumbra of illnesses and patients who are no less sick or disabled than those whose symptoms fit a text book case.

Should we say in such cases that the patient's testimony is untrustworthy, that their pain is imaginary? Or should we recognize that the distinction between illness and disease is less categorical, more opaque and more open to culturally variable influences than medical discourse suggests? This latter view is taken by the psychiatrist and social anthropologist, Arthur Kleinman, who challenges conventional interpretations and approaches to 'unexplained' pain by exploring the ways in which 'illness idioms crystallize out of the dynamic between bodily processes and cultural categories, between experience and meaning' (Kleinman, 1988, p. 14; see also DelVecchio Good et al., 1992). In a classic study of the personal consequences of China's Cultural Revolution, Kleinman observed the tendency for political disaffection to be articulated through illness which transformed existential problems into physical pain (Kleinman 1986). Headaches, listlessness, lack of concentration, hypersensitivity, fatigue and persistent pain were diagnosed by Chinese physicians as symptoms of 'neurasthenia', which is attributed in modern China to a physical disease.

Whilst in the west such symptoms might be indicative of an affective disorder, the Cultural Revolution revived a tradition of stigma towards mental disorders by associating emotional and psychological problems with 'incorrect political thinking'. Hence, a diagnosis of neurasthenia provided 'the legitimation of a putative physical disease for bodily expressions of personal and social distress that would otherwise go unauthorised' (Kleinman, 1986, p. 108). In one such case, Kleinman describes how symptoms of 'neurasthenia' developed and progressed as the patient, a young woman (Comrade Yen), confronted overwhelming social and political changes and a succession of 'demoralising' personal losses, including forced migration, ideological exclusion, poverty, an unhappy marriage and the stigma of giving birth to an unwanted and physically disabled daughter. To illustrate how social and cultural practices shape interpretations of pain, this case is compared with a young American woman with similar symptoms who had also suffered a number of personal set-backs which thwarted her ambition to become a professional musician. After separating from her partner, she had to endure the 'daily drudgery of uninspiring work' and live out her evenings 'desperately alone'.

Kleinman argues each case mirrors 'the culture and local social systems of its distinctive society' (1986, p. 104) in that perceptions and representations of pain are constituted by a specific set of cultural practices and social expectations. In both cases, the recognition and interpretation of illness, and what would bring effective relief, are framed by different medical conceptions of the relationship of the individual to society and the body to the self. In the Chinese case, the body is regarded as a microcosm symbolically expressing the socio-political and (in traditional medicine) the cosmic order. Health is a harmony of spiritual, physical, social forces, whereas illness represents dissonance and the loss of vital energy (qi). Accordingly, Comrade Yen's neurasthenia is seen as bodily expression of her ideological dislocation from the revolutionary cultural and social changes in Chinese society. She is resigned to her harsh existence and enduring pain which she believes will only remit when the tensions between her life and the wider social system are ideologically resolved.

In contrast, the American patient, Eliza, expects her symptoms to disappear once she has resolved the problems of her inner self. She blames her parents for her condition in as much as they failed to prepare her for the competitive pressures and set-backs of adult life. Psychotherapy, she hopes, will make good the deficit, giving her the self-confidence, assertiveness and toughness needed to pursue a successful career and a supportive emotional life. Both cases illustrate in different idioms the reciprocal relationship between medical categories and social processes, yet the dynamics between body, self and society are reversed. In China the body is seen as an 'open system linking social relations to the self', whereas in western medicine the body is thought of as a separate entity, distinct from the self, and separate again from the challenging demands of modern life. These cultural differences have implications for the perception and meaning of chronic pain and the point at which treatment should intervene: unlike Comrade Yen who accepts her illness as a fate beyond her control, Eliza's pragmatic individualism leads her to believe her problems can be overcome by a therapeutic reconstruction of her 'inner self'.

The management of chronic pain

Kleinman's ethnographies illustrate his view of chronic pain as bodily 'expressions of distress' arising from existential problems which people have neither the personal nor social resources to resolve (DelVecchio Good et al., 1992). Confronted with intractable obstacles, unexplained pain may express a form of resistance against destructive social relationships or unrealizable goals. At times, it may be the only language available for resisting oppressive professional, organizational or political demands, including discordant medical categories and treatment regimes. Like many critics of biomedical approaches to pain, Kleinman holds that a categorical dichotomy between mind and body, illness and disease is 'invalid and unavailing' and is likely to lead to treatment policies which amplify and perpetuate rather than relieve the patient's distress. In their place, he recommends a multidisciplinary orientation to treatment which recognizes that the persistence of physical pain 'is created out of the dialectic between cultural categories and personal signification on the one side, and the brute materiality of disordered processes on the other' (Kleinman, 1988, p. 55). To break the vicious circle in which pain may come to express political vulnerability, marginality, resistance, guilt or frustrated and thwarted lives, Kleinman proposes an alternative approach to therapy based upon a shared 'explanatory model' of the disorder in which the patient's narrative becomes integral to the management of their pain.

The underlying principles of this approach involve 'empathic witnessing' of the existential experience of suffering, and secondly, 'practical coping' of the psychosocial crises that constitute the menacing chronicity of that experience. The work of the practitioner includes the sensitive exploration of the patient's and the family's stories of the illness, constructing a 'mini-ethnography' of the changing contexts of chronicity, and what amounts to brief psychotherapy 'for the multiple, ongoing threats and losses that make chronic illness so profoundly disruptive' (Kleinman, 1988, p. 10). In particular, close attention to the patient's narrative offers both the physician and patient a common discourse for organizing and communicating thoughts, feelings and bodily processes. It shifts the point of medical intervention away from 'a morbid preoccupation with painful bodily processes' and consequent 'narrow, dehumanizing treatments' towards a recognition that the relationship of the body to self is mediated by powerful emotional, social and cultural reactions to being in pain.

The emphasis here upon disrupted biographies and explanatory narratives challenges conventional distinctions between mind, body and society, and differs markedly from the continuing tendency to 'medicalize' chronic pain in clinical practice and research. Yet despite earlier enlightened attempts to reorient the prevalent culture of medical care (Balint, 1968; Engel, 1959), and its associated forms of therapy (Mayou and Sharpe, 1995; Speckens et al., 1995), there appears to be lasting resistance in western medicine to genuinely holistic, biocultural approaches to pain which tend to be seen as 'soft' and oddly unmedical. Mayou and Sharpe (1997) argue the main reason for this is the stubborn persistence of a mind/body dualism in medical discourse which has remained an obstacle to both therapeutic innovation and theoretical advance (see also, Bendelow and Williams, 1995; Turner, 1984; Williams and Bendelow 1998, p. 155).

However, pressure for change may come from another direction: with some 32 million prescriptions each year for anti-inflammatory drugs alone, there is a growing realization that chronic pain is becoming one of the biggest drains upon the resources of the NHS. This growing burden of expenditure may move innovative, more cost-effective treatments higher up the political agenda and provide the professional impetus to mitigate not only the public but also the personal costs of medically intractable pain.

Further reading

Bendelow, G., and S. Williams, 'Transcending the Dualisms: Towards a Sociology of Pain', *Sociology of Health and Illness*, 17: 2 (1995) 139–65.
    An excellent overview of biomedical assumptions and emerging sociological perspectives on pain.

Morris, D., *The Culture of Pain* (Berkley and Los Angeles: University of California Press, 1991).

    A classic study that draws upon literature, art, psychology and medicine to explore the meaning of pain 'as an experience in search of an interpretation'.

Scarry, E., *The Body in Pain: The Making and Unmaking of the World* (Oxford: Oxford University Press, 1985).

    An influential analysis of the unrecognized significance of pain in western culture.

Wall, P., *Pain: The Science of Suffering* (London: Weidenfeld and Nicholson, 1999).

    An accessible account of recent advances in unravelling the neurophysiology of pain.

7

The Child's Body

Jo Bridgeman

Our own experiences as children and our current relationships with children may appear to render theorizing about the child unnecessary. Childhood appears a natural and normal period through which we all pass in preparation for adulthood. In common sense understandings what identifies the child is physical and mental immaturity which gradually develops with the transition from newborn, to infant, toddler, child and adolescent. At any and all stages, the child is understood in relation to and in contrast with the adult: the child stands as 'other' to the adult norm. The adult is mature, rational and competent; the child immature, irrational and incompetent.

Common sense understandings of the child are reflected in political debate about children and media representations of children where children are cast in contradictory terms as both pure and innocent and as inherently evil (Davis and Bourhill, 1997, p. 31). The former characterization focuses upon the need to protect children from danger and from corruption by the adult world (James, Jenks and Prout, 1998, pp. 13–15). The dilemma to be resolved by 'anxious' parents is the reality of the danger presented to their children by traffic and strangers, against the extent to which, in their efforts to protect, they harm their children by denying them the freedom to explore the boundaries of safety for themselves (Collier, 2000). Similarly, stories about 12-year-old mothers and moral panic surrounding the teenage pregnancy rate decry the loss of innocence (Worrall, 2000).

In contrast is the notion that within every child lurks the potential for evil which must be contained by adult control: 'Children are demonic, harbourers of potentially dark forces which risk being mobilised if, by dereliction or inattention, the adult world allows them to veer away from the 'straight and narrow' path that civilisation has bequeathed to them' (James, Jenks and Prout, 1998, pp. 10–13). Reports of crimes perpetrated by children exposed to violence on the television and/or lacking parental control appear to demonstrate the potential for the unleashed evil within children to disrupt civilised society. The contradictory nature of these understandings of children were brought into focus by the killing in 1993 of two-year-old Jamie Bulger by 10-year-old Robert Thompson and Jon Venables in the UK: the toddler paradigmatic of trusting innocence, his killers the embodiment of the evil which lurks within.

Within the social sciences, understandings of the child have been dominated by theories of developmental psychology and socialisation. In developmental psychology the work of Piaget has had a wide-reaching impact influencing a range of disciplines including theories of education, practical advice for parents and legal concepts such as the welfare principle. The immaturity of children is accepted as natural and their development as inevitable:

> Piaget lays out for us some inevitable and clearly defined stages of growth which are well signposted. Beginning immediately after birth with sensory-motor intelligence, children progress through preconceptual and intuitive thought to the final achievement of the 'normal' person in formal operations. Within the model, these stages are ordered temporally and arranged hierarchically along a continuum from infantile 'figurative' thought, which has relatively low status, up to adult, 'operative' intelligence, which has high status (James, Jenks and Prout, 1998, p. 18).

Children are monitored in order to gauge whether the developmental milestone towards the adult norm is achieved at the appropriate age, their progress is charted and judgements are made:

> Piaget's genetic epistemology has, through its measuring, grading, ranking and assessing of children, instilled a deep-seated positivism and rigid empiricism into our contemporary understandings of the child. Under the hegemony of developmental stage monitoring it is not just iniquitous comparison with their peers which children suffer … but also a constant evaluation against a 'gold standard' of the normal child (James, Jenks and Prout, 1998, p. 19).

An alternative analysis, albeit one which is framed by the same reference points of childhood as a period of apprenticeship for adulthood, is one which presents childhood as a period of socialisation. From this perspective, the task for adults caring for children is to teach them the skills, behaviour and characteristics appropriate to adult-hood (Prout and James, 1997, p. 12).

The 'new' sociology of the child, of which Chris Jenks is a leading exponent, takes a quite different approach. It is premised upon an understanding of childhood as socially constructed:

> To describe childhood, or indeed any phenomenon, as socially constructed is to suspend a belief in or willing reception of its taken-for-granted meanings. Thus, though quite obviously we all know what children are and what childhood is like, for social constructionists this is not a knowledge that can reliably be drawn on. Such knowledge of the child and its lifeworld depends on the predispositions of a consciousness constituted in relation to our social, political, historical and moral context (James, Jenks and Prout, 1998, p. 27).

Whilst children are physically and mentally immature and whilst children are dependent upon adults for 'the fulfilment of some or all of [their] needs' (Campbell, 1991, p. 107), biological differences and practical dependency do not alone explain the different treatment meted out to children (Jenks, 1996, p. 7).

This social constructionist perspective avoids biological reduction-ism and is based upon the premise that the institution of childhood – what characterizes children, what children do, where they go, how they occupy their time, the contribution they make, their abilities – is socially constructed. It contends that through analyzing the discursive construction of childhood, space can be created for alternative presentations. Childhood, currently characterized within western societies, as a period of innocence, happiness and freedom, protected by adults who serve their interests and meet their needs, as a time for play, without responsibility or worry is not universal, timeless or enduring. Childhood is not static but contingent, contested and changing over time and between cultures.

The construction of childhood, at a particular time in a particular culture, impacts upon the lives of real children as adults treat children accordingly and as children conform to the expectations of them:

> Because notions such as socialisation, the family, parenthood, protection, and education are inscribed in the practices of contemporary institutions of childhood – school, family, day care, state welfare institutions, etc. – the institutional ways of thinking produce self-conscious subjects (teachers, parents, care-takers, children) who think and feel about themselves in terms of those ways of thinking. The 'truth' (in the Foucauldian sense)

about themselves, their activities, situation, and relations with others is self-validating; and the more tightly the truth-producing discourses inter-sect and penetrate each other, the more difficult it is for alternative "truths" about children and childhood to break into the contemporary institutional realities in which children live (Alanen, 1994, p. 41).

As with childhood, the body, previously accepted as a natural bio-logical given, has been analyzed as socially constructed (Prout, 2000, p. 1). That is, as other chapters in this volume discuss, attitudes towards, treatment of and values given to the body are understood as discursively produced, and rather than being universal differ depending upon his-torical, cultural and social context (Gatens, 1996, p. viii). As James, Jenks and Prout remind us, a social constructivist approach must not reduce children's bodies to nothing but a discursive construct by excluding the material reality of children's bodies: 'social action is (generally speaking) embodied action, performed not only by texts but by real, living corporeal persons' (James, Jenks and Prout, 1998, p. 147; see also Prout, 2000, p. 2). Analysis of the effect of discourses upon our understandings of children's bodies should keep in sight children's experiences of their bodies.

At any one time, understandings of childhood and the body may be constructed in contradictory or conflicting ways by competing dis-courses. These may coexist or one may come to dominate in a partic-ular situation. In this chapter, I consider the ways in which legal discourse produces meanings, ascribes value and accordingly regu-lates the bodies of young children.

Bodies in law

The law plays a role in protecting the mental and bodily integrity of the subject ensuring that decisions are reached without, for example, coercion or undue pressure and the boundaries of the body are not invaded without consent. Furthermore, as Priscilla Alderson argues, adults are assumed to possess personal integrity which, 'moves on from mainly negative concepts of protecting territory against viola-tion, to more positive examination of what lies within the boundaries: the countless aspects of each personality interrelate and integrate to form each unique whole' (Alderson, 1994, pp. 46–7).

Analysis of the construction, by law, of the young child is a recent enterprise but one which can draw upon the insights of feminist legal theory. As Kylie Stephen explained in Chapter 3, feminist analysis of the law has revealed how, despite the appearance of gender neutrality, the normative legal subject is a rational, autonomous, isolated, disembodied individual crafted in accordance with 'male' values and modes of behaviour. Against this ideal, the 'female' stands as 'other', a comparator associated with devalued characteristics of irrationality, connectivity, emotions and nature (Bordo, 1993; Butler, 1990; Gatens, 1996; Stychin, 1998). Furthermore, feminist analysis of the law has revealed how the law is productive of different ideal subjects against which, when the individual comes before the law, the individual is judged. Feminists have also begun to explore the way in which legal discourse does not merely regulate the body but rather is productive of understandings of, meanings given to and values ascribed to the body (Butler, 1990; Gatens, 1996; Grosz, 1994).

For example, Ngaire Naffine provides a persuasive critique of the boundaried body constructed within the criminal law. The law imposes limits upon the ability of adults to consent to bodily invasion where it is not in the public interest, yet 'despite the liberal criminal legal rhetoric of universal rights of the individual to sovereignty over his own physical person, there has been in truth a highly selective casting of boundaries around persons' – one clear example being the exception which permits boxing 'in the public interest' (Naffine, 1997, p. 93). Naffine also argues that bodily integrity is denied to bodies which are different by, in her example, lacking clear boundaries (1997, pp. 82–4).

What I hope to illustrate in this chapter is how the law, influenced by developmental psychology, produces an understanding of the child's body as a body with potential. Consequently, decisions made within law about children's bodies, in the name of protection and employing the legal tool of 'best interests' are determined by consideration of the future embodied by the child and without reference to his or her present experiences. The next section sketches out the legal framework for making decisions about the welfare of the child. I then outline research which identifies different understandings of the child held by parents and professionals before turning to some examples from the law.

Parental responsibilities, professional perspectives

The primary responsibility for caring for children falls upon parents (or, more accurately, those with parental responsibility) and, in the majority of cases, upon mothers. Decisions about a child's welfare, across the spectrum from everyday matters of diet, exercise and treatment for childhood illnesses to consent to medical treatment for a serious ill-ness or life-threatening condition, are determined by parental assess-ments of the 'best interests' of their child. The parameters of parental discretion in determining best interests are set by the criminal law. The offence of child neglect contrary to the Children and Young Persons Act 1933 exists alongside offences of general applicability contrary to the Offences Against the Person Act 1861 and, in the event of the death of the child, as in a legal case known as *R.* v. *Senior* (1899), murder and manslaughter. Examples of criminal neglect include deliberately inflicted injury, failure to seek medical help for accidental injury – relevant legal cases here are *R.* v. *Ace* (1990), *R.* v. *Lavell* (1997), *R.* v. *Moore* (1995) – 'inadequate' parenting (*R.* v. *Sheppard* 1981), and adopting non-mainstream views about, for example, medical treatment (*R.* v. *Senior* 1899).

In addition to the punitive measures imposed by the state in the event of serious neglect, parents are provided with guidance and assistance in the task of caring for children. Alongside general health services, health visitors provide advice and practical help to parents of all children under the age of five. Current government policy is to extend the role of the health visitor, into the ante-natal period and through into the teenage years, in the belief that they are 'ideally placed for advising families on all kinds of problems' and 'no one feels they are a bad parent or their family has failed because they take the advice of a health visitor' (Home Office 1998, para. 1.27).

A recent, allied, innovation is the creation of the National Family and Parenting Institute, established in November 1999 by the new Labour government, to provide support, advice and information to parents. The provision of these support services sends the message that parents may need assistance with seemingly simple matters such as feeding, establishing sleeping patterns or the provision of a stimu-lating environment. However, their function is not solely to support but also to monitor the development of all children extending, in Armstrong's words, 'a constant normalising gaze ... over the growth and development of all children' (Armstrong, 1983, p. 63).

Research by Debra Westlake and Maggie Pearson has identified tensions arising from the health visitor functions of both providing support and advice and undertaking the surveillance and monitoring of child development. The mothers in their research experienced this tension as a sense of being policed in the quality of the care which they gave to their children (Westlake and Pearson, 1997). Developmental checks, for example, were experienced as surveillance of their parenting skills as their own knowledge of their child was irrelevant. Furthermore, the ability of the health visitor to give advice and assistance was undermined by the sense of mothers that health visitors were judgmental. For example, mothers felt that giving their child the freedom to explore and to learn meant running measured risk of accidental injury. Yet, rather than benefit from the support of health visitors in assessing risks, mothers feared that they would be judged an irresponsible parent should their child suffer accidental injury: 'This fear of reprisals inhibited a number of women from sharing their frustrations or needs for support with children, so that the very 'dangers' that the health-visiting service seeks to uncover, identify and ameliorate are likely to remain invisible to it' (Westlake and Pearson, 1997, p. 151). The professional status of the health visitor may explain, in part, the sense of mothers that they were policing their care. Research by Berry Mayall and Marie-Claude Foster identified clear differences in the way children were understood by health visitors and by mothers which may explain differences in expectation between professional and parent when it comes to caring for children (Mayall and Foster, 1989).

Parental and professional perspectives

The research discussed above indicates that professional knowledge about children is grounded in developmental psychology, which positions children as potential beings progressing towards adulthood. From this standpoint, childhood is a period of progression through a series of stages of development towards adulthood and a time in which children are taught, by their mothers, appropriate adult behaviour (Mayall and Foster, 1989, pp. 26–30). In contrast, and based upon their experiences of caring, the mothers saw their children (aged 21 months) as complete persons:

> [M]others indicate that from the earliest days they regard their baby as a person with individual character and wishes. They recognise their child's right and wish to make her own way, to establish her own space and to construct a social life within the family and beyond (Mayall, 1994, p. 115).

To the mothers in this study, their children had a clearly defined personality, actively developed affectionate relationships, sought to learn by questioning, involved adults and made demands of them in play and took the initiative in seeking to take responsibility for personal care (Mayall and Foster, 1989, pp. 25–6). This understanding of their child was grounded in the experience of caring for him or her:

> It is based on knowledge of the individual child and of others in the family: the child's character, history, the way her mind works, her likes and dislikes. It is knowledge that develops and deepens as the child grows, in response to the child's behaviour and development (Mayall and Foster, 1989, p. 18).

The research by Berry Mayall and Marie-Claude Foster identifies the influence of developmental psychology upon the advice provided by health visitors and their expectations of both mothers and children. Thus, the description which developmental psychology provides of children becomes a way of understanding children and establishes attitudes towards, expectations of and values ascribed to children with direct effect upon the way in which they are treated.

I now turn to consider some examples from case law, and from silences within the law. Through my discussion, I demonstrate that within law, children's bodies are constructed as potential, and what is permitted by the law is determined by consideration of the future which the child embodies and without consideration of the present reality of the child.

Ways of seeing children's bodies

The court is confronted with extremely difficult decisions when asked to decide whether medical treatment should be provided to or withheld from children with disabilities. Legal scholars Mason and McCall Smith note that, despite the particular vulnerability of newborns, who 'cannot express their feelings for the present or future and whose surrogates have no experience on which to base their health care decisions', the courts are rarely called upon to make treatment decisions concerning them (Mason and McCall Smith, 1999, p. 367). They suggest that it is not until the child is a little older that parents have any evidence upon which to disagree with treatment or non-treatment as recommended by the medical professional.

Yet, when the court is asked to decide, decisions about the appropriate treatment of young children with, for example, severe brain damage (see the case *Re J*, 1990) microcephaly, cerebral palsy and epilepsy (*Re J*, 1992) or spinal muscular atrophy (*Re C*, 1998), are made with regard to the future but without consideration of the present reality of life for the child. Whilst medical prognosis of anticipated physical condition and mental capacity, with or without the treatment, and future life prospects are relevant to determining the best interests of young children with disabilities so are the embodied experiences of these young children identified by those caring for them. The court decides the best interests of the child without evidence from those caring for the child, as parents or professionals, about their character, personality or experience of life, such as how they tolerate their condition or whether they gain comfort from those caring for them. Children are constructed as bodies with(out) potential and decisions guided by assessment of their future and without consideration of the immediate consequences of treatment or non-treatment for the individual in the light of their particular personality.

A specific illustration is provided by the legal judgement in the case of conjoined twins, Jodie and Mary, which gained much media attention in the UK in summer 2000 (*A 'Children'*, 22 September 2000). The twin girls each had a brain, heart, lungs, other vital organs, arms, and legs but were joined at the lower abdomen with a fused pelvis, spines and spinal cord and sharing a bladder. The judge in this case, Lord Justice Ward, considered evidence of the expected mental capacity and physical abilities of Mary and Jodie, with and without surgery, to determine whether separation surgery was in the best interests of each. Mary's heart functioned poorly and she had virtually no functioning lung tissue. The medical evidence was that if she had been born a singleton she would not have survived birth but that she owed her survival to the oxygenated blood she received from her twin and separation was clearly not in her best interests. The medical evidence was that the operation would permit Jodie to develop normally both mentally and physically. Although she would require further surgery, the operation was in her best interests. Having considered the best interests of each twin, the judge had to determine how to deal with a conflict between those best interests. Ward LJ noted that, at three weeks old, Jodie was 'very sparkling ... wriggling, very alert ... very much a with it sort of baby'. The paediatric surgeon who gave evidence before the Court of Appeal described both twins as 'very contented' although the only insight into Mary's experience of life is provided by discussion of the uncertainty as to whether she experienced pleasure or pain given that her reaction to both was the same. Aware that the proposed surgery would have the immediate effect of ending Mary's life, Ward LJ in this case does acknowledge the twins as living persons. However, evidence from parents and those caring for the twins about their individual personalities, character and spirit would have assisted the court to determine the best interests of the twins in a way which respected them as living beings and not in terms of the potential they embodied.

The construction of children's bodies in law as bodies with potential echoes the professional understanding of children as mere potential. This same perception is discernible in the attitudes of professionals implicated in the recent scandal in the UK concerning the removal and retention of organs from children following post-mortem examination and stands in contrast to the understanding of parents.

The practice of removing and retaining tissue including complete organs, brains, kidneys and lungs as well as hearts from deceased children following post-mortem examinations without parental consent or understanding, but in some cases arguably within the law, was exposed in evidence given to the *Inquiry into the Management of Care of Children Receiving Complex Heart Surgery at Bristol Royal Infirmary*. The discovery of this practice caused public outcry and extreme distress to parents which was compounded by mistakes made in informing parents whether any 'tissue' had been retained from their child (Kennedy, 2000, para. 6, fn. 7; Boseley, 2000). The *Interim Report* of the Bristol Royal Infirmary Inquiry (Kennedy, 2000) details a climate which can be described at best as medical detachment necessary for dealing with the sad loss at the death of any child and at worst professional arrogance in the form of a self-centred pursuit in the interests of medical science.

Failure to seek the permission of parents for the retention of organs was justified by legal uncertainty, with reference to sensitivity in dealing with parents who had just learned of the death of their child and to the value of organs for medical research and education. These justifications were described in the *Interim Report* as 'well-meaning' but ultimately 'self-serving' (Kennedy, 2000, para. 103), since the overriding aim was to secure organs for medical use and because, to the professionals, the bodies of young children were just bodies, the whole made up of constituent parts of medical interest. Professor Kennedy, in the *Interim Report*, identifies the different value ascribed to children's bodies by professionals and parents:

> There was a social and ethical time bomb waiting to go off. It is no surprise that the explosion of anger, when it came, was huge. The cause lay in two conflicting attitudes. For the parents of a recently deceased child, human material, certainly substantial specimens such as organs and parts of organs and even smaller samples, are still thought of as an integral part of the child's body and, thus, are still the child. For the pathologist and clinician, the material is regarded as a specimen or an object. It is de-humanised (Kennedy, 2000, para. 33).

For the professional the child's body was valuable as a specimen:

> Our generally held view as pathologists was that tissue lawfully obtained
> and no longer required for original purposes could ethically be used for
> the greater good and further retained rather than destroying it (Berry,
> 1999).

In contrast, the view of the parent was as follows:

> It might be considered over the top but we cannot help how we feel: we
> felt it was criminal, what was done ... that it was contemptuous to the dig-
> nity of our child, that her body had been as we see it, invaded and body
> parts stolen (Bradley, 2000).

Parents giving evidence to the Royal Liverpool Children's Inquiry
expressed their anguish at the failure to treat the bodies of their children with dignity or respect. The mother of Alexandra, stillborn,
explained to this Inquiry that she felt deceived and betrayed, and as
the Report explained:

> The third and most compelling reason for her emotion as a parent is that
> she would have done anything and everything in her power to protect her
> child. That was what she was there to do even more so in death because it
> was the only thing she could do for her child at that stage. She had put her
> trust in the doctors, the midwives, the pathologists that they would respect
> her child and that they would deal with her in the way one would wish to
> deal with a dead person. They did not, they desecrated her. She feels let
> down. There was only one thing she could do and that was to protect her
> in death and she did not do it and she has to live with that (*Royal Liverpool
> Children's Inquiry Report*, 2001, p. 408).

Parents expressed the need to protect their child even in death and
guilt at having let their child down by, as the mother of Laura, stillborn, put it 'letting the pathologist "butcher" her' (*Royal Liverpool
Children's Inquiry Report*, 2001, p. 410). The Bristol Heart Children's
Action Group expressed the feelings of parents similarly, in their contribution to the Chief Medical Officer's Summit: 'When a child dies
that child is still the parents' child – not a specimen, not a case, not
an unfortunate casualty of a failed procedure, but someone's baby,
someone's child' (CMO: *Summit Proceedings*, 2001, p. 6).

In all these instances, body parts of young children were valued by
the professionals as material of scientific interest. The anger and distress felt by parents of children from whom organs were removed and
retained arises from very different values ascribed to their bodies
arising from an understanding of children as persons with personal

integrity entitled to respect. As the *Interim Report* of the Bristol Royal
Infirmary Inquiry put it, parents considered their children's bodies as
'human beings rather than an extension of specimens' (*Rex*, quoted
in the *Interim Report*, 2000, p. 139).

Responsibility of carers

Young children are reliant upon those caring for them to respond to
their needs, wishes and feelings. This is not to suggest that young children are merely passive recipients of the care meted out to them. On
the contrary, they make demands, express their wishes and guide
those caring for them. As the Court of Appeal emphasized in the case
of conjoined twins, Jodie and Mary, when an issue of the welfare of
the child is brought before the court, it is the responsibility of the
court to decide where those interests lie in light of all the evidence,
not to choose between professional and parental views.

On the face of it, the case of *Re T* (1997) appears to be an unprece-
dented case in which the court rejected the weight of medical opinion
in favour of the views of the child's mother. However, the case demonstrates the need to distinguish carefully between parental accounts of
the child's experiences and the views, interests and preferences of the
parents themselves.

The mother in this case had refused her consent to the performance of a liver transplant operation upon her son, known as 'C'. 'C'
had been born with biliary atresia, a life-threatening liver condition.
He had undergone an operation at the age of three and a half weeks,
which had been unsuccessful, and three consultants formed the view
that unless a transplant operation was carried out 'C' would not live
beyond the age of two and a half. 'C's' mother refused to consent to
the operation, and the judge in the case, Lady Justice Butler-Sloss,
noted that in reaching this decision:

> She was focusing, it seems to me, on the present peaceful life of the child
> who had the chance to spend the rest of his short life without the pain,
> stress and upset of intrusive surgery against the future with the operation
> and treatment taking place.

His mother's understanding of the pain, distress and suffering 'C'
had experienced as a result of the earlier surgery is relevant to the
decision whether it was in his present best interests to undergo
further surgery as is her account of his experience of life at the time

without surgery. To this extent, the mother's account provides an insight into 'C's' character, tolerance and approach to his life. Likewise, her professional experience of children who had undergone transplants was relevant to assessment of his best interests.

However, the court failed to distinguish between the insight which the mother, as 'C's' carer, could provide into *his* best interests and the interests of the mother herself, as the court considered 'the practicalities' for the mother. These practicalities included 'coercing' the mother into caring for her child when she felt the course of action was wrong, the need to return to England either without the father and thus his support or requiring him to give up his job.

The court expressed the view that 'this mother and this child are one for the purpose of this unusual case', accepting 'C's' interests to be those expressed by his mother. Yet, when one consideration in reaching the conclusion that the transplant operation was not in his best interests was the impact upon his future health of care meted out by a reluctant carer their interests could be seen as directly opposed:

> Dr P maintained a very clear view that – even assuming that the operation proved wholly successful in surgical terms – the child's subsequent development could be injuriously affected if his day to day care depended upon the commitment of a mother who had suffered the turmoil of having her child being compelled against her will to undergo, as a result of a coercive order from the court, a major operation against which her own medical and maternal judgement wholeheartedly rebelled.

In his analysis of this case, Andrew Bainham emphasizes that children have interests which are distinct from those of their parents and with which they may 'clash' (Bainham, 1997). He suggests that the weight accorded to parental views means that: 'Life or death for these children can therefore be something of a lottery depending not on their medical best interests but on the values and preferences of their parents' (Bainham, 1997, p. 50). The focus of the court's assessment was misplaced in the weight which it gave to the 'values and preferences' of the mother, as opposed to the insight which she could provide into the best interests of the child.

The views of parents and carers as to the best interests of the child are essential to reaching a decision which respects the individual child. The responsibility which this places upon those caring for young children is to be alert to the individual character, wishes and spirit of the child so that decisions are made on their behalf which respect the individuality of the child.

At the discretion of parents

I finish with three specific examples – immunization, smacking and body piercing – in which the boundaries of the bodies of young children are invaded, their bodily integrity infringed and their personal integrity denied with the sanction of the law. My argument is that in permitting immunization, smacking and body piercing the construction of children as beings with potential and without current interests deserving of protection is created and continued.

The aim of the childhood immunization programme is to ensure the prevention of infectious disease amongst children (Health Promotion England for the NHS and Department of Health, 2001). In the first year of life in the UK, babies are immunized against Polio, Hib, Diphtheria, Tetanus, and Whooping Cough (at two, three and four months respectively). Between 12 and 15 months the MMR (measles, mumps, and rubella) vaccination is given. Older children receive boosters – MMR (pre-school), Diphtheria/Tetanus (pre-school and between 13 and 18) – and tuberculosis (BCG) immunisation between the ages of 10 and 14. The low incidence of these diseases is a consequence of and dependent upon the success of widespread immunization. These diseases are more prevalent in other countries and thus immunisation is necessary to protect the child who travels and from exposure by those who may have been infected abroad. Furthermore, 'Immunisation doesn't just protect your child and your family, it protects the whole community, especially those children who can't be immunised' (Health Promotion England for the NHS and Department of Health, 2001).

Young children cannot decide for themselves whether to accept the immediate distress, discomfort and risk of side effects to protect themselves from possible infection and for the benefit of the wider community. The decision is one to be made by parents, focusing as the law demands upon the best interests of *their* child. Whether, in a context of pressure to ensure participation, parents are provided with sufficient information about the risks, symptoms and appropriate response to uncomfortable, distressing or severe side-effects of vaccines and of research into links, for example, between MMR and Crohn's disease, MMR and autism, whooping cough and brain damage, is an important question beyond the scope of this chapter.

However, as Priscilla Alderson has identified there is a 'credibility gap between the child's perception of harm, and the adult's intention to benefit' (Alderson, 1994, p. 60). This arises from the pain and distress caused by the unexpected administration of an injection to a child exacerbated where it is done with the collusion of someone they trust. For pre-school children this might be addressed by a careful explanation, involving him or her in the decision to immunize, helping understanding and preparation for the experience. But the question remains whether sufficient consideration has been given to the child's experience of pain or 'sense of self' in the development of methods of administration or in judgements about the best interests of the child. It is questionable whether it would be lawful to administer an injection to an adult who was unable to give a valid consent in order to prevent possible infection with disease and in the interests of the wider community.

This question does not appear to be asked of young children as a focus upon the future of the child and the well-being of the community precludes consideration of current experiences. Whilst we may have moved on from a perception that children could not suffer harm, it is worth noting that what is harmful is not 'a transcendental notion which is automatically knowable and recognisable at any moment in history by any member of a culture' (Smart, 1999), but is defined as such within law by those with the power to give harm definition.

Parents (or anyone else with care and control of a child) are currently permitted to inflict reasonable punishment upon children without committing a criminal offence contrary to the Children and Young Persons Act 1933, the Offences Against the Person Act 1861 or a civil battery (*Collins* v. *Wilcock*, 1984). The European Court of Human Rights, in a case called *A.* v. *United Kingdom* (1998), held that English law was in breach of Article 3 of the Convention as it permitted the infliction of degrading treatment. In response, the government consultation paper, *Protecting Children, Supporting Parents: A Consultation Document on the Physical Punishment of Children* (DoH 2000) seeks a compromise which permits parents to physically punish their children whilst preventing them from inflicting inhuman and degrading treatment upon them. It states: 'There is a common sense distinction to be made between the sort of mild physical rebuke which occurs in families and which most loving parents consider acceptable, and the beating of children' (DoH 2000, para. 1.5).

Children appear not to make this common sense distinction. Instead, a further 'credibility gap' opens up: '[A smack is] parents trying to hit you [but] instead of calling [it] a hit they call it a smack' (Willow and Hyde, 2000, p. 18), where smacking of children is permitted, children are denied the protection extended to adults.

The physical and emotional pain, and the hurt to the 'sense of self', is not recognized for children as harmful, as it is for adults, by the law. Justified as educative or corrective, this exception is premised upon a perception of children as bodies with potential. This viewpoint allows the immediate hurt inflicted by physical violence to be effaced by a focus upon correcting childish misdeamours to guide the child towards appropriate adult behaviour.

That the law permits body piercing at all seems to be anomalous and the Law Commission could only explain the exception in terms of no-one wishing to challenge its existence (Law Commission, 1994, para. 11.22). Specific legislative action in the form of the Tattooing of Minors Act 1969 has made it a criminal offence to tattoo the body of a young child but the law does not appear to prevent the piercing of the bodies of young children. Where the body of a young child is pierced with parental consent, it must be justified in law as an act carried out in the best interests of the child. The Royal College of Nursing have expressed their concern at the practice (Brindle, 2000), which can result in infection and scarring and risks children with piercings hurting themselves. The Law Commission sought the views of consultees as to whether legislation should criminalize piercing *below the neck* of the bodies of children under the age of 18 (Law Commission, 1995, para. 9.24). In the unchallenged assumption that the bodies of young children may lawfully, that is in their best interests, be pierced, the law fails to protect the bodily integrity of the child. This silence constructs the body of the child as a mere container of potential which does not have personal integrity – it is not a self with feelings deserving of respect.

In the name of correction, young children are denied bodily integrity. In making judgements about the best interests of children, the assumption is that children lack personal integrity, 'a sense of the self', so that their present feelings, emotions and experiences are ignored. What is given legal sanction, in the name of protection, is intrusive, invasive and may be experienced as harmful. At present, the silence of the law in relation to immunization, smacking and piercing constructs the body of the young child as a body with potential. Whether the child is immunized unexpectedly or care taken to involve and ensure the child understands why they are being immunized and what it involves; whether the child is smacked; whether the child's body is adorned with decorative piercings depends upon the child's parents. The respect accorded to the bodily and personal integrity of the child depends upon the understanding which the child's parents have of childhood and how responsive they are to the individuality of the child. In the absence of legal regulation, the treatment of individual children depends upon the values and preferences of their parents.

Conclusion

Ann Oakley has argued that 'judgments about the welfare of ... children are based not on asking them what they want or need, but on what other people consider to be the case. It is a philosophy of exclusion and control dressed up as protection' (Oakley, 1994, p. 16). Recognition that adults do not know better than the child where his or her best interests lie, has resulted in a growing awareness of the importance of listening to children, and of ensuring that children participate in decisions affecting their lives to the extent that they want to and are able to. This also means challenging the preconceptions which adults have of children and childhood so that conclusions are not determined by our own hazy recollections of childhood reinterpreted through adult experiences or by a desire to protect (Qvortrup, 1994, p. 2).

A good example is Pia Christensen's research into adult responses to and children's experiences of everyday illness and minor accidents. The response of adults depended upon how serious the illness or injury appeared externally, frequently resulting in exhortations to stop making a fuss. Whilst the children's reaction reflected a more profound injury:

> In observations of everyday illness episodes or minor accidents at school and the after-school centres, it became apparent that children's concern was with the interruption of their body and their connections with the social and material world, not with, for example, the penetration of the body skin or naming the body part that hurt. They experienced the situations in which they were involved and the associated interactions as an integrated process. Thus children's accounts showed that experiencing vulnerability also related to the experience of losing their social position, activities and relationships and changes in their environment ... Children, then, spoke from the perspective of the body incarnate, the body as experience, in action, involved with the environment as well as in interactions with others (Christensen, 2000, pp. 46–7).

Christensen notes the importance of being aware of our own expectations of and concerns about children so that they do not affect interpretation of the opinions expressed and experiences outlined by children:

> Adults attempting to understand children's experiences by translating them into those of adults highlight particular problems in the interpretation of childhood illness. These problems may not be constituted from the adults' own experiences, but could be seen as arising from ... the limitations of adults' imaginative abilities ... An anthropological understanding of children must be achieved by replacing adults' images of children as social persons and of their vulnerability and instead firmly contextualising children in their own social worlds (Christensen, 2000, pp. 57–8).

Young children are dependent upon others to provide for their physical and emotional well-being. Lacking the capacity for autonomous decision-making young children are dependent upon others to make decisions about their welfare. Yet understandings of, meanings given to and values ascribed to children affect the way in which children are treated. Within the law, young children are understood and treated as bodies with potential, but not as persons with bodily integrity entitled to respect or with a 'sense of self'. The recognition within sociology that childhood is a social construction and consequently, contested and contingent not static, given and universal has resulted in an appreciation of the value of other accounts. Accounts given by those caring for and living with young children provide an understanding of children as persons with emotions, experiences, feelings, with spirit. In making decisions about their welfare, the responsibility is upon adults caring for children to be alert to the character, spirit and experiences of the child. When decisions are made by others, such as the court, the best interests of the child can only be determined if those caring for the child provide insights into the unique nature of the individual.

Cases

A (Children) 22 September 2000
A. v. United Kingdom [1998] 2 FLR 959
Collins v. Wilcock [1984] 1 WLR 1172
Re C [1998] 6 Med L Rev 99
Re J [1990] 3 All ER 930, CA
Re J [1992] 3 WLR 507, CA
Re T [1997] 1 WLR 242
R. v. Ace [1990] 12 Cr A R 533
R. v. Lavell [1997] 2 Cr A Rep S 91

R. v. *Moore* [1995] 16 Cr A R 65
R. v. *Senior* [1899] 1 QB 283
R. v. *Sheppard* [1981] AC 394

Further reading

Bridgeman Jo, and Daniel Monk, *Feminist Perspectives on Child Law* (London, 2000: Cavendish Publishing).

A collection of essays on Child Law considering areas of law going beyond this chapter including human rights, education law and criminal justice from a variety of feminist and critical theoretical perspectives including discourse analysis.

James, Allison, Chris Jenks and Alan Prout, *Theorising Childhood* (Cambridge, 1998: Polity Press with Blackwell Publishers Ltd).

Developing the social construction of childhood to accommodate the material realities of children's lives across a range of issues.

Jenks, Chris, *Childhood* (London: Routledge, 1996).

An introduction to approaches to childhood within sociology and addressing contemporary concerns through a social constructionist perspective.

Prout, Alan (ed.), *The Body, Childhood and Society* (Basingstoke: Macmillan Press – now Palgrave, 2000).

A collection of essays on children's bodies with a useful introduction to the theoretical perspectives.

8

The Pregnant Body

Ellie Lee and Emily Jackson

Whilst pregnancy can be defined biologically as the implantation of a fertilized ovum in a woman's uterus, the meaning and significance of pregnancy can be considered social. As Hartouni has argued, pregnancy can be viewed as an 'historically specific set of social practices, an activity that is socially and politically constructed and conditioned by relations of power, and that differs according to class, race, history and culture' (Hartouni, 1997, p. 30). In this chapter our focus is upon how some of the 'social practices' that define pregnancy might *regulate* the pregnant body. Our purpose is to consider whether a Foucauldian analysis of the body – as a product of *medicalized discourses* and as a site for the exercise of *disciplinary power* – has any resonance for the experiences of pregnancy.

When a woman discovers that she is pregnant she may decide to have an abortion or to carry the pregnancy to term. In either situation, she will encounter various distinctive regulatory processes. Invoking a Foucauldian understanding of power as subtle, dispersed and continuous, we suggest that pregnant women may in fact be controlled by practices which at first sight appear to benefit and empower them. We first consider how both pregnancy and abortion have become the province of *experts*, thus subjecting the pregnant body to the minute scrutiny of the medical gaze. Second, we explore the construction of pregnant women as *self-disciplined* and *productive* subjects.

In concluding our discussion, we argue that, while Foucault's writings may offer an illuminating and nuanced account of power, a theoretical approach which leans too heavily upon Foucault's work may have some important limitations. In relation to pregnancy, we will argue that an analysis that relies upon the impossibility of concepts such as self-determination and autonomy may undermine practical strategies which aim to expand the options available to pregnant women.

Foucault, medicine and biopower

Biopower was the name given by Michel Foucault to a series of new and distinct mechanisms of social regulation that emerged during the late eighteenth century. He explained:

> there was ... the emergence, in the field of political practices and economic observation, of the problems of birthrate, longevity, public health, housing and migration. Hence there was an explosion of numerous and diverse techniques for achieving the subjugation of bodies and the control of populations, marking the beginning of an era of 'biopower' (Foucault, 1978, p. 140).

Biopower is thus concerned both with controlling individual bodies, and with controlling the population as a whole. Many writers (Albury, 1999; Jones and Porter, 1994; Lupton, 1997; Sheldon, 1997) have identified medicine as one of the principal mechanisms through which biopower is exercised. Medical knowledge, in this analysis, has a crucial role in the regulation of both bodies and populations. For example, Deborah Lupton, with reference to Foucault's *The Birth of the Clinic*, has explained that:

> medical power may be viewed as the underlying resource by which illnesses are identified and dealt with. This perspective fits into the broader social constructionist approach in understanding medical knowledge not simply as a given and objective set of 'facts' but as a belief system shaped through social and political relations (Lupton, 1997, p. 99).

Central to medicine's role in the production of biopower is its capacity to define and delimit what counts as illness and what does not. Doctors are charged both with deciding what does or does not constitute pathology, and with identifying which bodies require medical intervention. And, in order to manage the whole population's health effectively, all bodies must be routinely subjected to the 'medical gaze'.

This point has been developed explicitly by feminist writers in their analyses of medicine's capacity to control women's bodies. For example, with reference to Foucault, Rebecca Albury has argued that the medical profession has:

> provided the language in which we speak of bodies, and the practices that interrogate and report bodily experience ... experience has to be

'medicalized' in order to be recognized; that is, it must be turned into a problem that is capable of being addressed in a medical way (Albury, 1999, p. 39).

According to this analysis, medicine plays a pivotal role in generating understanding about the body. We speak of bodies in the language of medicine, and it is through the prism of medicine that we decide whether or not there is a 'problem' with our bodies.

In this chapter we explore how its grounding in apparently neutral and objective scientific methodology lends special authority to medical knowledge about pregnancy. The medical profession's ability to produce apparently verifiable truths about the body gives it a central role in the production of 'the disciplinary society' (Foucault, 1977, p. 209). First we consider how expert medical knowledge has become the dominant grid through which women's choices in relation to both abortion and their prenatal behaviour can be understood.

It is, however, important to remember that the exercise of biopower does not involve explicit domination of passive patients by dominant doctors; rather power is located in techniques of surveillance and in the production of knowledge. Biopower is not, therefore, the subjugation of a docile population, but consists instead in the subtle, ubiquitous and continuous promotion of *self-discipline*. So while medical discourse may have played a crucial role in the social construction of the pregnant body, it would be rash and over-simplistic to assume that the pregnant body is simply repressed by the continuous accumulation of expert medical knowledge about pregnancy and abortion. Hence, in the second half of this chapter we also examine practices that constitute the pregnant woman as an agent responsible for exercising self-discipline over her own body. As we see, power exercised through these non-coercive regulatory practices may be both invisible and effective.

One way in which power is inscribed upon the body is through the process of *normalization*. The mapping out and scrutinizing of 'abnormal' behaviour (for example smoking during pregnancy, or not using contraception during recreational sexual intercourse) operates as an extremely powerful process of socialization through which normality is implicitly defined, celebrated and encouraged. In the regulation of the body, coercive legal sanctions to penalize aberrant behaviour may be unnecessary because we have each learned to become our own 'sternest and most constant critic' (Rose, 1989, p. 239). Vikki Bell describes how this normalization process has two complementary effects: on the one hand it produces homogeneity, or at least a strong pull towards conformity; yet on the other it individualizes issues so that each citizen is judged according to her ability to be 'normal' (Bell, 1993). In relation to pregnancy and abortion, medical expertize has assumed a critical role in defining normal and abnormal behaviour, while simultaneously pregnant women's agency in, and responsibility for the outcome of their pregnancies is assuming ever greater importance.

It should be noted that in conceptualizing the body in this way, as continuously subject to the practices of biopower, a Foucauldian analysis directly challenges the liberal conception of the body as autonomous and as the property or possession of the individual (Grimshaw, 1993; Ransom, 1993; Sawicki, 1991). Rather, for Foucault, the all-pervasive and productive effects of power render fully autonomous action a logical impossibility. In our conclusion, we will return to some specific problems this rejection of the notion of bodily autonomy poses for pregnant women.

Medical expertize

Abortion

As we have noted already, Foucault believed that the development of disciplines such as medicine (and psychology and psychiatry) and the establishment of a coordinated, accredited and increasingly specialized medical profession were key elements in the emergence of biopower. The expanding field of obstetrics, as many feminist writers have pointed out, was in part responsible for the *pathologizing* of pregnancy which has in turn led to the routine surveillance of the pregnant body (Brook, 1999).

On the one hand, increasingly sophisticated medical knowledge about pregnancy, and the development of reproductive technologies have undoubtedly been positive developments. As the introductory chapter of this collection argued, scientific and medical advances in the area of reproduction (for example the advent of the oral contraceptive pill, the development of new, simple abortion methods, such as the 'abortion pill', and the introduction of assisted conception techniques such as *in vitro* fertilization) have been of great benefit to women by giving them greater control over their fertility. Medical knowledge and interventions in pregnancy and childbirth were, at least in part, responsible for the drastic reduction in maternal mortality rates during the twentieth century.

On the other hand, these positive developments emerged alongside the construction of the pregnant body as potentially unhealthy, and in need of extensive medical scrutiny and intervention. Pregnancy becomes a state that is achieved by design rather than accident, and which, whether it ends in abortion or results in the birth of a child, is assumed both to pose a potential risk to health and to require medical attention. Whilst women are increasingly freed from the problems of nature (such as pregnancy-related illness and pregnancy as an inevitable risk of sexual intercourse), at the same time their bodies have become subject to intensive clinical surveillance.

In relation to abortion, one example of the medicalization of the pregnant body is the delegation of decision-making authority to medical professionals. In almost all countries where abortion has been legalized, its legality is dependent upon the approval of one or more doctors. As we discuss in more detail below, British law allows abortion *only* where it has been authorized by two doctors. In France, a woman seeking an abortion after the tenth week of pregnancy must obtain certification from two doctors that for serious medical reasons, the abortion should be carried out. In the German state of Bavaria, a woman must explain why she is seeking an abortion before she can obtain a medical note for a pre-abortion consultation. The United States is an exception because in the first three months of pregnancy the Supreme Court has declared access to abortion to be an aspect of women's constitutional right to privacy, and thus decision-making authority lies with the woman alone. Yet, even in the USA, for an abortion to be legal after three months, medical verification is required and an abortion will be permitted only where doctors judge that continuing the pregnancy would prejudice the woman's health.

Before the legalization of abortion in Scotland, England and Wales in 1967, under sections 58 and 59 of the 1861 Offences Against the Person Act anyone, including the woman herself, who attempted to procure an abortion was guilty of a criminal offence punishable by imprisonment. Although sometimes assumed to be a permissive piece of legislation, the Abortion Act 1967 did not in fact abolish the criminal offences contained in sections 58 and 59, nor did it give women the right to terminate an unwanted pregnancy. Rather the Act simply created a defence to the crime of procuring an abortion provided that two medical practitioners agreed that the woman's circumstances were sufficiently grave to justify termination (Bridgeman, 1998; Simms, 1985). So in order to comply with the terms of the Act, two doctors must agree of a woman who wants an abortion, that her health, or that of her children is endangered by the pregnancy, or that, if born, the baby would be seriously handicapped.

For our purposes, the significance of the Abortion Act lies in its insistence that abortion is only lawful if two medical experts consider that there are compelling *health* reasons to terminate the pregnancy. So, for example, an abortion can be carried out if two doctors consider that continuing the pregnancy may jeopardize the woman's physical or mental health. As Sally Sheldon (1997) has pointed out, if the grounds for abortion require a clinical diagnosis of potential pathology arising from the continuation of the pregnancy, the technical expertise of a doctor becomes essential in deciding whether or not a pregnancy should be terminated. Thus the pregnant body is pathologized, and an unwanted pregnancy must be constructed as a source of ill health in order to be lawfully terminable.

We do not want to give the impression that the Abortion Act always makes it very difficult for women to obtain abortions. Undoubtedly some doctors interpret the Act strictly and demand that women prove that their health would be damaged if they were to have a child. Where they can, such doctors may deny women's requests for abortion (Marie Stopes International, 1999). More often, however, doctors interpret the Act in order to make it relatively easy for women to terminate their unwanted pregnancies. For example, David Paintin, a gynaecologist active in providing abortion both before and after the passing of the 1967 legislation has argued 'the Act can be interpreted so that abortion can be provided virtually on request' (Paintin, 1998, p. 17). He suggests that even when the Act came into force in 1968, there proved to be a significant minority of doctors who were willing to interpret the Act as 'allowing them to provide abortion to women stressed by unwanted pregnancies' (Paintin, 1998, p. 18). Since 1968, Paintin contends, doctors have increasingly relied upon the World Health Organisation definition of health: 'a state of complete physical and social wellbeing and not merely the absence of disease or infirmity'. As a result, doctors can certify 'that there is a risk of injury to mental health if they can identify factors in the woman's life that would stress her mental well-being if the pregnancy were to continue'. Since 'such factors are present in the lives of all women who are motivated enough to consult a doctor about abortion', any woman can qualify for an abortion on this ground (Paintin, 1998, p. 17).

In the first full year after the Abortion Act came into force, 50 000 legal abortions were notified in England and Wales. This number doubled over the next two years, to reach a total of between 100 000 and 130 000 abortions for the next 12 years (Simms, 1985). The abortion rate currently stands at around 180 000 per year in England and

Wales. Between one in three and a quarter of all women will have an abortion at some point. Nevertheless, the fact remains that it is doctors' interpretation of the effects of pregnancy for a woman's health, rather than the woman's views about her pregnancy, that matter for the law. A woman must frame her reasons for wanting to terminate her unwanted pregnancy in terms of its risk to her health, and must submit to the scrutiny of medical experts before she can obtain a legal abortion. Women's relatively straightforward access to abortion in Scotland, England and Wales is therefore entirely contingent upon individual doctors' decisions to interpret the legislation in a broad and permissive way. We now turn to consider the example of pregnancies that are carried to term, where the pervasive control exercised through expert medical knowledge is not sanctioned by statute, but is nonetheless peculiarly far-reaching and effective.

Wanted pregnancy

If a pregnant woman decides to carry her pregnancy to term, the biological changes in her body will almost always be subject to the close attention of medical professionals. In addition to obstetricians' scrutiny of individual pregnant bodies, expert knowledge about pregnancy is also continually disseminated through health promotion campaigns, the media, and through the burgeoning market in self-help literature. In this section we see how the pregnant body is constructed as always potentially pathological, and we explore the ways in which this shapes women's experience of pregnancy.

For the last hundred years, the assumption that there is a simple causal relationship between new technology and better health outcomes has tended to dominate attitudes to pregnancy care. However, it is at least arguable that reductions in perinatal and maternal mortality rates over the last century owe at least as much to general improvements in women's standard of living. Since the late nineteenth century, when stethoscopes first enabled doctors to hear the fetus's heart beat, there has been an accelerating growth in technologies which supplant the pregnant woman's account of changes in her body with more 'objective' diagnostic techniques. Technological developments which allow a fetus to be seen, monitored, tested and treated mean that birth is no longer the point at which the new human life becomes visible and real to the doctors involved in its care.

Within contemporary obstetrics a new field of expertise has emerged in which the interests of the pregnant woman tend to be obscured by the fetus's status as a 'patient' in its own right. 'Fetal medicine' constructs the pregnant body as a vector through which this new patient can be reached. So rather than being a neutral description of a particular area of clinical practice, the new discipline of fetal medicine may reinforce the twin assumptions that the pregnant woman is simply a exceptionally sophisticated incubator, and that she should be prepared to sacrifice her bodily autonomy in order to allow the doctors to fulfil their primary duty to preserve the life of their tiny and vulnerable patient. The changing priorities of obstetric practice are also evident within new editions of textbooks that tend to devote progressively more of their pages to treatment of the fetus, and fewer to the care of the pregnant woman (Kolker and Burke, 1994).

As monitoring techniques have become more sophisticated, the obstetrician has been involved not only in salvaging problem pregnancies, but also in anticipating and preventing abnormalities. Prenatal testing, most notably ultrasonography and the alpha fetoprotein (AFP) test, is now a routine aspect of prenatal care in the UK, with fewer than one per cent of pregnant women receiving no prenatal tests. The received wisdom is that by subjecting normal physiology to rigorous supervision, obstetricians can minimize pathological deviations from the norm. It could be argued that routine deployment of diagnostic techniques which are overwhelmingly likely to give a normal result wastes both time and scarce NHS resources; does nothing to improve infant health; and reinforces the perception that every pregnancy is potentially abnormal and must therefore be subject to intense scrutiny and sophisticated technological intervention. Paradoxically then, despite falling birth rates and falling mortality rates, the number of pregnancies regarded as 'abnormal', and requiring medical intervention continues to rise, a trend undoubtedly exacerbated by the increasing possibility of malpractice suits against obstetricians for failing to intervene in pregnancy.

Medical expertise has thus redefined the 'normal' pregnant body, with two principal effects. First, despite its roots in seemingly objective medical knowledge, normality is revealed to be a judgement rather than a neutral, scientifically verifiable description. For example, new editions of obstetrics textbooks have steadily reduced the length of a 'normal' labour, with the result that a higher proportion of deliveries will now be defined as abnormally long and therefore in need of medical intervention. Second, since every pregnancy and its delivery is potentially pathological, it is not possible to define a pregnancy as completely normal until after the baby has been safely delivered. The normal, pathology-free pregnancy exists only with the benefit of hindsight. Since risk is inherently unpredictable, all pregnant women tend to be treated as if things might go wrong: so, for example, less than one per cent of all births now take place at home. Obstetric practice is then concerned primarily with the management of risk in *all* pregnancies, rather than with interventions in exceptional cases *after* complications have developed.

Contemporary obstetrics facilitates the identification of abnormalities while simultaneously expanding the range of indications which lead to a diagnosis of abnormality. A more potent example of the process of 'normalization' would be hard to imagine. If every pregnancy is potentially abnormal, meticulous attention to fetal development and its continuous comparison with the normal or ideal pregnancy is essential during *every* pregnancy. There is a clear parallel with a Foucauldian analysis of power. The universal monitoring of pregnant bodies takes place through:

> mechanisms that analyse gaps, series, combinations, and which use instruments that render visible, record, differentiate and compare: a physics of a relational and multiple power which has its maximum intensity not in the person of the king, but in the bodies that can be individualized by these relations (Foucault, 1977, p. 208).

Almost all pregnant women are scrutinized in minute detail, and unlike the prisoner in the panopticon (Foucault, 1977), surveillance of the pregnant body is not confined to externally observable conduct. Instead, the most intimate internal workings of the pregnant woman's body are visualized, assessed and recorded.

Medical knowledge, embodied in experts such as doctors and other medical professionals, thus acts as a powerful source of control over the pregnant body. As we saw earlier however, a Foucauldian analysis considers power to be constructive, rather than repressive. Power does not act against the will of those subject to it, instead individuals' behaviour is controlled and regulated through a web of practices which construct the citizen as a self-disciplined subject. In relation to pregnancy, this sort of power relies not upon the existence of penalties for women who fail to follow medical advice, rather it generates pregnant women's active engagement in the medicalization of their pregnancies. As Sarah Nettleton has explained, a Foucauldian reading of modern health-care policies identifies ways in which individuals are encouraged to take responsibility for their own health. So 'individuals are recruited to take care of themselves, but the techniques that are deployed by the "experts" of human conduct must in turn invariably shape how individuals come to think about them*selves*' (Nettleton, 1997, p. 212). In the next section we shall explore women's active participation in the regulation of their pregnant bodies.

Self-regulation

Pregnancy

It is important to remember that the pregnant body is not simply constructed as a passive object of the medical gaze but is instead an active participant in the production of optimum fetal health. The weight of expert knowledge about the impact of the pregnant woman's lifestyle upon the future health and well-being of her children will often prompt women to self-regulate their conduct during pregnancy (Bertin, 1995). Through the wide dissemination of health promotion information, pregnant women are continually encouraged to act responsibly in order to promote normal fetal development.

In the United States, women have been subject to both criminal and civil actions for harming their fetuses. In *State ex rel. Angela M.W.* v. *Kruzicki* 541 N.W. 2d 482 (Wis. Ct. App. 1995) a woman who was five months pregnant tested positive for drugs. She had refused voluntary inpatient treatment and the court interpreted Wisconsin's child welfare statute to include 'fetus' within the statutory definition of 'child'. A protective child custody order was granted which allowed the court to detain the woman without her consent. On 17 May 2001, a 24-year-old woman from South Carolina was sentenced to 12 years in prison for killing her fetus by smoking crack cocaine. Regina McKnight was convicted of homicide by child abuse.

Under the Congenital Disabilities (Civil Liability) Act 1976, women in the United Kingdom cannot be held liable for injuries caused *in utero*, with the exception of road traffic accidents in which the presence of compulsory insurance means that liability is in the interests of both the woman and her disabled child. But while the law cannot be used to stop women from, for example, drinking heavily or smoking while pregnant, a more refined source of control might be the proliferation of advice about how to behave during pregnancy in order to optimize the future well-being of one's offspring. By alerting the pregnant population to ways in which they can prevent disease and abnormality, illness is subtly transformed from an unavoidable misfortune into a failure of personal responsibility (Crawford, 1994). So if a pregnant women does not regulate her own lifestyle and modify her risky behaviour, she is constructed as someone who exhibits a morally reprehensible lack of self-control, rather than as a free agent exercising her right to make decisions about her body and lifestyle (Greco, 1993).

Insofar as good health is increasingly perceived to be key obligation of productive or virtuous citizenship, pregnant women are charged with performing a particularly vital civic function in promoting the health of future generations by exercising self-discipline over their immoderate appetites or desires. As Petersen and Lupton have explained 'the woman as 'healthy' citizen ... is understood as a resource for the reproduction and maintenance of other 'healthy' citizens' (Peterson and Lupton, 1996, p. 73). The provision of information to pregnant women about the best ways to maximize fetal health is a good example of health education's dual function as a provider of information which assists the exercise of informed decision-making, and as a refined and pervasive system of control. The dissemination of vast and detailed expertise about how to optimize fetal development may help pregnant women to make choices about their lifestyle, but it simultaneously represents a powerful stimulus towards self-discipline (Martin, 1987). Significantly, there tends to be more interest in studies that find a negative correlation between prenatal behaviour and fetal development than those which indicate that prenatal exposure to a particular toxin has no discernible impact upon fetal well-being. So, for example, studies that found women's prenatal cocaine use had had no adverse effect upon fetal well-being were, according to one survey, five times less likely to be accepted for publication than studies that had identified a negative impact upon fetal health (Bertin, 1995, p. 388). Any bias in medical journals will then be amplified by the media's indifference to research with no headline-grabbing potential.

The accumulation of techniques which can monitor fetal development multiply the opportunities for pregnant women to feel anxiety about fetal progress (Gallagher, 1995). New research into factors affecting fetal development is published in medical journals each week. The identification both of risk factors, and of appropriate tactics for risk-avoidance is, therefore, in a constant state of flux. Sociologists have analyzed some of the consequences of our increased awareness of risk in relation to pregnancy, childbirth and child rearing (Furedi, 1997; 2001). In relation to pregnancy, women are not only supposed to follow medical advice, but also to be alert to the possibility of new guidance, and endlessly receptive to it.

While it is undoubtedly true that fetal development is affected by the conduct of the pregnant woman, it could be argued that women's responsibility for the health and well-being of the next generation is frequently overstated, in comparison with a widespread underestimation of the impact of socioeconomic circumstances and of 'paternal behaviour' (Bertin, 1995). As Sally Sheldon argued in a previous chapter, differences exist in the regulation of male and female exposure to reproductive hazards in the workplace. Evidence that an individual's future health may be adversely affected by toxic environments which damage sperm quality (Bertin, 1995), or by exposure *in utero* to affected seminal fluid (Narayan, 1995) does not tend to result in attempts to restrict the workforce participation of men, although it may lead to claims for compensation (Daniels, 1999). Instead 'fetal protection policies' have concentrated upon the hazards posed by *women's* participation in traditionally *male* working environments. So there has been much less interest in the toxicity of poorly paid and traditionally female occupations, such as nursing or cleaning (Narayan, 1995). This discrepancy is particularly striking in the light of the correlation between parental affluence and fetal well-being: exclusion from well-paid employment may cause fetal harm just as serious as an environmental toxin.

It is perhaps interesting that preventative health programmes have tended to individualize the problem of prenatal harm by concentrating almost exclusively upon steps that a pregnant woman can take to ensure a healthy baby, rather than addressing collective responsibility for toxic environments and inadequate social care. For example, the development of Fetal Alcohol Syndrome is closely associated with the socioeconomic class of the pregnant woman, and it is actually relatively uncommon among the children of wealthy women who drink heavily during pregnancy but who have other material advantages such as good nutrition and prenatal care. So while advising women not to drink excessively during pregnancy may help to prevent Fetal Alcohol Syndrome, improving the living standards of poorer women would actually be a more effective strategy.

We have seen how the concept of fetal medicine and the proliferation of prenatal health advice acts upon the body of the pregnant woman. She is constructed both as a docile subject, submitting to invasive medical scrutiny, and as an active agent responsible for optimizing fetal health. Although it would be contrary to legal principle for a fetus's well-being to take precedence over the pregnant woman's freedom and bodily integrity (McLean, 1999, p. 69), the extent to which women are realistically able to refuse medical intervention in pregnancy, or to reject prenatal health advice is questionable.

Bringing about enthusiastic participation in fetal health promotion is clearly a much more sophisticated and successful way to control behaviour than coercive legal sanctions.

Abortion

We have already seen how the privileging of medical expertise, evident in abortion law and policy, is one way in which pregnant bodies are regulated. A Foucauldian analysis of power should also prompt us to examine ways in which women seeking abortions may discipline themselves. We now consider women's active participation in the construction of the decision to have an abortion. However, in highlighting the ways in which women have internalized dominant cultural understandings about abortion, our aim is not to present women as unimaginative, passive victims. Rather it is simply to draw attention to the profound and inevitable influence cultural norms exert upon the ways in which women experience their unwanted pregnancies (Albury, 1999).

As we saw earlier, abortion is lawful only if two doctors agree that one of the four specified grounds exists. In addition to the assumption that doctors are better qualified than pregnant women to decide whether a pregnancy should be terminated, the Abortion Act also distinguishes between 'good' and 'bad' or 'deserving' and 'undeserving' justifications for abortion (Boyle, 1997). So within the terms of the Act, a woman has a 'good' reason for abortion if termination is necessary on health grounds. By implication, reasons for abortion which are not based upon a threat to the health of the pregnant woman or her children are perceived to be both inadequate and morally deficient.

The idea that it is possible to distinguish between 'good' and 'bad' reasons for termination has had a profound impact upon popular understandings of abortion, and we suggest, has generated a powerful imperative towards self-discipline on the part of women. Our focus here is upon the relationship between contraceptive use and abortion, and we explore how the dominant assumption that women need abortion because they have failed to control their fertility helps to construct women as self-regulating subjects.

New developments in contraceptive technology have led to the prevalent belief that pregnancy is now effectively optional. The wide availability of the contraceptive pill and other forms of hormonal contraception is supposed to mean that the need for abortion services will wither away. If almost failsafe forms of contraception are available to women, an unwanted pregnancy is assumed to result from the woman's failure to exercise proper control over her body's reproductive potential. We would contend that this perception of the reliability of contraception is fundamentally flawed. The pill is believed to be the most reliable method of contraception: it is 99 per cent effective. However, this means that of the 3 million women currently using the pill in Britain, even where they use it according to manufacturers' instructions, 30 000 will get pregnant each year. In practice, many more will. In one study, a fifth of all women referred for abortion claimed to have been using the pill (Furedi, 1996). The most common reason for the pill's failure to prevent pregnancy, according to Furedi, is that women sometimes forget to take it. She notes a recent MORI poll that found that 60 per cent of pill users had forgotten to take their pill at least once during the preceding 12 months, and that on average, a woman forgets to take the pill eight times a year. This level of human error and its resulting unwanted pregnancies and abortions could be regarded as an inevitable hazard of pill use. Instead it is commonly cited as evidence of women's carelessness or irresponsibility.

As a result of this assumption that fertility is always controllable, conception has become something that people are expected to achieve by design. If medical science has enabled every woman to avoid unplanned conception, a woman's need for abortion becomes a sign of weakness or incompetence. As Albury has pointed out, 'pregnancy is often regarded as a moral failure of control and personal responsibility, rather than a failure of the contraceptive methods or plain bad luck' (Albury, 1999, p. 38). If pregnancy should always be preventable through contraceptive vigilance, it is unsurprising that feelings of irresponsibility, stupidity, failure and guilt have come to be associated with the experience of abortion.

The assumption that responsible women are always able to use contraception effectively serves to stigmatize women who want to terminate their unwanted pregnancies, and this in turn shapes their experience of abortion. The feminist writer, Marge Berer, has explained that 'the prevailing belief is that no matter how responsible an act it is to use contraception, it is only responsible enough if the contraception doesn't fail you, or you don't fail with it. In other words, if you end up pregnant and you didn't want to be, it's probably all your own fault' (Berer, 1993, p. 41). Women can internalize these norms of responsible contraceptive behaviour, and construct themselves as either justified in seeking abortion if they had assiduously tried to prevent pregnancy through contraceptive use, or ashamed about their need for abortion if they had failed to use contraception effectively (Stotland, 1998).

As many researchers of women's accounts of abortion have noted (Davies, 1991; Furedi, 1996; Pipes, 1998), women often feel guilty if their pregnancy is a result of unprotected sexual intercourse. Some women are too embarrassed to admit that they have not used contraception, others apologize to the health care professionals with whom they discuss their request for abortion. According to Lattimer (1998), women's accounts of their reasons for seeking abortion are produced by a dominant discourse which assumes that there is no excuse for unplanned pregnancy. The disciplinary impact of this construction of 'good' and 'bad' reasons for abortion has been also been noted by Lee (2000) in her account of an interview study with women who have had abortions. One interviewee, Anne-Marie explained:

> the guilt I felt, the guilt I felt at having got pregnant ... I just couldn't believe it, I was so mad at myself. I was so mad at everything. I felt awful, I felt guilty, I felt ashamed of myself. I felt awful for having got pregnant ... you feel that you should have taken every single precaution necessary to ensure you never have to go through that (Lee, 2000).

Similarly Emma, a student in her early twenties, was determined that her contraception should never fail again: 'now, even if I get a bit of sperm near me, I get a morning after pill. I'm so cautious.'

Increased knowledge about contraception, and its widespread promotion by many public health agencies has normalized contraceptive use. At the same time, however, we contend that it has generated a powerful imperative towards the self-regulation of the pregnant body. So, in addition to the Abortion Act vesting doctors with the power to determine whether the woman has a sufficient, health-based reason for terminating her pregnancy, the division between 'good' and 'bad' reasons for abortion is further reinforced by the prevailing assumption that an unwanted pregnancy represents a personal failure. Power is then exercised over pregnant bodies both by the dispassionate external authority of the medical expert, and by the woman herself whose internalization of norms of contraceptive responsibility acts as an effective stimulus towards her own self-discipline.

Conclusion

As we have seen, a Foucauldian analysis of power has considerable resonance for the legal and extra-legal disciplinary practices that regulate the pregnant body. The experiences of both pregnancy and abortion have been so thoroughly saturated with professional expertise that their medicalization has become simply the way things are. It is now almost unimaginable for a pregnant woman to carry her pregnancy to term without undergoing any high-tech monitoring. And law which rests on medical control over the decision to terminate a pregnancy has similarly become a non-negotiable aspect of abortion provision. Power which consists in the generation of expert knowledge and in the surveillance of the population is undoubtedly evident within the disciplinary practices to which the pregnant body is subjected.

As a descriptive tool, then, a Foucauldian understanding of power may have much to offer an analysis of the regulation of the pregnant body. But while Foucault does suggest that some resistance is the inevitable by-product of power, and that fostering such resistance should be the principal task of those who advocate radical social change, it is not clear that this is necessarily the only or even the optimum practical strategy for those in favour of disrupting the web of disciplinary norms which construct the pregnant body.

It is, as we have seen, true that there may be pockets of resistance to dominant understandings about the proper management of pregnancy and abortion. For example, in relation to women's experiences of pregnancy, Albury has pointed out that 'women's subjectivity is not completely constituted in relation to medical discourses ... feminist ideas have contributed to the recognition of women as experts in their own lives' (Albury, 1999, p. 52). Medical authority in relation to abortion, for example, has by no means been left unchallenged. The Women's Movement of the 1970s adopted the slogan 'Not the doctors, not the state, women must decide their fate', in order to indicate their outrage at the assumption that doctors were better placed than women to decide the outcome of a pregnancy. Such campaigns for women's reproductive freedom have offered a powerful resource for women seeking to resist dominant assumptions about abortion.

But according to Foucault, the all-pervasiveness and inescapability of these diffused and often imperceptible mechanisms of biopower means that individual agency can exist only in the weakest possible sense. So, as we saw earlier, pregnant women are encouraged to act 'autonomously' in choosing a healthy lifestyle, but a Foucauldian analysis would consider that their choices are not the result of free will and reflect, instead, the profound penetration of the disciplinary society. As a result, there is little scope within Foucauldian theory for arguments based upon principles of autonomy or self-determination.

The liberal conception of autonomy is rooted in the idea that an individual should be able to pursue their own goals according to their own values, beliefs and desires. According to a Foucauldian analysis, however, the 'perfection of power should tend to render its actual exercise unnecessary' (Foucault, 1977, p. 201) because the individual has been 'carefully fabricated ... according to a whole technique of forces and bodies' (Foucault, 1977, p. 217). If power has thus created an individual's preferences, respecting them is simply another way in which the omniscience of biopower manifests itself. In this framework, the choices people make are simply evidence of biopower's penetration.

It is obviously important to acknowledge that our preferences may reflect the internalization of cultural norms. In our view, however, by effectively effacing the notion of free will, Foucauldian analysis offers an inadequate basis for constructive social change. The right of every adult to have a sphere of self-determination or self-government is central to the exercise of both freedom and responsibility, and may in fact be especially important for pregnant women.

Recognizing the pregnant woman as the primary decision-maker in relation to her prenatal behaviour, or her decision to have an abortion, may fail to capture the rich network of disciplinary practices which operate upon the pregnant body. Nevertheless, it may offer a pragmatically useful starting point for legal reform. Insofar as the pregnant body is subject to especially profound control, comparing its regulation with the priority usually given to individual autonomy, particularly in relation to medical treatment, reveals that pregnant women are subjected to levels of scrutiny and intervention which would be unthinkable in any other context (Jackson, 2000). At the very least, given that induced abortion and obstetric care are medical procedures to which only female bodies are subject, it might be worth drawing attention to the conspicuous absence of a robust conception of the pregnant woman's bodily autonomy (Sheldon and Thomson, 1998).

Further reading

Brook, Barbara, *Feminist Perspectives on the Body* (London and New York; Longman, 1999).
    A very accessible introduction to feminist approaches to the body. Chapter 2, 'Reproducing Bodies' deals with some of the themes discussed in this chapter.
Peterson, Alan and Lupton, Deborah, *The New Public Health: Health and Self in the Age of Risk* (London: Sage, 1996), Chapter 1 'The New Public Health: A New Morality', pp. 1–26, and Chapter 3 'The Healthy Citizen', pp. 61–88.

These chapters offer a clear and persuasive account of the ways in which the discourses of the new public health seek to transform individuals into self-regulating and productive citizens.

Young, Iris Marion, *Intersecting Voices: Dilemmas of Gender, Political Philosophy and Policy* (Princeton: Princeton University Press, 1997), Chapter IV 'Punishment, Treatment, Empowerment: Three Approaches to Policy for Pregnant Addicts', pp. 75–94.

In this stimulating chapter, Young uses Foucault's notions of disciplinary power to criticize an alternative treatment model for pregnant drug addicts based around a supposedly feminist ethic of care, on the grounds that this treatment programme tends to individualize the social problem of drug use.

9

The Dressed Body

Joanne Entwistle

Dress has an intimate relationship to the body. The materials we hang at the margins of our body – fabric, jewellery, paint or feathers – enjoy a close proximity to the flesh, outlining, emphasizing, obscuring or extending the body. Choosing leather as opposed to silk, Lycra as opposed to cotton, denim rather than wool, will affect the way the body looks and feels. Umberto Eco captures this close relationship between dress and the body very well when he describes wearing jeans, which are still too tight after losing some weight. He describes how the jeans feel on his body, how they pinch and restrict his movement, how they make him aware of the lower half of his body; indeed, how they come to constitute what he calls an 'epidermic self-awareness' which he had not felt before:

> As a result, I lived in the knowledge that I had jeans on, whereas normally we live forgetting that we're wearing undershorts or trousers. I lived for my jeans and as a result I assumed an exterior behaviour of one who wears jeans. In any case, I assumed a demeanor … Not only did the garment impose a demeanor on me; by focusing my attention on demeanor it obliged me to live towards the exterior world (Eco, 1986, pp. 192–4).

Dress, then, forms part of our epidermis – it lies on the boundary between self and other. The fact that we do not normally develop epidermal self-awareness tells us a lot about our routine relationship to dress, that is, that it forms a second skin which is not usually an object of consciousness. Our consciousness of dress is heightened when something is out of place – when either our clothes do not fit us, as Eco describes, or they do not fit the situation, for example, when we

133

find ourselves dressed too casually at a formal situation or too formally at a casual situation. In the first instance, when clothes do not fit us, the experience is very private and sensual – an experience of the body. To understand the relationship between dress and the body one must acknowledge the very private and very visceral nature of dress which imposes itself on our experience of the body, expressing or constraining it, making us aware of the girth of our waist as Eco describes, or the breadth of our shoulder blades, the length of our arms or legs, and so on. In the second instance, the experience is about the relationship of dress to the social world. It tells us that our dress does not only belong to our bodies but to the social world as well. Thus, any understanding of the dressed body must acknowledge the social nature of it – how it is shaped by techniques, attitudes, aesthetics and so on, which are socially and historically located.

Different techniques of dress produce different bodies. A body dressed in *Commes des Garçons* is very different to a body dressed in a Vivienne Westwood corset and skirt. Many Japanese designers have, in recent years, deconstructed the dressed body familiar to the west, draping it in garments of fluid cloth, which do not conform to the conventions of western tailoring. In contrast, Westwood plays with the conventions of traditional English tailoring by exaggerating them. In each case, the dressed body takes on very different shapes and forms, largely as a result of the tailoring of the cloth: *Commes des Garçon* clothes often obscure the line of the body, creating space between the body and the fabric, while Westwood's tailoring exaggerates the body's lines and curves. Cloth, and the tailoring practices that shape it, give form to the body's presentation in culture. These practices are always historically and culturally located: the fact that we can locate a particular 'Japanese' as opposed to 'English' style of tailoring is indicative of this. Such labels are, of course, imaginary in the way that Benedict Anderson (1986) suggests – constructive of national communities rather than unproblematically reflecting them. Nevertheless these imaginary constructions, once in place, have an historical, political and cultural reality to them.

What I hope these examples suggest is that dress and the body exist in dialectic relationship to one another. Dress operates on the phenomenal body; it is a very crucial aspect of our everyday experience of embodiment, while the body is a dynamic field, which gives life and fullness to dress (Entwistle and Wilson, 1998). Dress is a ubiquitous aspect of our social embodiment, a basic fact of all social life. The social world demands that we appear dressed and there are no examples of cultures that leave the body unadorned, although what constitutes 'dress' varies from culture to culture. Bodies can be dressed in a variety of ways with fabric, body paint, tattoos, jewellery and make-up being some of the more common forms of adornment. Any number of these might be worn by bodies within a culture, since what is considered appropriate dress will vary according to the situation or occasion.

In this chapter, I want to explore this relationship between dress and the body, examining how each shapes the other. As a sociologist, I examine the dressed body as a *situated object* within the social world. The dressed body is not only a uniquely individual, private and sensual body, it is a social phenomenon too, since our understandings and techniques of dress and our relationship to cloth, are socially and historically constituted. However, I posit that the dressed body is a fleshy, phenomenological entity that is so much a part of our experience of the social world and so thoroughly embedded within the micro-dynamics of social order, as to be entirely taken for granted. While it would seem obvious that dress cannot be understood without reference to the body, and while the body has always and everywhere to be dressed, there has been a surprising lack of concrete analysis of the relationship between them. With the exception of anthropology, which has long investigated the body's centrality to culture, much social theory has ignored or repressed the body.

Classical social theory failed to acknowledge the significance of dress because it neglected the body and the things that bodies do (Turner, 1984). The emergence of studies of the body in sociology, cultural studies and other fields in the last 20 years or so, would seem an obvious place to look for literature on dress and fashion, but this research has also tended not to examine dress. The reasons for this are not clear, but it may perhaps have something to do with a long-felt antipathy towards fashion and dress which are seen as frivolous and not worthy of serious, scholarly attention (see for example Veblen, 1953). This absence of the dressed body within classic and modern social theory is surprising considering the importance of dress to bodily social order. Questions of social order are, in essence, questions of bodily order.

This point is made forcefully by Bryan Turner in his now classic study *The Body and Society* (1984). Turner's book helped to establish the 'sociology of the body' and place it firmly on the academic map within contemporary social theory. He argues that all societies, however large or small, have to control, contain and manage bodies, and the mechanisms and techniques for coordinating bodies are many and varied. He argues, therefore, that much classic social theory, which has typically been concerned with social order, can be reframed to consider the body as the thing that is controlled and managed. He notes, in particular, the influence of French theorist Michel Foucault as crucial to the inauguration of sociology of the body (a point borne out by the influence of a Foucauldian approach in chapters in this volume). As previous and following chapters detail, Foucault (1977, 1978, 1980) argues that the institutions and disciplines of modernity were centrally concerned with the control and manipulation of bodies and his work therefore provides for a historical account that renders visible the body in social life. However, to date, there has been little consideration of the role played by techniques of dress in the establishment and maintenance of social order. Turner does not consider the role of dress in social order, nor does Foucault, although, as I will argue below, the latter's work can be utilized to analyze the dressed body.

There is another absence too in the literature on fashion and dress produced by history, cultural studies and other fields. This has, until relatively recently, paid little attention to the body, focusing instead on the communicative aspects of dress and adornment, sometimes adopting the rather abstract, and disembodied linguistic model of structural linguistics (see for example, Barthes, 1985; Hebdige, 1979; Lurie, 1981), and examining the spectacular, creative and expressive aspects of dress rather than the mundane and routine part it plays in reproducing social order (for example, Clarke et al., 1992; Polhemus, 1994).

Between these bodies of literature, between the theorists of the classical tradition and theorists of the body who tend to overlook fashion and dress as trivial, and those theorists of fashion and dress who have focused rather too much attention on the articles of clothing, the *dressed body* as a discursive and phenomenological field vanishes and dress is disembodied. Either the body is thought to be self evidently dressed (and therefore beyond discussion) or the clothes are assumed to stand up on their own, possibly even speaking for themselves without the aid of the body. And yet, the importance of the body to dress is such that encounters with dress, divorced from the body, are strangely alienating. Wilson (1985) grasps this when she describes the unease one feels in the presence of mannequins in the costume museum and, likewise, the clothes of dead relatives are often the most poignant of objects left behind, particularly when the shape of the arm or the imprint of the foot is still visible. These encounters with clothes, haunted by the bodies of the dead, point to the ways in which we 'normally' experience dress as alive and 'fleshy': once removed from the body, dress lacks fullness and seems strange, almost alien, and all the more poignant to us if we can remember the person who once breathed life into the fabric.

In this chapter, I therefore want to flesh out some ways of thinking about the dressed body, which capture the dynamic relationship between body and dress – in other words, an account that tries to embody dress. In doing so, I am arguing for ways of thinking about the dressed body which bridge the gap between theories of the body, which often overlook dress, and theories of fashion and dress, which too frequently leave out the body. I want to explore a number of ways of thinking through the body in culture and I suggest how these may be extended to the analysis of dress. I discuss the work of a number of theorists whose work sheds some light on the relationship between the body and dress. In most cases, these theorists have not recognized the role of dress but I want to draw out the implications of their analysis for understanding the dressed body. However, I hope to avoid giving an overly theoretical and abstract discussion by illustrating these theories through a number of examples, some of them drawn from my own research, as well as that of others.

The two bodies

As I have already suggested, the body is both an intimate and social object: intimate in that, as Fred Davis (1994) puts it, it comes 'to serve as a kind of visual metaphor for identity'; social in that, it is structured by social forces and subject to social and moral pressures. It is no surprise to note, therefore, that the body's margins and boundaries are rich in symbolic meaning and the focal point of cultural and individual anxieties. The body, as we know, is subject to moral pronouncements and social regulations from the macro to the micro level. As Foucault (1977, 1978, 1980) argues, Church, state and other modern institutions, such as prisons, hospitals and family, seek to control and coordinate bodies, rendering them meaningful and productive in the process. Other aesthetic and moral practices, such as tailoring and the fashion system, also operate on the body, coordinating, managing bodies and imposing ways of being on the body that come to constitute the common sense of our everyday embodiment. Since all cultures 'dress' the body in some way or another, it is therefore no surprise either to find individuals concerned with what to hang at the body's margins. Thus, as the historian and theorist Mikhail Bakhtin

(1984) and the anthropologist Mary Douglas (1973, 1984) have demonstrated, the body's physiological properties and boundaries are a rich repository of cultural meaning. The boundaries of the body are potentially dangerous since they are 'leaky' – the body is semi-permeable, open and therefore must be managed by culture.

Douglas (1973, 1984) has provided a most compelling account of what she calls the 'two bodies' which constitute the totality of our experience of embodiment – the physical body (the biological, individual body) and the social body (the body demanded by our culture). The latter gives meaning to the former, shaping our understandings of our embodiment. She summarizes the relationship between them in *Natural Symbols*:

> The social body constrains the way the physical body is perceived. The physical experience of the body, always modified by the social categories through which it is known, sustains a particular view of society. There is a continual exchange of meanings between the two kinds of bodily experience so that each reinforces the categories of the other (Douglas, 1973, p. 93).

In other words, our experience of embodiment is thus always mediated by the culture we live in. According to Douglas, the body is a highly restricted medium of expression that expresses the social pressure brought to bear on it. Our ways of being in the body are crucially shaped by the social practices of our culture. Thus, the social situation imposes itself upon the body and constrains it to act in particular ways. Indeed, the body becomes a symbol of the situation. Douglas gives the example of laughing to illustrate this. Laughter is a physiological experience, which starts in the face but can infuse the entire body. Douglas asks, 'what is being communicated?' by laughter and says, in answer, 'information from the social system' (Douglas, 1979, p. 87). To put it another way, she is arguing that the social situation determines the degree to which the body can laugh: the looser the social constraints, the freer the body is to laugh out loud. In this way, the body and its functions and boundaries symbolically articulate the concerns of the particular group in which it is found and, indeed, become a symbol of the situation: the social imprints itself onto the body in such a way that the individual body symbolically expresses that situation. Groups that are worried about threats to their cultural or national boundaries might articulate this fear through rituals around the body, particularly pollution rituals and ideas about purity (Douglas, 1984). These rituals have a strong moral component to them. If we follow them, we demonstrate ourselves to be respectful citizens of our culture, if we fail to meet them, we risk censure, criticism, condemnation or exclusion.

In the work of the sociologist Erving Goffman (1971, 1972), the moral dimension of embodiment is brought to the fore. For Goffman, as for Douglas, the body is both the property of the individual and the social world: it is the vehicle of identity but this identity has to be 'managed' in terms of the definitions of the social situation which impose particular ways of being on the body. Thus, the individual feels a social and moral imperative to perform their identity in particular ways and this includes learning appropriate ways of dressing. Learning to keep our clothes on while in public is something parents have to enforce upon unruly young children who are so fond of taking them off, especially if there is an audience. Pre-school toddlers can get away with stripping in public, but as they approach school age, parents may become anxious to ensure children learn shame and do not risk ridicule in public by stripping off at school. Obvious though this seems, it is a taken-for-granted aspect of social life that illustrates the centrality of dress to our experiences of embodiment and to the moral order of the social world. Like so much bodily behaviour, codes of dress come to be taken for granted and are routinely and unreflexively employed, although some occasions, generally formal ones (like weddings and funerals) set tighter constraints around the body, and lend themselves to more conscious reflection on dress. I will return to this point below.

Dress is the way in which individuals learn to live in their bodies and feel at home in them. Wearing the right clothes and looking our best, we feel at ease with our body, and the opposite is true also: turning up for a situation inappropriately dressed, we feel ill at ease in our bodies, out of place and vulnerable. Dress is, therefore, a fundamentally moral phenomenon. Goffman's work thus adds to Douglas's account of the 'two bodies' by bringing actual bodily practices into the frame, describing how individuals manage their bodies in concrete settings – on the street, in bars and restaurants, asylums and hospitals.

Douglas and Goffman do not talk in detail about dress in their analysis of bodily practices but their ideas can be extended to the interpretation of dress and adornment. Goffman's ideas can be extended to discussion of the ways in which dress is routinely attended to as part of the 'presentation of self in everyday life'. Most situations, even the most informal, have a code of dress and these impose particular ways of being on bodies in such a way as to have a social and moral imperative to them. Quentin Bell gives the example of a five-day-old beard which could not be worn to the theatre without censure and disapproval 'exactly comparable to that occasioned by dishonourable conduct' (Bell, 1976, pp. 18–19). Indeed, clothes are often spoken of in moral terms, using words like 'faultless', 'good', 'correct'. Few are immune to this social pressure and most people are embarrassed by certain mistakes of dress, such as finding one's flies undone or discovering a stain on a jacket.

However, the embarrassment of such mistakes of dress is not simply that of a personal faux pas, but the shame of failing to meet the standards required by the moral order of the social space. When we talk of someone's 'slip showing' we are, according to Wilson, speaking of something 'more than slight sartorial sloppiness' – 'the exposure of something much more profoundly ambiguous and disturbing ... the naked body underneath the clothes' (Wilson, 1985, p. 8) and such nakedness is closely associated with our feelings of shame. A commonly cited dream, for many people, is the experience of suddenly finding oneself naked in a public place: dress, or the lack of it in this case, serves as a metaphor for feelings of shame, embarrassment and vulnerability in our culture as well as indicating the way in which the moral order demands that the body be covered in some way. These examples illustrate the way in which dress is part of the micro-order of social interaction and intimately connected to our (rather fragile) sense of self, which is, in turn, threatened if we fail to conform to the standards governing a particular social situation.

Thus, as Bell puts it, 'our clothes are too much a part of us for most of us to be entirely indifferent to their condition: it is as though the fabric were indeed a natural extension of the body, or even of the soul' (Bell, 1976, p. 19). Thus, in the presentation of self in social interaction, ideas of embarrassment and stigma play a crucial role and are managed, in part, through dress.

If we extend Douglas's analysis we can understand dress as expressive of the concerns of the particular cultural milieu and social situation in which it is found. Dress conveys information about a situation, providing what Douglas calls 'feedback' about that situation. Formal events, such as, weddings, funerals and job interviews, impose themselves more forcefully on the body, making more demands of it than do informal ones and this generally translates into a more highly regulated body in terms of dress. At a wedding one must not wear white unless one is the bride and it would be inappropriate to dress in jogging pants or jeans to a job interview. Such rules are relaxed in more informal situations, although they are not without any rules. Informal situations, such as a party, require a casual appearance and not being dressed in clothing that is in keeping can generate embarrassment. For example, in the film, *Bridget Jones's Diary*, the central character, Bridget Jones, turns up for a party she thinks is on the theme 'tarts and vicars', dressed in a skimpy bunny-girl outfit, only to find out that this theme has been dropped and everyone is in regular clothes. Her embarrassment is shared by other party members and made worse by the fact that she is dressed in a sexually provocative way. What these examples highlight is that the dress we wear in different situations is to some extent governed by the codes of that situation, to such an extent that, as Douglas suggests, the dressed body can symbolize the rules of each.

Let me illustrate Douglas's point with my own research on career women. In my analysis of the dress practices of career women, this contrast between formal and informal situations and the way the body articulates these implicit rules of such situations, becomes very apparent. The women I interviewed all spoke of two different bodies, one appropriate to work, the other to home. These two bodies were very much defined in terms of a sharp distinction between tailored or structured dress worn to work and untailored or unstructured dress at home. The dressed body at work, described by my respondents, was a public body, dressed for the formal conditions of the professional workplace. This formal body was more tightly constrained in terms of its visual appearance, its contours firmly demarcated by tailored clothing, especially by the tailored jacket which marks a clear boundary around the body in much the same way as a man's suit jacket does. I have argued elsewhere (Entwistle, 1997, 2000) that this structured dress gives visible form to the professional woman, marking her out as a businesswoman, lawyer, and manager, as opposed to a secretary or other clerical worker. Thus, the sharp skirt or trouser suit articulates a very particular kind of body: one that is feminine *and* professional at the same time. Such a public body is a relatively recent historical invention since only recently have women become visible as professional women. This is not to say that women had never before been seen in tailored clothing. The appearance of tailored dress for the professional woman in the 1970s and 1980s can be compared to the first fashions in tailored dress worn by women at the end of the nineteenth century and early twentieth century. This dress reflected the increasing visibility of women in public in the late Victorian era, as sportswomen in riding garb or on bicycles and, later, as clerks and secretaries in offices. These ancestors of the career woman adopted tailored jackets and waistcoats, mannish hats and neckties similar to that worn by men at the time. It marked a new fashion for women, adapted to meet newly expanding opportunities for women to appear in public. Similarly, in the late

1970s and early 1980s, the growth of professional and businesswomen, in relatively male-dominated occupations and spheres of work required a new way of dressing for increasing visibility at work *as* professionals. This resulted in the adaptation of the male business suit, known as the 'power suit', because of its associations with a new breed of career-orientated and increasingly powerful women in the professions, powerful symbolically, and to some extent, in real economic terms too.

This particular female, dressed body was articulated in a number of sites: in new self-help manuals on how to 'dress for success' and by a relatively new group of 'experts' or dress consultants who gave advice on how to 'dress for success'. This female body was also articulated in the design and manufacture of dress for working women, most notably by designers such as Donna Karan, Georgio Armani, as well as by retailers such as Jigsaw and Next during the 1980s, and she figured in a whole range of representations in magazines (*Cosmopolitan*), newspapers, film (*Working Girl*, 1988) and television (*Thirtysomething*). The tailored, female body, found in increasing numbers since the 1980s, thus constituted a new kind of public body which took shape against the backdrop of very particular social, economic and political circumstances.

In contrast to the tailored body at work, the professional women I spoke to described a very different body at home. This was a body dressed not for *visibility* in sharp suits in clear, tailored lines but for *comfort* in jeans, jogging pants and T-shirts. This dressed body, unlike the professionally dressed body, was defined in terms of unstructured clothing, loose as opposed to tailored.

To return to Douglas's notion of the body as symbolic of the social situation, it would seem, from these examples, that the body in the formal situation at work and the informality of the home, becomes a symbol of the implicit 'rules' or norms of the situation. The formal conditions of work require a formality in the body and set tighter constraints around it. The body at work, then, is a more formal, highly structured body and sharply outlined in tailored dress. At home, bodily constraints are loosened and this quite literally is expressed in terms of 'loose' clothing, such as jeans and T-shirts, designed for comfort and movement. In this way, we can see how fabric gives form to the body, producing it as formal or informal, tailored or casual.

Fabric and embodiment

As this example illustrates, the cut and shape of cloth, and the overall practices of tailoring, constitute an important part of the social and historical context of the dressed body. These practices frame the meanings given to cloth and mediate the relationship between dress and the body. As Christopher Breward (1999) has argued, the introduction of new techniques in tailoring from the 1820s, such as the tape measure and developing standardisation in measuring and cutting techniques, can be correlated very closely to emerging ideas about the fashionable male, and, to a lesser extent and a little later perhaps, to emerging ideas about the female body in public. Tailoring techniques articulate cultural attitudes to the body which are historically and culturally specific and which have a moral imperative to them, since any practice that works so closely on the body touches on questions of morality.

I want to say a little more about the relationship between fabric and embodiment and how these relate to one another to constitute part of our experience and understanding of embodiment. Relatively recent developments in fabric production can be analyzed in relation to ideas and ideals of the body. Let me illustrate with some examples. Our relationship to fabric has a historical dimension to it. If we examine evidence as to fabric fetishism, it would seem that different fabrics have been endowed with erotic content. The early twentieth-century psychoanalyst William Sketel (1930) documented some rare examples of female fetishism, many of which focused on fabrics such as silk and satin. For these women, the sensual properties of silk were the focus of intense sexual pleasure, leading, one young woman, a silk weaver's daughter, to steal silk from shops. However, as Valerie Steele (1996) has noted in her analysis of fetishism, the 'soft' fabrics like silk, satin and also fur, popularly fetishized in the nineteenth and early twentieth century, have been supplanted by the emergence of new technologies for the production of 'hard' fabrics in recent years, such as leather, PVC and rubber. Today's fetishists are more likely to focus on plastic, PVC, rubber or leather than satin or fur. The erotic content of these softer fabrics has not, of course, been emptied out, since lingerie, often the focus of fetishistic desires, is still largely made from soft fabrics like silk. However, there are few documented cases of silk or satin fetishists today: fetishists are more likely to eroticize the feeling and smell of rubber or leather. This would seem to suggest that the eroticism of fabric and the relationship of fabric to the sexual and sensual body, is in part historically constituted as well as culturally variable. In other words, our understandings of dress and the relationship of fabric to the body, are the products of our time.

New technologies of fabric production are also altering other relationships between cloth and the body and are indicative of the dynamic relationship between the dressed body and broader social and cultural developments. For example, Lycra has the ability to mould the body in such a way as to promote a body that looks fit, lean and muscular, enabling the production of a more streamlined body. Initially used in sportswear, Lycra has become so popular that it is now used in a wide range of garment production. It suggests how bodily matters, such as comfort, flexibility and movement, are important aspects of the modern dressed body, as is the aesthetic concern to look fit and toned. Compared to the dressed bodies of the nineteenth and early twentieth century, the contemporary body dressed in Lycra is an altogether different body. In the realm of sportswear, new intelligent fabrics are utilized to produce bodies that look leaner and more lithe and have helped to promote new body aesthetics. Similarly, the 'fast skins' worn by the Australian swimmers at the last Olympic games promoted a new kind of swimming body, one that provoked considerable controversy as to whether or not such a totally encasing suit of special fabric constituted inappropriate technology or apparatus. It also changed the image of the swimming body, which is conventionally dressed in the tiniest of fabric, in such a way as to threaten understandings of the Australian body, so closely associated with sport, and especially with the image of the swimmer. Fabric then, in its close proximity to the body, carries enormous social, cultural, political and moral weight. It is closely bound up with individual anxieties and broader social and historical concerns about the regulation of bodies in social space.

If fabric can be said to constitute a 'technology', then the work of anthropologist Marcel Mauss (1973) is pertinent here, for he describes how the physical body is shaped by culture when he elaborates on mundane 'techniques of the body'. Mauss's work has some potential for understanding the situated nature of the dressed body. The techniques he outlines are not 'natural' but the product of particular ways of being in the body, which are embedded within culture, and his examples also point to the ways in which these are gendered. Ways of walking, moving, making a fist, and so on, are different for men and women because, in the making of 'masculine' and 'feminine', culture inscribes the bodies of men and women with different physical capacities. Mauss's 'techniques of the body' has obvious application to dress and the way in which dress modifies the body, embellishing it and inflecting it with meanings, which, in the first instance, are gendered. Although he says little about dress, he does note how women learn to walk in high heels which would be difficult and uncomfortable for men who are generally unaccustomed to such shoes. Mauss's idea of 'techniques of the body' is therefore useful for understanding how dress works on the body, requiring particular forms of knowledge, skills and producing various sorts of body movement which gender the body in the process.

Haug et al. (1987) provide ample evidence of the ways in which feminity is reproduced through various techniques, bodily and sartorial. They argue that the female body and its ways of being and adorning are the product of particular discourses of the body, which are inherently gendered. Take for example the fact that women learn to pluck their eyebrows while men shave their faces, both these techniques are far from 'natural' (that is, there is no reason why men and women have to do either) and thus point to the cultural meanings and practices surrounding the male and female body. Other techniques include the various skills required to apply make-up or style one's hair, all of which are gendered, as are various other techniques of dress such as knotting a tie or walking in short or tight skirts. All of these have to be learned, but the chances of one learning one or other technique is largely dependent upon our gender.

This argument that techniques of the body are closely bound up with the reproduction of gender is taken much further in the work of Judith Butler (1990, 1993). Butler's notion of gender performativity argues that it is in, and through, techniques of the body that sex/gender is reproduced. In other words, there is no prior 'natural' sex, only performances of male and female that are always cultural. In this way, as previous chapters have explained using examples other than dress, according to Butler, sex is the product of cultural inscriptions and discourses that constantly call upon us to act as 'masculine' or 'feminine' through techniques and strategies of the body/dress. Drag artists draw attention to the artificiality of such codes by adopting the dress of the opposite 'sex', many of them successfully 'passing' as the opposite sex, but if all such acts of the body are 'unnatural', that is in no way determined by some essential qualities of our 'sex', then we are all wearing 'drag'.

Dress, social structures and bodily order

Butler draws much inspiration for her analysis of performativity from the work of Foucault. Foucault, as argued earlier, has been very influential in demonstrating the social significance of the body to the social world. In *Discipline and Punish* Foucault (1977) argues that bodily practices are part of the capillary-like operations of power which work to render bodies docile and obedient. His concept of power is novel in that it argues that modern power works not by repressing or forbidding things, but by inducing ways of acting and being, so that individual bodies come to manage themselves. In this way, power is productive of subjectivity: modern prisons produce the 'criminal', psychoanalysis produces the 'hysteric' and so on. Power is at work in discourses which, in turn, are put into practice: so, for example, the eighteenth-century discourse of liberalism was important in producing the idea of the 'criminal' as reformable and was put into practice through the building of prisons. This discourse and system of punishment was enforced through panoptical surveillance and had obvious implications for bodies, which were incarcerated. The panopticon was a design for a prison produced by social theorist and reformer, Jeremy Bentham. The cells of the prison were organized around a central watch tower which remained in darkness. The design enforced the principle of self-surveillance: since prisoners could not know when they were being observed, they would be forced to monitor their behaviour at all times. This prison, though never built in this form, has informed the design of many modern institutions, such as the hospitals, schools and indeed, prisons that we may have all encountered at some point in our lives.

While feminists such as McNay (1992) and Diamond and Quniby (1988) argue that Foucault ignores the issue of gender, they point out that his theoretical concepts can provide feminists with a framework for understanding the ways in which the body is acted on by power/knowledge. Indeed, Foucault's notion of discourse can enable the analysis of fashion as a discursive domain which sets significant parameters around the body and its presentation. Fashion (defined here as a system of continually changing styles), which sets out an array of competing discourses on image and is the dominant system governing dress in the west, has been linked to the operations of power, initially marking out class divisions but, more recently, playing a crucial role in policing the boundaries of sexual difference. For example, fashion magazines frequently proclaim '*vive la difference!*' when fashions for men and women conform to dominant stereotypes of 'masculine' and 'feminine', but this can and does get replaced from time to time by proclamations about androgyny. However, even androgynous fashions rely on the idea of some a priori sexual difference for their clothing, even while they appear to unsettle or challenge fixed ideas about male/masculine, female/feminine.

Although utilized by Wilson (1992), Foucault's work on the body has not been usefully employed in the analysis of fashion as a textual site for the construction of the body although it would seem that it would have some application. Fashion, particularly as it is laid out in the fashion magazine, is 'obsessed with gender' (Wilson, 1985, p. 117) and constantly shifts the boundary between the genders. This preoccupation with gender starts with babies and is played out through the life cycle so that styles of dress at significant moments are very clearly gendered (weddings and other formal occasions are the most obvious examples). Such styles enable the repetitious production of gender, even when gender appears to break down as with androgynous fashion, and are aided, in part, by the repetition of gendered styles of bodily posture routinely reproduced in fashion magazines. While these styles of being reproduce gender as a body style, they are also open to subversion through exaggeration and parody, as Butler (1990, 1993) has forcefully suggested.

Foucault's insights into the ways in which bodies are subject to power and discursively constituted can also be utilized to show how institutional and discursive practices of dress act upon the body, marking it and rendering it meaningful and productive. The idea of surveillance through self-surveillance is one that has also been extended to describe the emergence of a new modern self who is increasingly called upon to monitor behaviour, often by technologies of the body, such as, diet, exercise and plastic surgery, to name but a few. It can also be used to describe technologies of dress and how they are one means of managing bodies in public. Institutions and corporations often use dress codes and uniforms as part of the establishment of a corporate discipline. Carla Freeman (1993, 2000) describes how a smart dress code was utilized by one data-processing corporation in Barbados as part of the surveillance and discipline of its largely female staff. Similarly, institutions such as prisons and hospitals impose uniforms which erase the individual features of the wearers' bodies and produce a uniform image of the institution or corporation. Likewise, some shops may also enforce a dress code or require their workers to wear a uniform to project an appropriate image: indeed, to ensure that workers *embody* the image the corporation seeks to project. On the other hand, professional occupations, by and large, do not lay down a specific uniform, but they generally expect professional staff to have inculcated a 'professional' dress and wear smart, suited dress. In this way, Foucault's ideas about the relationship between institutions and the discipline of the body can be extended to the examination of dress in a wide range of social settings.

However, while Foucault's insights on the body and the way it is shaped by society are useful, there are limitations to his analysis. In particular, he has been criticized for seeing bodies as 'passive' and thereby failing to explain how individuals may act in an autonomous fashion (see McNay 1992, 1999) – a criticism endorsed by Lee and Jackson in this volume. His analysis might, therefore, lead to the discussion of fashion and dress as merely constraining social forces and neglects the way individuals can be active in the choices they make from fashion discourse in their everyday experience of dress. His overly poststructuralist perspective produces an account of bodies as if they were texts, acted upon by social forces, rather than the flesh and blood material of our embodied existence. If the dressed body is to be understood not only as always situated and structured by culture, but also as an intimate aspect of embodied experience, we have to look elsewhere for a fuller account of dress as a 'fleshy' practice, that is, one that involves real flesh and blood bodies. How can one begin to understand the experience of choosing and wearing clothes that forms so significant a part of our daily practice, a crucial experience of our body/self? Thomas Csordas (1993, 1996) argues that the structuralist and poststructuralist paradigm of Douglas and Foucault is inadequate because it does not tell us what people do with their bodies in daily life – it neglects to account for embodiment. He posits a 'paradigm of embodiment', which examines *what the body does* to supplement the 'paradigm of the body' which examines, as do Douglas and Foucault, *what is done to the body*. He looks to the phenomenology of Maurice Merleau-Ponty and the sociologist Pierre Bourdieu as offering ways of thinking about embodiment. Merleau-Ponty puts embodiment at the centre of his philosophical approach. Embodiment is an a priori fact of existence and it is through the body that we come to know and act in the world. This philosophical tradition does not easily lend itself to application but has been translated into a more sociological approach through the work of Bourdieu, as Csordas suggests, and also Goffman, as Nick Crossley (1995a, 1995b, 1996), has argued. In his account, Goffman describes how people embody space, how they improvise within space, much like actors do. Thus, while space imposes itself on us to some extent (the spaces of work dictating how we should dress/appear) we are active in producing this space and can transform space through our active engagement with it. As a symbolic integrationist, Goffman sees space as something produced through the actions of individuals, not as something a priori to them.

Pierre Bourdieu's (1984, 1989) work has also demonstrated how embodied social agents orientate themselves to situations. Although he ultimately produces a rather too structuralist account of embodiment, that is, one that focuses rather too much attention on social structure rather than agency in his account of the world, Bourdieu's methodological framework does lend itself to an account of embodiment in everyday life. There is much potential in his idea of the 'habitus' as a concept for thinking through embodiment. The habitus is used to describe the way we come to live in our bodies and how our body is both structured by our social situation, primarily our social class, but also produced through our own embodied activities. It is, therefore, a concept that can provide a link between the individual and the social. According to Bourdieu, our social class structures our 'tastes' which are themselves bodily experiences, but these structures are only brought into being through the embodied actions of individuals. Once we have acquired the appropriate habitus, we have the capacity to generate practice. The important point is that these practices or embodied activities are constantly adaptable to the conditions it meets. Class taste, then, is something that is reproduced through our intimate relationships to the body.

This analysis seems far removed from dress but, as with the other theorists I have discussed here, it is possible to extend Bourdieu's analysis to dress. It can be argued that the habitus predisposes individuals to particular ways of dressing: for example, the middle-class notion of 'quality not quantity' generally translates into a concern with quality fabrics such as cashmere, leather and silk which, due to cost, may mean buying fewer garments. On the other hand, working-class dress may favour quantity not quality. Our class position may therefore orientate us to particular kinds of cloth, for example, silk as opposed to nylon, and to particular styles of dress, such as the middle-class style of Laura Ashley.

Conclusion

To conclude, I have tried to suggest how understandings of the dressed body need to explore the dynamic relationship between the body and dress, rather than abstract the body from dress. I have drawn on the work of a number of theorists who examine the body in the social world and sought to extend their analysis to the study of the dressed body. I have argued that the dressed body is a crucial component in micro-social order and that, in order to understand the forces at work in dressing the body, a range of theoretical resources are needed. Although I have discussed theorists of the body, rather more than theorists of dress, I have done so in order to bring these theoretical resources to bear on how we dress the body in the social world. I have also used them to examine the role that dress plays in the production and reproduction of bodily and social order. I would argue that the close relationship of fabric and flesh is one that can be explored through the analysis of the attitudes to cloth and tailoring practices that shape it. There is not the space to give anything more than a glimpse at some of the possibilities for analyzing the dressed body and it is hoped that future research might extend the preliminary thoughts laid down here.

Further reading

Breward, C. *The Culture of Fashion: A History of Fashionable Dress* (Manchester: Manchester University Press, 1995).

   This gives a very good comprehensive history of fashion from its beginnings in the fourteenth century.

Davis, F. *Fashion, Culture and Identity* (Chicago: University of Chicago Press, 1994).

   This book offers a good analysis of the relationship between fashion and identity within contemporary culture.

Entwistle, J. *The Fashioned Body* (Cambridge: Polity Press, 2000).

   This book offers a comprehensive overview of theories of fashion and dress from a sociological perspective, as well as connecting these with theories about the body and identity in modern society.

Steele, V. *Paris Fashion: A Cultural History* (Oxford: Berg, 1998).

   A book that offers a very full account of the emergence of the fashion system within nineteenth- and twentieth-century modernity, focusing on the historical 'centre' of modern fashion, Paris.

10

Feeding the Body

Janet Sayers

In common with other factors affecting our bodies, feeding is very much socially conditioned. Our bodies are what we feed them, but what we feed them is conditioned by economic, historical, biographical, ideological, and discursive factors. These, in turn, vary systematically with culture, class, and sex. This is particularly evident in conditions of food scarcity and abundance. I will accordingly focus on these conditions in this chapter. I will begin with ways in which scarcity has varied, and continues to vary, with class and sex in Europe and Asia. I will then consider how class and sex, as well as ideological and discursive factors, including fantasy, mediate what women and men feed their bodies in conditions of abundance. Finally I will consider the implications of all this for feminism.

Scarcity

First, then, let us consider how feeding the body is affected by scarcity. Food scarcity is mediated by wealth and power. Even when food is most scarce – even when its scarcity reaches famine proportions – it is available to those who can command it through rights of property, exchange, and employment. Noting this, Mennell (1991) goes on to argue that, from 1750 onwards, the increasing reliability of food production and distribution resulted in famine occurring less often in western Europe.

Nevertheless concern about the quantity and quality of food and water supplies continued and still continue in the west. Following the industrial revolution, philanthropists and others in the British ruling class, concerned for the welfare of the urban poor, and fearful of contagion by the diseases of urbanization (such as cholera), and wanting to minimize the tax burden of those rendered incapable by illness and disease, pressed for improvements in the supply of food and water. Anxiety about the bodily debility of men recruited to the army during the Crimean, Boer and First and Second World Wars also led to pressure to improve the otherwise scant or inadequate food intake of the poor. It led, among other things, to the introduction of meals for children at school. Sociological research also contributed, earlier in the twentieth century, to increasing pressure to alleviate food scarcity among the working class. Particularly notable in this respect was Charles Booth's seventeen-volume study, *The Life and Labour of the People in London*, published in 1903, and Seebohm Rowntree's 1902 book, *Poverty, a Study of Town Life*, in which Rowntree concluded from investigating the calorie requirements of the average working man that:

> The diet of the 'servant-keeping class' is in excess of that necessary for health, the food supply for the artisan class is satisfactory if there is no 'wasteful expenditure on drink', and the diet of 'the labouring classes, upon whom the bulk of the muscular work falls, and who form so large a proportion of the industrial population are seriously underfed' (Rowntree, 1902, p. 28, quoted in Turner, 1992, p. 191).

By the end of the twentieth century, however, some sociologists assumed that inequalities between classes as regards food scarcity had been eliminated in Europe. Mennell (1991) claims that equality and interdependence between social classes in western Europe had been achieved to such an extent by this time, that scarcity had become a thing of the past. He maintains there was now considerably greater equal distribution of food, and similarity of cuisine between classes, and that there were considerably less extreme differences between the food consumed on ordinary and festive occasions.

Yet food scarcity persists in the west. And it continues to be medi-ated unequally both by class and sex. In England and Ireland those who are poorest, as measured by their dependence on welfare bene-fits, often suffer dietary deficiency, with women often suffering worse deficiency than men. In the 1990s, Lobstein (1991) and Dowler and Calvert (1995) reported that a significant proportion of women claimant households in London had a diet deficient in key nutrients. As regards differences between women and men in what they ate, Hilary Graham (1993) reported that a study, published in 1989, of people living on a Dublin housing estate suffering scarcity of food because many of the residents were unemployed, demonstrated that women fared significantly worse than the men in terms of the recommended daily food amount (RDA) deemed necessary for optimum health. Three times as many women as men in the study were found to be consuming less than 75 per cent of the RDA of vitamin C. And only half the lone mothers achieved even half the RDA for iron. Men, by contrast, suffered little in this respect.

Graham argues that women's food deficiency relative to men in conditions of scarcity is due, at least in part, to their doing without food in favour of giving it to their children and men. She quotes one mother in the above-cited Dublin study saying:

> I'll cut down myself on food. Sometimes if we're running out the back end of the second week and there's not a lot for us to eat, I'll sort of give the kids it first and then see what's left (Graham, 1993, p. 160).

She also quotes a mother from a study conducted in 1990 of women living on benefit, who said:

> I buy half a pound of stewing meat or something and give that to Sid and the kiddies and then I just have the gravy – before I used to buy soya things and substitutes to meat but I can't afford that now (Graham, 1993, p. 160).

Similar inequalities between women and men, and between upper and lower classes, in conditions of food scarcity prevail in the developing world where, according to McGuire and Popkin (1990), women generally meet a smaller percentage of their current RDA than men, and often consume lower quality vegetable protein, with men often consuming a larger proportion of whatever animal protein is available. This sex difference, report McGuire and Popkin, is particularly marked in the African country, Burkina Faso (in the former Upper Volta). Here women not only consume a lower proportion of what is deemed necessary as regards gross daily protein intake. They also consume only 0.8 grams of animal protein compared to men's consumption of 10.3 grams daily. McGuire and Popkin also note that women's vitamin and mineral intake in the developing world is inadequate both absolutely and relative to men's intake.

Jiggins (1994) reports similar sex inequalities. She notes that, in self-provisioning households in South Asia, men tend to have preferential access to whatever food is available. Furthermore, she observes, as the amount or quality of food deteriorates, differences in male and female health and nutritional status increase, with women and girls tending to have a lower nutritional and health status than men and boys even in wealthier households. Gittelsohn (1991) reports similar sex inequalities in the distribution of food to women and men (but not to girls and boys) in rural Nepal.

Again we find that in the South, as in the North, sex inequalities in food consumption in conditions of scarcity vary by class. In India, for instance, one study reports that, while rich women consumed a daily average of 2500 calories, and increased their weight by an average of 12.5 kg during pregnancy, poor women consumed a daily average of 1400 calories, and only increased their weight by an average of 1.5 kg during pregnancy (Anon, 1985, p. 43).

Where women suffer inadequate food intake because of prevailing food scarcity in their class, this often begins at birth. Perhaps due to the greater social value attached by patriarchy to men in the family – as providers and rulers – boys are breast-fed more often and for longer periods than girls in India. Or at least this is the claim of one report (UNICEF, 1988). The same report speculates that the desire for a son may prompt mothers quickly to discontinue breast-feeding their daughters so as to ovulate and conceive again as soon as possible. The report also notes that, again in India, girls under five were more likely to suffer malnutrition, and more severe malnutrition, than boys. Even in privileged families, it was observed, boys ate better, and were more likely than girls to be given milk, eggs, meat, and fruit. Further-more, the report pointed out, when boys grow up and get jobs, they spend part of their earnings on food and snacks while girls, having no such disposable income, continue to be subject to the unvaried diet of their families at home.

Evidence regarding sex inequalities in infant feeding in conditions of food scarcity in the East is more unclear. Harriss (1989) found no differences in South Asia between boys and girls in the amount they were breast-fed. Santow (1995), by contrast, reports that in rural Uttar Pradesh girls are sometimes breast-fed for a shorter time and less intensely than boys. Chatterjee and Lambert (1989) report similar inequalities in breast-feeding of girls and boys in India and Pakistan generally. There is also evidence in the rural Punjab that, although ordinary food is divided equally between boys and girls, more nutri-tious food goes disproportionately to boys (Das Gupta, 1987). In another study of children in rural Bangladesh the calorie consump-tion of boys exceeded that of girls by 16 per cent in children under five years old, with protein intake averaging 14 per cent more in boys (Chen et al., 1981). On the other hand, while Abdullah and Wheeler

(1985) report significantly lower food intake by girls aged one to four years in one village in Bangladesh, Chaudhury (1984) found greater intake of nutrition for pre-school Bangladeshi girls.

The evidence is also conflicting as regards sex differences in infant malnutrition and mortality. One factor contributing to conflict in the data is the effect of the position and number of girls in the family. In Bangladesh, for instance, it has been found that the risk of infant mortality was 84 per cent in girls with older sisters compared to a risk of 14 per cent in girls without sisters (Rousham, 1999). Another factor is whether the girl's family own land. Rousham reports that, among two- to six-year-olds in a remote rural area of Bangladesh, girls in landless families had a worse nutritional status than all other children during the monsoon, but that this difference was no longer significant following the end of the monsoon and a successful late October rice harvest. Children from landless families still ate significantly fewer meals per day than children from landowning households. But there was no difference between boys and girls in the frequency of their meals. In sum, Rousham's study indicates that cultural bias against feeding girls only has a significant impact at times of food scarcity when its impact is worst on girls growing up in landless families unable to access and control its supply.

Sex bias in infant feeding in conditions of food scarcity can, of course, be fatal. Biology, however, seemingly favours the survival of girls through the first year of life, concludes a recent United Nations (2000) report. But the report also notes that discriminatory food and health care practices against girls can offset this advantage in one- to five-year-old girls. It is in these terms that the report explains the higher infant mortality of girls compared to boys in recent statistics collected for Guam, Papua New Guinea, and Samoa. On the other hand Sommerfelt and Arnold (1998) argue that, despite evidence of discrimination against girls in feeding practices and medical treatment in countries in which there is a strong preference for sons, this is not reflected in differences between boys and girls in their nutritional status, at least up to the age of five. Whatever their impact, sex and class inequalities in feeding persist not only in conditions of food scarcity. They also obtain in conditions of food abundance, as we will now see.

Abundance

In western Europe, writes Mennell (1991), the economically and socially most powerful classes sought, in earlier centuries, to distinguish themselves from less powerful classes by the quantities they ate. He also argues that psychological pressure to overeat was linked to fear of food scarcity. In the past, he notes, the state sought to suppress gluttony. More effective however in this respect, he adds, was increasing reliability in the abundance and availability of food. This, says Mennell, led to court cuisine becoming more delicate and refined, and to the middle classes imitating the food delicacy and refinement of the upper class, at least in France.

Food intake in conditions of abundance has also been shaped by what the Marxist theorist, Louis Althusser, dubbed 'ideological state apparatuses', and by what followers of Michel Foucault refer to as 'discursive practices'. Particularly important in this respect in the Middle Ages was religious doctrine concerning the virtues of limiting food intake. This doctrine persisted into the Renaissance and beyond. In 1558, for instance, an influential Italian book, *Trattato della vita sobria*, preached the virtues of foregoing feasting as a defence against the temptations of the flesh. Its author, Luigi Cornaro, who had cured his own ills through dieting and sobriety, recommended the same for his readers. He had learnt, he wrote, 'never to cloy my stomach with eating and drinking, but constantly to rise from table with a disposition to eat and drink still more' (Turner, 1991, p. 161).

An English edition, translated by the religious poet George Herbert, was published in 1634. It may, in turn, have been read by George Cheyne who, the next century, wrote several books advocating diet which became very influential and popular among the London elite with whom Cheyne lived and worked. Having studied medicine in Edinburgh and taught in Leyden, he had, by 1724, become a fashionable London doctor. His appetite, it seems, was gargantuan. He ate and drank so much his weight rose to a staggering 448 lb (203 kg)! Not surprisingly he had difficulty walking and became severely depressed. To cure himself he tried various diets, and ended up drinking milk and eating vegetables, drinking less alcohol, and riding and sleeping regularly. His health improved and he lived a long life for the time. He died, aged 70, in 1743.

In his books, he recommended his readers to follow the same recipe he believed had cured him. He portrayed disciplined food intake as a religious duty, and condemned gluttony as tantamount to suicide. He blamed excessive eating in his class on expanding trade having brought exotic food, drink, spices, and a general surplus of food to England. He also condemned, as contrary to nature and digestion, the changing eating habits and cuisine of his class. He said they wrongly stimulated the appetite. Attributing the ills of his class to over-abundance and inactivity, he advocated abstinence, temperance, and exercise. He also advocated purging, or, as the medical sociologist, Bryan Turner, puts it:

> For the 'learned professions', he recommended regular use of his 'dome-stick purge' – a mixture of rhubarb, wormwood, nutmeg and orange peel … Once a proper, regular diet has been established [Cheyne wrote], the pro-fessional man has only two further requirements for sound health – (1) 'A Vomit, that can work briskly, quickly and safely' by 'cleaning, squeezeing and compressing the knotted and tumified Glands of the Primae Viae'; (2) 'Great, frequent and continued Exercise, especially on Horseback' (Turner, 1992, p. 189).

Cheyne's claims regarding the healthful effects of dieting spread, in turn, to other social classes through being canvassed by the religious preacher, John Wesley, in his popular 1752 book, *Primitive Physic*. In this book, and following Cheyne, Wesley advocated a regime of regularity and moderation, more as a matter of right conduct than of diet, for which this was hardly relevant, at least for his readers and listeners from the working class in so far as it was still at risk of famine and starvation. Nevertheless, the emphasis of Cheyne, Wesley, and others on diet, hygiene, and exercise was taken up by all classes, arguably because of its ideological value to the ruling class in inculcating discipline in its workers and their children. As such it shaped education, work, and health up to our own times, embracing all social classes in what Turner calls 'a framework of organized eating, drinking and physical training' (Turner, 1992, p. 192).

Alongside discourses of religion and diet, a discourse of taste has also shaped similarities and differences between social classes in what they eat in conditions of food abundance. Sociologist, Pierre Bourdieu, for instance, notes the following, class-related effects of this discourse:

> The taste of the professionals or senior executives defines the popular taste, by negation, as the taste for the heavy, the fat and the coarse, by tending towards the light, the refined and the delicate … [meanwhile] the teach-ers, richer in cultural capital than in economic capital, and therefore inclined to ascetic consumption in all areas, pursue originality at the low-est economic cost and go in for exoticisms (Italian, Chinese cooking etc.) and culinary populism (peasant dishes) (Bourdieu, 1984, p. 185; see also Shilling, 1993).

But eating is not only shaped by class-related discourses concerning religion, diet, and taste. It is also shaped by these and other discourses concerning gender, as I will seek to highlight next through turning to women's fasting and feasting, and its medical construction as symptomatic of anorexia and bulimia nervosa.

Fasting and feasting

Fasting is not, of course, confined to women. It has been an ascetic discipline for both sexes in virtually all religions. A frequently quoted example, at least in recent books about anorexia (for example, Hepworth, 1999), is Catherine Benincasa, who lived from 1347 to 1380. Resisting pressure from her family to marry against her will, she took refuge in fasting, which she justified in religious terms as divinely inspired, and as a means of securing her parents' salvation. She accordingly courted scarcity, and, as one commentator puts it:

> From the age of fifteen ... consumed nothing but bread, uncooked veg-
> etables, and water; from the age of twenty-five she simply chewed on bitter
> herbs, spitting out the substance ... In the end she refused even to drink
> water and so, in her early thirties, put an end to her life (Cohn, 1986, p. 3).

While her parents, apparently, construed her fasting as rebellion against them, the Church made her into a saint, and it is by her sanctified name – Saint Catherine of Siena – that she is now usually known.

The sociologist, Arthur Frank (1991), argues that this contradictory disapproval and approval of fasting (as in Catherine's case) became general following the Renaissance, with some equating fasting with purity and holiness, and others regarding it as heresy inspired by the devil. In the nineteenth century, this religious construction of fasting was gradually supplanted by a scientific and medical discourse which, in the case of fasting, made women its object. Fasting came to be diagnosed as a symptom of hysteria (linked to the wandering of women's wombs).

Addressing a meeting of the British Medical Association in Oxford in the autumn of 1868, William Gull, a London-based specialist in gastric disorders, spoke of 'young women emaciated to the last degree through apepsia hysterica' (Hepworth, 1999, p. 2). Later, in 1874, he introduced the term 'anorexia nervosa' to describe women patients in whom there was no evidence of gastric dysfunction, whose emaciation he attributed to loss of appetite due to a morbid mental state. Their emaciation was not seemingly due to poverty, or lack of available food. Gull's patients evidently came from the wealthier classes. Their families could evidently afford to travel, as in the following case, of whom Gull wrote:

> Miss B., aged 18, was brought to me Oct. 8, 1868, as a case of latent tubercle. Her friends had been advised accordingly to take her for the coming winter to the South of Europe. The extremely emaciated look, much greater indeed than occurs for the most part in tubercular cases where patients are still going about, impressed me at once with the probability that I should find no visceral disease. Pulse 50, Reps. L6. Physical examination of the chest and abdomen discovered nothing abnormal. All the viscera were apparently healthy. Notwithstanding the great emaciation and apparent weakness, there was a peculiar restlessness, difficult, I was informed, to control. The mother added, 'She is never tired.' Amenorrhoea since Christmas 1866. The clinical details of this case were in fact almost identical with the preceding one, even to the number of the pulse and respirations (Gull quoted in Hepworth, 1999, p. 2).

Just as Gull wrote about women's emaciation in terms of then received scientific and medical discourse, so did Charles Lasègue, a physician in France who, in 1873, assimilated this symptom of emaciation, as had Gull initially, to hysteria. He called it *l'anorexia hysterique*, and attributed it to sexual frustration or unfulfilled sexual expectations in courtship and early married life. Other doctors, notably Charcot and Freud, similarly linked anorexia to sex. Freud initially attributed it to the patient having been sexually abused – or 'seduced', as he called it – in early childhood. Later he described anorexia as expressing, in the form of oral disgust, repressed, and therefore unconscious, sexual desire for oral sex with the father. It was in these terms that he described the anorexic and other hysterical symptoms of his 18-year-old patient, Dora (Freud, 1977). His immediate followers similarly diagnosed anorexia as an illness. They claimed it was the pathological effect of regression from adolescent genital desire to the oral desires of infancy (see Sayers, 1988).

More recently psychoanalytically-minded writers have diagnosed anorexia less in terms of genital or oral sexuality, and more in terms of feeding and its control. They also note that it involves self-imposed scarcity in conditions of abundance. One writer calls his book about anorexia, *Starving to Death in a Sea of Objects* (Sours, 1980). Another writer, Hilde Bruch (1977), calls her book about anorexia, *The Golden Cage*. She characterizes anorexia as a curious form of gilded existence involving disturbed body image, disturbed perception of hunger stimuli, and a paralyzing sense of ineffectiveness. Her characterization of anorexia has, in turn, informed the American Psychiatric Association's

(APA) definition of this condition (Busfield, 1996). In the fourth edition of its *Diagnostic and Statistical Manual* the APA characterizes anorexia as involving:

A. Refusal to maintain body weight at or above a minimally normal weight for age and height ...
B. Intense fear of gaining weight or becoming fat, even though under-weight.
C. Disturbance in the way in which one's body weight or shape is experi-enced (APA, 2000, p. 4).

Meanwhile the World Health Organization (WHO) has defined anorexia as a 'disorder characterized by deliberate weight loss, induced and/or sustained by the patient' (Busfield, 1996, p. 176).

Alongside the scientific and medical construction by the APA and WHO, of self-imposed lack of food as evidence of anorexia, both organizations have also constructed bingeing and purging, in scien-tific and medical terms, as warranting the diagnosis 'bulimia nervosa'. WHO defines it as 'characterized by repeated bouts of overeating and an excessive preoccupation with the control of body weight' (Busfield, 1996, p. 177). The APA defines it as including:

A. Recurrent episodes of binge eating ...
B. Recurrent inappropriate compensatory behavior in order to prevent weight gain, such as self-induced vomiting (APA, 2000, p. 4).

The APA adds that, to warrant the diagnosis of bulimia nervosa, the patient's 'binge eating and inappropriate compensatory behaviors [must] both occur, on average, at least twice a week for 3 months' (APA, 2000, p. 4).

Just as Gull and Lasègue construed anorexia as a female condition in so far as they characterized it as a form of hysteria, so too does the APA. In its most recent pronouncements on the subject it notes that anorexia and bulimia are six to ten times more prevalent in women than in men (APA, 2000). And, like Gull and Lasègue, the APA also diagnoses these conditions in scientific, publicly observable, behav-ioural terms. So too do Bruch and other psychoanalytically-minded US ego psychologists. Others, by contrast, understand these condi-tions in terms of more inward-looking fantasy.

Fantasy

Whereas Freud and his immediate followers linked anorexia with sex-ual fantasy, post-Freudians, particularly in England, link anorexia and other eating disorders with fantasies they imply are universal in infancy regarding feeding and being fed. In this they often draw on the development of Freud's theory by Melanie Klein. On the basis of her work in pioneering child analysis, Klein hypothesized that, in feeding from the breast or bottle, babies fantasize incorporating the mother as a loved and hated figure within them. They imagine her as super-abundant. They also imagine emptying her. They imagine greedily robbing and scooping her out, and enviously spoiling and destroying everything inside her, thereby voiding her of all goodness, food, and love. This, in turn, gives rise to other fantasies in children of their mothers retaliating by devouring them, as in the fairy tale of Hansel and Gretel fed and fattened with all manner of sweets by a witch so she can eat them up.

Explaining eating disorders in these terms, and to illustrate the everyday occurrence of such fantasies, art therapist, Mary Levens, quotes the following conversation:

> *Dinah* 'Where did I live before I was born? I don't know'
> *Mother* 'In my tummy.'
> *Dinah* 'And did you eat me up?'
> *Mother* 'No.'
> *Dinah* 'And what did I eat?'
> *Mother* 'Some of my food, because you were in my tummy' (Levens, 1995, p. 49).

To this fantasy Levens adds others. She quotes Freud's colleague, Karl Abraham's account of a man expressing his childhood fantasy equation of love and food. He recalled imagining swallowing his beloved nurse – 'skin, hair, clothes and all' (Levens, 1995, p. 51). Levens argues that eating-disordered patients today similarly equate loving and eating with all the fantasies of destroying and being destroyed to which this equation can give rise. She quotes an anorexic patient imagining her mother ordering herself: 'Eat the child, bind the child, claw the child … Never let it go' (Levens, 1995, p. 56).

Levens notes that the novelist, Margaret Attwood, attributes the following cannibalistic fantasy to an anorexic character in her 1980 novel, *The Edible Woman*:

> She cut into the [pink heart-shaped] cake. She was surprised to find that it was pink in the inside too. She put a forkful into her mouth and chewed slowly. It felt spongy and cellular against her tongue, like the bursting of thousands of tiny lungs. She shuddered and spat the cake out into her napkin (Levens, 1995, p. 61).

Levens also quotes a contrary fantasy of this same character baking a cake to resemble a woman's body, and telling it: 'You look delicious ... very appetising ... that's what you get for being food' (Levens, 1995, p. 61).

Returning to non-fictional data, Levens quotes a young boy, playing at swallowing his foster mother, triumphantly saying, 'Now you can't talk', and then immediately vomiting her out (Levens, 1995, p. 62). As further evidence of the ubiquity of children's fantasies about feeding and being fed, Levens cites the case of a boy, disgusted by his greed, describing runner beans on his plate as 'crawling green snakes' (Levens, 1995, p. 63). She also cites one of her patients painting a picture of spaghetti and then imagining it climbing off the plate and wrapping itself around her throat to throttle her.

Klein's colleague, Susan Isaacs, described in her diary similar fantasies in children attending the progressive nursery school she ran in Cambridge in the 1920s

> 25.2.25. Harold had accidentally kicked Mrs. I.'s foot under the table, and this led him to say, 'I'll undress you and take off your suspenders, and gobble you all up' ...
> 11.10.25. In the garden, Tommy ran after Mrs. I. and caught her. He said, 'I'll kill you,' and called Christopher and Penelope to 'come and help me push her down and kill her – and make her into ice-cream!' ...
> 2.2.26. At lunch there was some talk about 'cutting Mrs. I. up' and 'having her for dinner' (Isaacs, 1933, pp. 113, 114–15; see also Sayers, 2000).

But if these fantasies occur in both sexes why is it that anorexic and bulimic feasting and fasting occur so much more often in girls and women than in boys and men? What does this sex difference imply for sexual politics?

Feminism

In her 1984 book, *Fat is a Feminist Issue*, the feminist therapist, Susie Orbach, explains sex differences in the incidence of eating disorders as originating in sex inequalities in early infant feeding. Whereas I have cited data from Asia regarding these inequalities above, Orbach cites data from Italy. She puts this together with evidence that the buying and cooking of food is usually assigned to women and thus becomes part of their general role as providers of love, care, and concern for their families. This includes women subordinating their need for food to men and children in their families when food is scarce. In England this is also evident in women cooking what their husbands want rather than what they want, and in their not bothering to cook or even eat when their husbands or children are absent or gone (Murcott, 1983).

Generalizing from such findings, Orbach (1984) argues that women teach their daughters from earliest infancy to subordinate their needs – including their need for food – to others. This results, she says, in girls growing up alienated from, and unconscious of hunger signals arising within their bodies. Women's fatness, she argues, may be motivated by resistance to this process of socialization through indulging their needs and bingeing on whatever they want. Or, like the suffragettes at the beginning of the twentieth century, they may protest by fasting and going on hunger strike (Orbach, 1986).

But this explanation of women's fasting and feasting poses problems. Orbach advocates combatting women's alienation from, and unconsciousness of, their need for food by reconnecting them with this need so as to make them conscious of it. But this is to treat our need for food as though it existed within us unaffected by, and divorced from, the social factors which, as we have seen above, in fact shape and condition our feeding of our bodies from earliest infancy. Furthermore, claims Joan Busfield (1996), Orbach over-readily allies anorexic and bulimic starving and bingeing with political protest although this is rarely the woman's conscious intent.

Orbach's account also does not explain why anorexia, at least until recently, occurred more often in England among young women from upper middle-class, high-achieving families, whereas the prevalence of bulimia was distributed more evenly across all social classes. Nor can Orbach's account explain why, in the USA, eating disorders appear to be as common in young Hispanic as in Caucasian women, and appear to be more common in Native Americans and less common among Blacks and Asians. Nor does it explain why African-Americans are more likely to become bulimic than anorexic, nor why they are more likely to purge with laxatives than with vomiting. Nor can Orbach's account explain why eating disorders are rare in non-western cultures, apart from Japan where the prevalence of these disorders is substantial and increasing (for these and other data in the USA, UK, and elsewhere, see Lee, 1998; APA, 2000).

These national, ethnic, and class differences can be more adequately explained in terms of the theory of women's eating disorders put forward by the feminist philosopher, Susan Bordo. She argues that anorexia and bulimia are an effect of three dominant discursive practices – or 'axes' as she calls them – promulgated by the ruling class in western Europe and the USA.

The first axis she identifies is the mind/body dualism, discussed in detail in Chapter 6, associated with the philosophies of Plato and

Descartes, which, in effect, repudiates the body as alien to the mind. This philosophy, Bordo implies, contributes to both bulimia and anorexia. It is evident in the bulimic reviling her bingeing as 'an animalistic orgy ... whoring after food'. It is also evident in the psychoanalytic psychiatrist, Ludwig Binswanger's anorexic patient, Ellen West, describing herself as wanting to get out of her body, as wanting to be 'too thin ... *without a body*' (Bordo, 1993, pp. 147, 148). Binswinger's account of Ellen West was published in the 1930s. The previous decade, in 1921, the novelist, Aldous Huxley, described a young woman character in his novel, *Crome Yellow*, expressing the same horror of eating as Ellen West. He writes:

> 'Pray, don't talk to me of eating,' said Emmeline, drooping like a sensitive plant. 'We find it so unspiritual, my sisters and I. One can't think of one's soul when one is eating' (Lawrence, 1984, p. 36).

The second axis Bordo identifies concerns control. She notes western philosophy's celebration of will-power and its control. She argues that they are expressed in the bulimic's compulsive exercising, and in the anorexic using her scales, as one patient put it, to provide 'visible proof ... that I can exert control' (Bordo, 1993, p. 149). And, of course, this philosophy of control tallies with the self-control or self-discipline which Turner (1991, 1992), as we have seen, notes writers from the sixteenth century onwards in Europe enjoined on men in the ruling class in urging them to curb and control what they drank and ate.

Bordo's axis of control also tallies with Turner's account of the spread from the upper to the lower class of a discourse of diet and self-control in so far as it suited the interests of the ruling class to have the lower classes control and discipline themselves so as to become effective soldiers in war, and effective workers in agricultural and factory production. Not surprisingly, perhaps, given the greater benefits of this injunction to the ruling class, its pathological effect – in the form of anorexia – first occurred most frequently in this class, and only spread subsequently, through assimilation and globalization, to other cultures and classes. On the other hand, capitalist expansion also enjoins women and men of all classes to increase its profits by indulging themselves as much as they can as consumers. This arguably contributes to the prevalence of self-indulging bulimic bingeing across all classes, with the upper classes more often seeking to remedy its effects through vomiting as long ago preached by Cheyne to the elite for whom he wrote.

To explain why, despite this universalization across classes of feeding control, controlling bulimic purging and anorexic fasting occur more often in women than men, Bordo singles out a third axis. She calls it 'gender/power'. Noting the lack of power socially accorded women relative to men, she argues that this makes young women both fearful and disdainful of becoming powerless and oppressed like their mothers, and women generally in the generation before them. It also makes them fearful of embodying the mysogynist image of women, that is arguably a corollary of women's social powerlessness and oppression, which Bordo calls 'the archetypal image of the female: as hungering, voracious, all-needing, and all-wanting' (Bordo, 1993, p. 160).

Bordo implies that the way forward lies in feminism combatting the social inequalities reflected in this negative stereotype. She also implies that the reason this archetypal image contributes to the occurrence of anorexia and bulimia among women in the North but scarcely at all in women in the South is due to the equation of slenderness with moral and personal adequacy, and with will-power and control by the mind over the body, only being possible in societies enjoying food in abundant supply.

Conclusion

Over half a century ago a young social theorist, Simone Weil, died of starvation. Some claimed it was due to anorexia, stemming from a personal biography of poor bodily feeding even as a baby. Others argued that Weil starved herself out of solidarity with the working classes in German-occupied Paris who were then suffering terrible food shortages and scarcity. After Weil's death, aged 34, in Ashford on 24 August 1943, the Coroner's verdict recorded: 'The deceased did kill and slay herself by refusing to eat whilst the balance of her mind was disturbed'. By contrast, the *Kent Messenger* ran a story under the title: 'French Professor's curious sacrifice' (McLellan, 1990, p. 266).

This contradictory reaction to Weil's death nicely highlights a contradiction in the data I have discussed in this chapter. On the one hand it indicates the personal preoccupations of individuals, in conditions of abundance, with feeding and not feeding the body so as to maximize their pleasure and health, improve their appearance, and distinguish themselves from individuals in other cultures and classes. It also indicates our preoccupation as individuals, from earliest infancy, with fantasies about feeding and being fed. On the other hand the data I have discussed also testifies to the importance of sociological and collective forces, as opposed to individual factors, conditioning what we eat. It demonstrates the persistence of gross inequalities between North and South, upper- and lower-class girls and boys, and women and men in what they can and cannot feed their bodies. As I said at the outset: our bodies are what we feed them, but everywhere differently so according to class, culture, and sex.

Further reading

Bordo, Susan, *Unbearable Weight: Feminism, Western Culture and the Body* (Berkeley: University of California Press, 1993).

    An important text, which examines the relationship between dominant discursive practices in post-modernity, and body size and eating disorders.

Orbach, Susie, *Fat is a Feminist Issue* (London: Hamlyn, 1984).

    A classic, and controversial feminist text, which considers women's relationship to food and the body from a psychoanalytic perspective.

Turner, Bryan, *Regulating Bodies: Essays in Medical Sociology* (London: Routledge, 1992).

    A seminal work that examines the relationship between society and the body, with a particular focus on the role of medicalized and health-related discourses in the regulation of the body.

11

The Ageing Body

Hazel Biggs

In 1999 there were 10.6 million older people aged 65 and above in the UK, representing 18.11 per cent of the total population. Estimates suggest that by 2021 there will be in excess of 12 million such people. Predictions that over the next 30 years the number of people over 65 in Britain will increase by 50 per cent are regarded as broadly accurate, confirming that the proportion of the population that has retired from contributing to the economy is increasing year on year. Similar percentage figures apply to most other western countries and statistics like these have been used to describe a 'demographic time bomb' that will lead to the collapse of economies and state welfare provision as more and more older people make ever greater demands on welfare resources.

But ageing is not a linear process with universal effects. Chronological age can be distinguished from biological age and bodies age at different rates according to the social, biomedical and environmental influences they encounter (Kaim-Caudle et al., 1993). Also, while the physical integrity of the human body does inevitably decline over time, the process, and its effects, are variable. Some 90-year-olds are as healthy and vital as most 30-year-olds, while some much younger people are physically and intellectually frail.

Older people, however, are typically regarded as lacking rigour and intelligence, such that 'there is a common way of perceiving elders as a group who fit certain images and behave in particular ways' (Minichiello et al., 2000, p. 258). In the process, 'old soldiers' and 'wise old women' have been devalued, often to become objects of derision and ridicule. Yet, the reality is that not all old people exhibit the characteristics that social roles and expectations assign to them on the basis of their visual appearance, and socially constructed features of the older body are frequently at odds with the attributes of the real body. So how and why has the older body been problematized to such an extent that many people will go to extraordinary lengths to avoid or disguise the processes of ageing for fear of becoming old?

In his timely book, *The Imaginary Time Bomb*, Phil Mullan makes a persuasive argument that, with proper management and forecasting, world economies would be well equipped to cope with the impact of the growing population of older people (Mullan, 2000). He analyzes the dogma behind the construction of ageing as a social problem to identify its roots in the naturalization of the physical process. This, he argues, leads to the assumption that inevitably most people will live into old age and will need to draw heavily on welfare resources until ultimately they become totally dependent. Mullan describes these assumptions as mystification that arises when, 'biological assumptions about individual ageing falsely extend into the realm of ageing populations' (Mullan, 2000, p. 14). His interpretation of the issues is convincing and relevant, particularly with respect to constructing a Foucauldian analysis of the impact of stereotypical imagery on individuals, and on social and regulatory responses to the ageing body.

A range of inescapable experiences and often unpalatable realities dawn as the body ages. For women the experience of growing older can be associated with changes in social status as the ability to bear children fades and ultimately disappears, while men's experiences include the prospect of impotence and increasing physical frailty. Much scientific and medical research on the body has recently focused on the processes and effects of ageing, leading to greater understanding of its biological origins and physiological action. As a result, an array of techniques and products are now available to help reduce and disguise the effects of ageing. Hence today's bodies can be refashioned to mirror youth using surgical and pharmaceutical implements or devices, of which cosmetic surgery and hormone replacement therapy (HRT) are obvious examples. Numerous techniques also exist to permit childbirth after the onset of the menopause and to restore male potency. This widespread development and use of innovations designed to overcome the effects of ageing is perhaps indicative of the fact that an increasing proportion of the population are concerned about the impact of ageing upon their ability to live their lives in a manner they find acceptable.

Old age has come to be regarded as a distinct and separate stage of life and social perceptions of older people have been constructed in such a way that people now make stringent efforts to resist ageing and separate the ageing body from the old body it is progressing towards. The ageing body represents a dichotomy between the strength of wisdom and experience, and the fragility and vulnerability of physical and mental deterioration. Yet these descriptions reveal obvious contradictions. For how can a person be both wise and in the process of mental decline? Such ambiguities are indicative of the tensions prevalent in social attitudes and responses to the aged and ageing, and are depicted in the debate about access to medical treatments presented here. These social perceptions about older people are shaped by negative physical images of old people, who are frequently presented in modern western culture as frail, belligerent and demanding. Representing them in this way permits the operation of potentially discriminatory social, political and legal responses, and can induce some older people to use apparently extreme methods to limit the effects of ageing. Bodily deterioration, collapse and impending death are invariably associated with ageing, and increasing age is conspicuous because of its obvious and deleterious impact on the appearance. Disguising the visual signs of ageing, and retaining independence as long as possible, whilst shrinking from the prospect of becoming burdensome is therefore an understandable priority in a climate where the culmination of life is expected to be uncomfortable and lonely. Perhaps it is predictable, in these circumstances, that some people will consider taking control by actively courting death through euthanasia as a preferable option (Biggs, 1998).

Recent technological and medical advances can benefit older people through the provision of therapeutic regimes that can diminish the physical and visual impact of the ageing process, maintain youthful functions and improve the quality of life. However, while some of these benefits are readily available, access to others is limited through professional and regulatory controls. By first postulating that many of the poor experiences of older people, and the attitudes they reflect, are socially constructed, this chapter will argue that stereotypical media imagery has helped to generate the particular social, medical and legal responses under scrutiny here. Some explanations as to where the root of the 'problem' of ageing lies will then be suggested, along with some possible solutions.

Attitudes to ageing

There is limited consensus between sociologists and historians that the role and value of older people in society has altered and deteriorated during the course of the twentieth century. For example, Hall wrote in 1922 that 'there is a certain maturity of judgement about men, things, causes and life generally, that nothing in the world but years can bring, a real wisdom that only age can teach' (Hall, 1922, p. 366). According to this view, old age used to be a time of wisdom and consolidation, involving unique psychological processes which held sublime social significance, where increasing old age was something to be celebrated, an achievement. Furthermore, old age was a time of life that could not be mirrored elsewhere because only once life had been lived and experienced would it be possible to possess the knowledge and confidence to be wise. Not all commentators would agree, however, and clearly the position of elders in pre-industrial society should not be overly idealized. Prior to the introduction of institutionalized retirement ages and state-funded pension schemes, growing old would often have been associated with greater financial and social uncertainties than generally exist today.

Even so, the different stages of life familiar in twentieth-century society were less well demarcated in the past, with the result that the disruptive modern-day transitions between these periods were largely unnecessary. Of course, fewer people lived to 'a ripe old age', but for those who did continuity of status and value was often maintained throughout life, especially in rural communities where home and work environments were highly integrated. People remained useful and could retain control and social status all through their lives, especially as average longevity was rather shorter than it is today, and child rearing and employment extended until life's end. As a result, 'old people experienced economic and social segregation far less frequently ... and they retained their familial and economic positions until the end of their lives' (Hareven, 1995, p. 127). Hence growing old, and more particularly the unpleasant connotations associated with increasing age, such as dependence and institutionalization, can be regarded as a relatively recent phenomenon.

Economic factors and industrial development requiring employment and production, coupled with the introduction of a fixed retirement age prompting a reassessment of the status of older people within society, have gradually lead to the devaluation of their contribution. Studies have shown that elders themselves recognize these shifts in attitude and object to them with comments like, 'suddenly at 65, after functioning, working computers, having responsible jobs, you stop, like the click of your fingers' and 'you get that attitude as though you don't exist ... they think you're not as intelligent as you used to be' (Minichiello et al., 2000, p. 266). It is perhaps inevitable, in societies where individuals are characterized according to their participation in the labour market, that those who are excluded from that realm are regarded as inherently less valuable. Changing patterns of family life have accompanied these economic transformations. The family unit designed for child rearing has become more insular so that older people have become more isolated. In turn, this has 'added to the loss of power and influence of the old people in the family' (Hareven, 1995, p. 131). Many of the functions of the family have also been transferred to much larger social institutions so that the ethos of community caring prevalent in the pre-industrial era is now diminished. Older people have been effectively eliminated from the labour force and the family to become socially segregated, as they are cared for in homes and hospitals. They have been marginalized, both individually and as a group, and isolated groups of this kind are readily targeted for denigration and discrimination through the kind of negative stereotyping that can lead to devaluation.

In the context of ageing, philosopher John Harris has explored the premise that some lives are considered inherently more valuable than others. He compares a friendless widower in his later years with a 40-year-old married mother of three children, and wonders who is more likely to be provided with medical treatment if its availability is restricted? Similarly, he considers the situation where only half the people on a waiting list can be treated but all have an equal chance of making a full recovery. On the basis that young life is valued more highly than old because young adults are generally more productive to society and more likely to have dependants, he concludes that the old are likely to be discriminated against in these circumstances (Harris, 1994).

Often triggered by physical appearances, such prejudice echoes other discriminatory practices encountered throughout the ages and across cultures. Examples include those based on racial or gender bias, and that experienced by people with disabilities. The identification of older people with imagery representing them as unattractive, diffident and inefficient epitomizes this kind of stereotyping, but appearances are not always what they seem.

Ageing and imagery

In modern western culture older people are portrayed as feeble, weak, unfashionable, and outdated, and frequently regarded as burdensome.

Similar evidence is also emerging from other cultures (Gerasimova, 1996). Old age is presented and perceived as disempowering in a climate where, 'looking young is seen to be one of our main preoccupations' (Ussher, 1993, p. 116). Older people are generally represented as 'asexual, feeble and ridiculous' (Ward, 1983). Thus, older women are seen infrequently on television or in film and older female actors complain repeatedly about the dearth of roles suitable for them. Furthermore, when mature women are seen in the media they are seldom depicted as capable, independent or sexually attractive (Itzin, 1986). This may be attributable to the fact that 'our images of "ideal woman", against whom all women are judged and against which we judge ourselves, are primarily of young, slim, able-bodied, heterosexual, attractive women' (Ussher, 1993, p. 116). In some respects older men receive similar treatment with Sarah Grogan reporting that 'studies of media portrayal of men over 65 years old have tended to find that they are rarely portrayed on television (on average about five per cent of characters on television fall into this age range)' (Grogan, 1999, p. 129).

Conversely though, older men are seen significantly more frequently than are older women, and, when not playing grumpy old men, in film they are often represented as virile lovers of women considerably younger than themselves. Recent examples include Sean Connery who was depicted in the 1999 film *Entrapment* as the lover of Catherine Zeta-Jones, at least 30 years his junior. Such positive imagery is atypical, however, in a culture dominated by images of lovely young icons, and certainly it is almost unheard of for women. The enchanting film *Cocoon* (1985) serves to emphasize the point, recounting the story of a group of older people who find personal salvation by escaping the physical and emotional limitations of their ageing bodies. In this environment the pressure to 'keep young and beautiful' as a strategy for avoiding becoming sexually undesirable is enormous and the ageing body is perceived as something to be avoided at all costs.

Arguably these images and attitudes are largely responsible for the fact that many people today seek to modify their bodies through, sport, exercise, surgery and drugs in order to avoid growing old for as long as possible. And, because the physical signs of ageing provoke the prejudices associated with popular images of older people, some are prepared to go to almost any lengths to disguise them. Yet ultimately it is not possible to stop the clock. The effects of ageing can be disguised with cosmetic surgery or overcome through the therapeutic use of interventions like HRT, which gives symptomatic relief and helps maintain a youthful appearance, but ageing is inevitable. Furthermore, once the point of no return is passed, striving too hard to stay youthful and fit attracts further negative imagery epitomized by descriptions like 'the oldest swinger in town' and 'mutton dressed as lamb'. Attempts may be made to combat these discriminative tendencies through the construction of arguments based on 'anti-ageist' theories or around notions of a 'fair innings', but, at an individual level, the best response might be to try to avoid the ageing process through medical interventions of one kind or another.

Ageism in practice?

Medical science can assist in two main ways; it can alter the appearance to disguise the physical effects of ageing primarily through cosmetic surgery, and it can help improve the function of the ageing body to retain a youthful performance. Cosmetic surgery, designed to maintain youthful appearance, is socially acceptable and relatively easy to obtain. Aside from instances where there is a demonstrable clinical need, using it is largely a matter of individual choice, although it is rarely provided by state-funded healthcare services. There is little cause for regulatory intervention so long as quality of service is maintained. Some commentators have argued that technically there is little to distinguish cosmetic surgery from rather more nefarious practices like female circumcision, in that they represent physical modification through surgery legitimated by cultural norms and stereotypes (Bibbings, 1995). Legally, of course, the validity of any consent given for these procedures might be called into question if concerns are raised about the motivation and influences, cultural or personal, behind their selection. Anxieties amongst the elderly about the health and welfare implications of ageing, fuelled by concerns about dependence and neglect, are well known and widely reported. Further, gaining access to general health care services that might improve the function of an ageing body may present difficulties for older people due to stereotypical assumptions made about their understanding and needs.

Powerful influences operate within society to construct models of acceptable conduct which generate and legitimate social and medical responses to the body generally, and to the ageing body in particular. Over the last two centuries, the human body has been reconstructed to form a link between individual human beings and the body of society as a whole. As previous chapters have discussed, Michel Foucault explored the transformations that occurred during this period arguing that once those with power in society began to concentrate on life, rather than simply making decisions about death, the political and biological realms began to intertwine (Foucault, 1978). As a result, 'issues of sexual and reproductive conduct interconnect with issues of national policy and power' (Gastaldo, 1997) so that knowledge of and about the body could then be used to exert power. The concept of the body may then be manipulated so that at a collective and individual level it can be 'subjected, used, transformed and improved' (Foucault, 1977, p. 136) in politically useful narratives, as will be demonstrated below in the discussion of the application of the Human Fertilisation Embryology Act 1990.

Applying Foucault's philosophy, Turner has identified the source of power in medical decision-making precisely, stating that 'the clinical gaze enabled medical men to assume considerable social power in defining reality and hence in identifying deviance and social disorder' (Turner, 1987, p. 11). As Ellie Lee and Emily Jackson argued, when they considered the pregnant body in Chapter 8, the authority to determine who is eligible to receive treatment and who is considered competent to make healthcare decisions for themselves then resides with the medical professions. Thus, the ageing body can be readily identified as unsuitable for expensive treatments that are made easily available to the younger population, and media imagery reinforces perceptions that older bodies are not worthy of them.

At another level, professional medicine has widely disseminated information about the potential benefits of advanced medical techniques and products. The quest for answers to the biological problems of ageing now dominates the scientific, medical and popular media outlets with a constantly optimistic narrative about possible technological solutions. Repeated reports about the development of new methods to prevent ageing or reduce its effects bombard public consciousness to negatively influence perceptions of the nature of the ageing body and its deficiencies. Recently it was reported, for example, that genetically-altered mice can live a third longer than their non-modified contemporaries. Genetic modification of this type is revered as promising 'to have a considerable effect on life span, without apparent negative side-effects' so that 'we may be at a watershed in the study of ageing' (*BioNews*, 22 November 1999). Similarly American researchers based at the University of Illinois, Chicago, have identified a gene they say may be responsible for triggering many of the diseases of old age. Gaining control of this gene offers the potential to arrest the ageing process (*BioNews*, 17 April 2000).

The continual publicity surrounding scientific advancement coupled with images promoting youth and vitality as desirable goals has lead to a culture that expects biology to solve problems associated with health and life span. So important is the perceived need to overcome the ageing process, that these reports are prominently and hopefully recounted. Scant attention is paid to the fact that therapeutic intervention and genetic manipulation would be required before these techniques could be utilized in human beings. There is little, if any, questioning of whether there is an underlying need to correct the effects of ageing and why society might seek it. Thus biology acts as a powerful discourse to shape understandings of ageing and its social and medical implications. By presenting ageing as problematic, a social imperative is created, which prompts and expects people to take personal responsibility for their own health and well-being. In the context of ageing, the emphasis has been directed towards reducing the effects and appearance of advancing maturity and has masked the realities of ageing.

Avoiding and overcoming ageing

In an environment where ageing is perceived and presented as unwelcome and unattractive, publicity associated with scientific progress and miracle developments encourages people to seek out medical means to overcome or avoid the effects of ageing. While cosmetic surgery is relatively free of formal regulation, access to the rather more invasive procedures associated with restoring or enhancing declining bodily functions is more complex. The scope and operation of these regulatory mechanisms is highly informative about the nature of the relationship between cultural and legal attitudes towards the ageing body. An interesting example is provided by the regulation of fertility, in particular post-menopausal pregnancy, which can enable older women to bear children.

There are many reasons why a woman might wish to embark on a pregnancy after she has lost the natural ability so to do. One case that perhaps generates a sympathetic response concerns those women who have encountered an unusually early menopause. They find themselves unable to conceive a child naturally even though they are still in their twenties or early thirties because their bodily functions mimic those of somebody much older than their chronological age. An early menopause in these circumstances may be the result of hormonal insufficiency or due to the effects of disease or perhaps chemotherapy. Reproductive function can be artificially restored in these circumstances and is generally considered socially and morally unproblematic. Not so for those women aged 45 years or over, who seek interventional fertility treatment to have a child at or beyond the normal age of menopause. Such women may have avoided pregnancy in order to pursue a career, may have left their attempts at pregnancy until later only to discover they were unable to conceive, or may have simply failed to meet a suitable partner until their fertility was naturally declining. Their reasons are often regarded as much less deserving and depicted as selfish and unnatural and their access to fertility services is correspondingly limited both legally and practically – a further example of the construction noted in Chapter 8 of the distinction between 'good' and 'bad' reasons for requests for medical treatment in pregnancy.

The UK Human Fertilisation and Embryology Act 1990 (HFE Act) places no explicit restrictions on the age at which a woman is considered eligible to receive fertility treatment. But, through the interpretation of section 13, part 5 of this Act, and the operation of the Human Fertility and Embryology Authority's Code of Practice, it does influence the criteria used by licensed fertility centres in determining how suitable patients are selected. Under this section of the Act, clinicians are required by law to take account of the 'welfare of any child who may be born as a result of treatment'. The Code of Practice provides guidance on how this provision is implemented, suggesting that factors like the ages of prospective parents and their likely future ability to care for a child be considered. As a result, many fertility centres refuse to admit women over 45 for treatment. Double jeopardy operates here because couples of this age are also considered too old to adopt a child. Furthermore, few National Health Service (NHS) health authorities provide funding for fertility treatment to couples where the woman is over 35 years of age. So even if a centre does agree to conduct the treatment it will have to be paid for independently of the NHS.

The justification for refusing to fund these procedures is that they are costly and success rates are very low. Both of these statements are true. Fertility treatment is expensive – but no more so than very many other procedures that the NHS finances without question. Success rates are low, but not only for older women; all kinds of fertility treatments licensed by the HFE Authority have surprisingly low rates of success (HFE Authority, 2000). It is also true that the number of live births to women over 38 years is significantly lower than for younger women and virtually no successes are recorded in women over 40. However, the higher success rates in younger women are generally attributed to the biological age of their gametes. And, since women who have encountered the menopause will only be able to undergo treatment using donated eggs, their chances of success should be no lower than women in their thirties who are using their own gametes. Interestingly, no figures are published matching age to the number of births where donated eggs have been used. Could it be that the inherent prejudices expressed in the HFE Act and its Code of Practice are operating to discriminate against older women becoming parents?

Where people have confounded nature by producing children later in life without the need for medical assistance there is little significant evidence that their children suffer as a result. Women have given birth naturally in their late forties and even after 50 years of age, while men can father children throughout their lives with frequent reports of men in their eighties becoming fathers. Clearly there is a risk that older parents will become ill or die before their offspring are independent, but that is a risk that all parents share and many children confront, even if their parents are young. It is not a problem that is confined to parents with ageing bodies. Additionally, statistically people are generally living longer, which reduces these risks.

Similar arguments concerning access to treatment have recently been advanced in respect of the provision of therapy for the alleviation of erectile dysfunction in men. Impotence does tend to afflict predominantly older men but is also symptomatic of a range of medical conditions like diabetes, multiple sclerosis, injury to the spinal cord and radical pelvic surgery, which are encountered by relatively young men. Until recently, its treatment achieved only limited success, relying upon cumbersome mechanical devices. The advent of Viagra, and more recently developed similar products, offer a solution that requires no more effort than swallowing a small blue pill; an apparent panacea. Except that Viagra is, by comparison with many other drugs, very expensive. Its cost implications are compounded by the prospect of enormous demand because impotence is recognized as a very widespread problem, especially for older men. Partial or total impotence is reported as affecting around ten million men in the UK and 30 million in the USA with a proportionately similar incidence across the world. So while hailed as a revolutionary treatment likely to improve the quality of life of very many men, and women, this product, has been the subject of a carefully orchestrated campaign to devalue the significance of the disorder and its treatment.

Albeit with a rather different agenda, Germaine Greer has derided the furore surrounding the introduction of Viagra with claims that impotence is a 'naturally occurring variation of normal function' rather than a dysfunction and therefore requires no special attention from the medical profession (Greer, 1999). The media have been complicit in presenting the drug and its potential recipients, as smutty and undeserving. Jokes about elderly men flaunting their Viagra-induced erections in the dance halls fuelled by media anxiety and greeting-card humour all conspire to deter would-be beneficiaries from requesting the treatment. Even agony aunt Claire Rayner, usually an advocate of patient's rights, was vociferous in her condemnation in the tabloid medical press claiming that 'the hard pressed NHS should not fund the sexual desires of the elderly, who are very likely to regard this pill as the fountain of youth' (Rayner, 1998, p. 41). Rationing of such a medication is easily justified and accepted by the public in these circumstances.

Like fertility treatment for younger women, younger men who require Viagra to remedy a medically induced dysfunction can obtain it on prescription. Others, who seek it to enhance the quality of their lives by retaining the enjoyment of a bodily function taken for granted by most young people, are denied free access. In the absence of one of the triggering conditions defined by the National Institute for Clinical Excellence (NICE) Viagra is only available at a price, through private prescription. Hence, rather than being a panacea, Viagra may compound the insecurities and stresses of older age because of the limitations placed upon its availability. Once again, older users of nationally provided resources are discriminated against, this time because of concerns that demand will outstrip resources.

The law offers no effective remedy against this inequity. Healthcare providers have a legal duty under section 1 of the National Health Service Act 1977 to promote a 'comprehensive health service designed to secure improvement … in the prevention, diagnosis and treatment of illness [and] … to provide or secure the effective provision of services'. However, repeated precedents have failed to uphold the principle that the service should be comprehensive and inclusive. For example, in a legal case in 1992, *R* v. *Secretary of State ex parte Hinks*, it was held that 'the health service currently falls short of what everyone would regard as the optimum desirable standard. This is very largely a situation brought about by lack of resources, lack of suitable equipment, lack of suitably qualified personnel, and above all lack of adequate finance'. But this and numerous subsequent cases failed to address the inadequate health service resources because treatment provision must be 'determined in the light of current Government economic policy'.

Restricting the availability of treatment to alleviate the effects of old age in this way perhaps illustrates deep prejudices about ageing in our culture. But the existence and usage of the myriad of techniques that aim to overcome the ageing process, including those discussed here, is evidence of the importance with which many individuals view the need to retain a youthful appearance and outlook on life. Simultaneously, recent controversies in the UK generated by the use of so-called 'Do Not Resuscitate orders', especially in hospital wards designated for the care of older people clearly, demonstrate the moral significance of ageing and social value of the elderly. Medical staff and managers stand accused of making decisions not to revive patients who suffer cardiac or respiratory collapse solely on the basis of their age and often without proper consultation with patients or their families. The inescapable implication is that in the cash-limited NHS clinical decisions are being taken on the basis of costs and the inevitable victims are those who might be seen as a net drain on the system. Furthermore, because older patients are often frail and traditionally more compliant and deferential towards medical opinion they are frequently less able, or willing, to speak up against such policies. Institutional intolerance of the needs of the older people described by the failure to provide for their social and healthcare needs, including those associated with the avoidance of ageing, can therefore result in a desire to shun further dependence. In this environment, once the physical and functional effects of ageing can no longer be evaded, alternative strategies, like euthanasia and suicide, might become attractive (Biggs, 1998).

Lack of confidence in the medical profession's perceived approach to the specialism defined as 'care of the elderly', combined with the desire to avoid the worst features of dying and death has lead to euthanasia being increasingly regarded as an appropriate means of avoiding the extremes of old age. Infirmity, dependence and loss of control could be diminished or evaded by a timely death and support for legal reform to permit euthanasia is growing in response, frequently premised upon fears that healthcare choices will not be respected. However, calls for legislation to permit actions designed to terminate life by those who seek to avoid dependence and indignity seem to contradict perceptions that older people are often neglected by the medical profession, as exemplified in the controversy over 'Do Not

Resuscitate orders'. Perhaps perversely, however, they may represent two sides of the same coin because central to both arguments is the desire to maintain independence and exercise individual autonomy and choice throughout the full span of life.

The living will is viewed as one mechanism through which autonomy can be maintained over the process of dying. Increasing numbers of older people are drawing up living wills stipulating the kind of healthcare they would find acceptable should they be unable to speak for themselves. Theoretically, the living will provides a safeguard against unwanted medical intervention, but in practice the ability of a living will, or advance directive, to ensure that a person's healthcare choices are respected may be limited.

It is settled in law that 'Prima facie every adult has the right and capacity to decide whether or not he will accept medical treatment even if a refusal may risk permanent injury to his health or even lead to premature death' (the case in question was in 1992, called *Re T*). Similarly, a case known as *Re C* (1994) found that decisions taken when competent can be binding even after a person has lost the capacity to participate in medical decision-making. But the efficacy of a decision made in advance is dependent upon a range of practical, legal and sociological factors which will determine whether the living will is valid and can be applied in the circumstances that have arisen.

A living will only becomes operational once the individual who has instigated it is no longer able to decide for herself. An obvious and immediate shortcoming is that any documentary evidence representing a patient's wishes may not be visible at the time when a medical crisis requiring life and death decisions occurs. The patient may be away from home or in hospital and there may be no record of the relevant documentation. There is no requirement that a living will, or advance directive, be written down, or, if it is, that it conforms to a specific format. The law will uphold a person's considered wishes if they are known and certain but this of course depends upon the existence of evidence demonstrating that the views expressed are consistent and voluntary. Disputes may arise as to the validity of the 'will' based on concerns about whether the person was competent to make binding advance decisions at the time the 'will' was formulated. Here, it may be the professional or emotional carers who initiate the dispute based upon their own (competing) interests and concerns.

Many older people fear that their views may not be respected even while they are still capable of expressing their opinions, hence the furore over 'Do Not Resuscitate orders'. They often hope a living will to be an appropriate means of helping to ensure that their wishes are heard. Certainly, a properly designed living will can assist a still competent person to have her wishes upheld, particularly if it can be regarded as evidence of a real and continuing desire or opinion. Should such evidence be necessary, however, it is likely that the relevant medical decisions are already in dispute and the elder will be arguing from a position of relative weakness. The tendency within society and the medical professions to assume that older people suffer from impaired mental capacity is strong. Media imagery encourages such an approach depicting the aged as 'incapacitated, incompetent, pathetic and the subject of ridicule' (Grogan, 1999, p. 129) and justifying paternalistic responses. Questioning the capacity of older people to understand the implications of their living wills or their ability to give valid consent to surgical procedures designed to disguise ageing are of course representative of the problem.

The visual representations associated with the decline of the body during ageing are significant in the impact they have on social attitudes and cannot be divorced from the stereotypical images surrounding the intellectual capabilities of older people. In many cultures the experience and knowledge associated with older age is respected and revered, but modern western cultures tend to regard older people as lacking intellectual rigour. There is little recognition that while physical deterioration is inevitable and unmistakable, it is not inevitably accompanied by reduced mental capability. According to Age Concern estimates suggest that only five per cent of the population of people aged over 65 suffers from dementia, rising to 20 per cent of those aged over 80 years (Age Concern, 1999). Negative associations are drawn between physical, bodily appearance and mental capacity, even though the powers of reasoning and understanding are invisible and can only be detected and tested through interaction with others. The acceptance of these downbeat stereotypes goes a long way towards justifying the overly paternalistic responses with which those who exercise medical power often seem to approach the 'care of the elderly'. As a result, despite the protection offered by living wills, decisions concerning treatment for older people continue to be taken in the absence of consultation with them.

Tensions clearly exist between the rights of all individuals to act as autonomous agents and the therapeutic and regulatory responses described here as they relate to older people with ageing bodies who seek particular medical interventions. It is apparent from this discussion that despite the existence of medical techniques to overcome the functional deterioration, or disguise many of the problems associated with the ageing body, the people who inhabit those bodies do not always benefit from technological advancement. Furthermore, even though the law professes to support all adults in their healthcare choices, older people in particular may be denied choice and effective decision-making.

Conclusion

This chapter has observed some of the stereotypical images that can lead some people to seek to delay or limit the effects of ageing on their own body and its appearance. These stereotypes are undoubtedly informed by the political and economic influences that pervade society and influence policy-makers and have translated ageing into a social problem. Arguably, however, much of the political debate is premised on false assumptions.

Of course the problems associated with ageing are not all socially constructed. Ageing is a physical biological process that does impact poorly upon many bodily functions, so that, according to figures published by Age Concern, 52 per cent of people aged over 75 years complain that they have a long-standing illness that limits their life style (Age Concern, 1999). Similar conditions sometimes befall younger people, but because their condition is not age-related they can usually expect their health and welfare needs to be met. Not so far the visibly aged, whose real needs may be reconstructed to fit social stereotypes founded on imprecise assumptions, characterizing them as less deserving or less credible.

If Mullan is correct that 'the anxiety about ageing ... is misplaced' (Mullan, 2000, p. 215) then the stereotypes that generate people's needs to reconstruct themselves as younger and somehow more acceptable within society are similarly misplaced and arguably unnecessary. Yet overturning stereotypes is not an activity that can be performed by individuals, especially those who are designated as part of a homogeneous group that has negative connotations. Because of the pessimistic social response to ageing, old age is now inevitably associated with poor health, dependence and loss of status. This then becomes a realistic expectation.

Equating growing older with the decline into dying and death is not a new phenomenon. Neither is the preoccupation with novel methods of overcoming it, as Oscar Wilde's *Picture of Dorian Gray* testifies (Wilde, 1999). Equally pertinent is the fact that, while temporary solutions may be available and some functions can be restored in the short term, it is not possible to turn back the clock or to stop the march of time. People are living longer, fuller, more healthy lives but that in itself is not enough because the use of scientific and medical technology to preserve and extend life is meaningless if that life is not valued. Experience born of maturity is not apparently a quality that is highly valued, hence people seek to evade discrimination by disguising their longevity through cosmetic interventions and increasingly by calls for regulatory control. For example, in the USA, discrimination in employment on the basis of age is impermissible and calls are now being made in the UK for questions about chronological age to be removed from job application forms. Rather than adopt the 'top down' approach that such action would denote, what is really required is for the social value of experience and wisdom to be properly appreciated. As John Harris argues, 'the most moral and most honourable way of dealing with the difficulties ... is to try to ensure that we have sufficient resources ... so that we do not have to choose between people invidiously' (Harris, 1994, p. 110). Once we do that the ageing body could be accepted as representing a stage of life like any other. After all, there is rarely any negative stigma attached to the bodies of children, neonates or pregnant women, and the only distinguishing feature of the ageing body is that it represents a time of life that many people fear and find unacceptable. That is the reality.

Cases

R v. *Secretary of State ex-parte Hinks* [1992] 1 BMLR 93 (decided in 1980)
Re C (Adult Refusal of Treatment) [1994] 1 All ER 819
Re T (Adult: Refusal of Treatment) [1992] 4 All ER 649

Further reading

Featherstone M. and Wernick A. (eds), *Images of Ageing: Cultural Representations of Later Life* (London: Routledge, 1995).
  A collection of essays, from international contributors, which addresses themes such as images of ageing used by governments in health education campaigns, gender images of ageing, experience and identity in old age, and, illness and death.
Kaim-Caudle, P. Keithlry, J. and Mullender A. (eds), *Aspects of Ageing* (London: Whiting & Birch, 1993).
  Another collection of essays which provide intriguing and multicultural insights into a range of aspects and experiences of ageing.

Mullan, P. *The Imaginary Time Bomb: Why an Ageing Population is not a Social Problem* (London: I.B. Taurus, 2000).

A fascinating study of the socio-political implications of ageing, that challenges many contemporary concerns about the 'problem' of the ageing population.

Ageing and Society

An international journal published bimonthly, devoted to contributing to the understanding of human ageing, from the behavioural sciences and humanities.

Bibliography

Abberley, P. 'The Concept of Oppression and the Development of a Social Theory of Disability', *Disability, Handicap and Society* 2 (1987) 5–20.

Abberley, P. 'Work, Utopia and Impairment', in L. Barton (ed.) *Disability and Society: Emerging Issues and Insights* (London: Longman, 1996).

Abdullah, M. and Wheeler, E. F. 'Seasonal Variations, and the Intra-household Distribution of Food in a Bangladeshi Village', *American Journal of Clinical Nutrition* 41 (1985) 1305–13.

Age Concern. *Older People in the United Kingdom: Some Basic Statistics* (London: Age Concern, 1999).

Ahmed, S. 'Tanning the Body: Skin, Colour and Gender', *New Formations* 34 (1998) 27–42.

Ahmed, S. *Strange Encounters: Embodied Others in Post-Coloniality* (London: Routledge, 2000).

Alanen, L. 'Gender and Generation: Feminism and the "Child Question"' in J. Qvortrup, M. Bardy, G. Sgritta and H. Wintersberger (eds) *Childhood Matters: Social Theory, Practice and Politics* (Aldershot/ Vermont: Avebury, 1994).

Albury, Rebecca M. *Beyond the Slogans, the Politics of Reproduction* (St Leonards: Allen and Unwin, 1999).

Alderson, P. 'Researching Children's Right to Integrity', in B. Mayall (ed.) *Children's Childhoods: Observed and Experienced* (Falmer Press: London, 1994).

American Pain Society. *Chronic Pain in America: Roadblocks to Relief* (1999) http//www.ampainsoc.org/

Anderson, B. *Imagined Communities* (London: Verso, 1986).

Anon. *Women: A World Report* (New York: Methuen, 1985).

APA. 'Practice Guideline for the Treatment of Patients with Eating Disorders (revision)', *American Journal of Psychiatry* (Supplement) 157 (January 2000) 1–39.

Armstrong, D. *Political Anatomy of the Body: Medical Knowledge in Britain in the Twentieth Century* (Cambridge: Cambridge University Press, 1983).

Autton, N. *Pain: An Exploration* (Darton, Longmann and Todd, 1986).

Bainham, A. 'Do Babies have Rights?', *Cambridge Law Journal* 56 (1997) 48.

Bakhtin, M. M. *Rabelais and his World* (Bloomington and Indianapolis: Indiana University Press, 1984).

Balint, M. *The Doctor, his Patient and the Illness* (London: Pitman, 1968).

Barnes, C. *Disabled People in Britain and Discrimination* (London: Hurst & Co, 1991).

Barnes, C. and Mercer, G. (eds) *Exploring the Divide: Illness and Disability.* (Leeds: The Disability Press, 1996).

Barthes, R. *The Fashion System* (London: Cape, 1985).

Bartley, M., Blane, D. and Davey-Smith, G. (eds) *The Sociology of Health Inequalities* (Oxford: Blackwell, 1998).

Barton, L. and Oliver, M. (eds) *Disability Studies: Past, Present and Future* (Leeds: The Disability Press, 1997).

Bell, Q. *On Human Finery* (London: Hogarth Press, 1976).

Bell, V. *Interrogating Incest: Feminism, Foucault and the Law* (London: Routledge, 1993).

Bendelow, G. 'A "Failure" of Modern Medicine? Lay Perspectives on a Pain Relief Clinic', in S. Williams and M. Calnan (eds) *Modern Medicine: Lay perspectives and Experiences* (London: UCL Press, 1996).

Bendelow, G. and Williams, S. 'Transcending the Dualisms: Towards a Sociology of Pain', *Sociology of Health and Illness* 17: 2 (1995) 139–65.

Benhabib, S. 'Feminism, Postmodernism: An Uneasy Alliance', *Praxis International* 11: 2 (1991) 137–49.

Benhabib, S. et al. *Feminist Contentions: A Philosophical Exchange* (New York and London: Routledge, 1995).

Berer, M. 'Abortion: A Woman's Perspective', in K. Newman (ed.) *Progress Postponed: Abortion in the 1990s* (London: International Planned Parenthood Federation, Europe Region, 1993).

Berry, Peter, quoted on *BBC News Online*, 23 September 1999.

Bertin, J. 'Regulating Reproduction', in J. Callahan (ed.) *Reproduction, Ethics and the Law: Feminist Responses* (Bloomington and Indianapolis: Indiana University Press, 1995).

Best, S. and Kellner, D. *Postmodern Theory: Critical Interrogations* (London: Macmillan, 1991).

Bhabha, H. *The Location of Culture* (London: Routledge, 1994).

Bhavnani, Kum-Kum and Collins, D. 'Racism and Feminism: An Analysis of the Anita Hill and Clarence Thomas Hearings', *New Community* 19: 3 (1993) 493–505.

Bibbings, L. 'Female Circumcision: Mutilation or Modification?', in J. Bridgeman and S. Millns (eds) *Law and Body Politics: Regulating the Female Body* (Aldershot: Dartmouth, 1995).

Biggs, H. 'I Don't Want to be a Burden', in S. Sheldon and M. Thomson (eds) *Feminist Perspectives on Health Care Law* (London: Cavendish, 1998).

BioNews, vol. 35, 22 November 1999, 'GM Mice Aid Ageing Research', http://www.progress.org.uk/News/BioNewsSearch.html

BioNews, vol. 54, 17 April 2000, 'Gene Linked to Diseases of Old Age', http://www.progress.org.uk/News/BioNewsSearch.html

Blane, D., Brunner, E. and Wilkinson, R. (eds) *Health and Social Organization* (London: Routledge, 1996).

Blank, R. H. *Fetal Protection in the Workplace* (New York: Columbia University Press, 1993).

Blyth, F. M., March, L. M., Brnabic, A. J., Jorm, L. R., Williamson, M., Cousins, M. J., 'Chronic Pain in Australia', *Pain* 89, (2–3): (2001) 127–34.

Booth, C. *The Life and Labour of the People in London* (London: Macmillan, 1903).

Bordo, S. '"Maleness" Revisted', *Hypatia* 7: 3 (1992) 197–208.

Bordo, S. *Unbearable Weight: Feminism, Western Culture and the Body* (Berkeley, Los Angeles and London: University of California Press, 1993).

Boseley, S. 'Parents' Fury over New Organ Scandal', *The Guardian*, 16 August 2000.

Bourdieu, P. *Distinction: A Social Critique of the Judgement of Taste* (London: Routledge, 1984).

Bourdieu, P. *Outline of a Theory of Practice* (Cambridge: Cambridge University Press, 1989).

Boyle, M. *Re-thinking Abortion, Psychology, Gender, Power and the Law* (London: Routledge, 1997).

Bradley, Paul, quoted in *The Guardian*, 13 May 2000.

Breward, C. *The Culture of Fashion: A History of Fashionable Dress* (Manchester: Manchester University Press, 1995).

Breward, C. *The Hidden Consumer* (Manchester: Manchester University Press, 1999).

Bridgeman, J. 'A Woman's Right to Choose?', in E. Lee (ed.) *Abortion Law and Politics Today* (Basingstoke: Macmillan Press – now Palgrave, 1998).

Bridgeman, J. and Millns, S. (eds) *Law and Body Politics: Regulating the Female Body* (Aldershot: Dartmouth, 1995).

Bridgeman, J. and Monk, D. *Feminist Perspectives on Child Law* (London: Cavendish Publishing, 2000).

Brindle, D. 'Warning over Body Piercing', *The Guardian*, 5 April 2000.

Brook, B. *Feminist Perspectives on the Body* (London and New York: Longman, 1999).

Bruch, H. *The Golden Cage* (Cambridge: Harvard University Press, 1977).

Busfield, J. *Men, Women and Madness* (London: Macmillan Press – now Palgrave, 1996).

Butler, J. *Gender Trouble: Feminism and the Subversion of Identity* (London/New York: Routledge, 1990).

Butler, J. *Bodies that Matter. On the Discursive Limits of 'Sex'.* (New York and London: Routledge, 1993).

Butler, J. 'Contingent Foundations: Feminism and the Question of 'Postmodernism', in Benhabib, S. et al. *Feminist Contentions: A Philosophical Exchange* (New York and London: Routledge, 1995).

Butler, M. *Introduction to Frankenstein* (Oxford: Oxford University Press, 1998).

Cambier, J. 'A Modern View: Pain Today', in R. Rey (ed.) *The History of Pain* (trans. by L. E. Wallace, J. A. Cadden and S. W. Cadden) (Cambridge, MA: Harvard University Press, 1995).

Campbell, A. 'Dependency Revisited: The limits of Autonomy in Medical Ethics', in M. Brazier and M. Lobjoit (eds) *Protecting the Vulnerable: Autonomy and Consent in Health Care* (London: Routledge, 1991).

Campbell, J. and Oliver, M. *Disability Politics: Understanding our Past, Changing our Future* (London: Routledge, 1996).

Chatterjee, M. and Lambert, J. 'Women and Nutrition', *Food and Nutrition Bulletin* 11 (1989) 13–28.

Chaudhury, R. H. 'Determinants of Dietary Intake and Dietary Adequacy for Pre-school Children in Bangladesh', *Food and Nutrition Bulletin* 6 (1984) 24–33.

Chen, L. C. et al. 'Sex Bias in the Allocation of Food and Health Care in Rural Bangladesh, *Population and Development Review* 7 (1981) 55–70.

Chief Medical Officer (CMO), *Summit Proceedings*, 11 January 2001 www.cmo-summit.org.uk

Christensen, P. H. 'Childhood and the Cultural Constitution of Vulnerable Bodies', in Prout, A. (ed.). *The Body, Childhood and Society* (Basingstoke: Macmillan Press – now Palgrave, 2000).

Clarke, J., Hall, S. et al. 'Subcultures, Cultures and Class', in T. Bennett, G. Martin, C. Mercer and J. Woollacott (eds) *Culture, Ideology and Social Process: A Reader* (Milton Keynes: Open University Press, 1992).

Cohn, N. 'By Love Possessed', *The New York Review*, 30 January 1986, 3–4.

Collier, R. *Masculinity, Law and the Family* (London: Routledge, 1995).

Collier, R. 'Anxious Parenthood, The Vulnerable Child and the "Good Father": Reflections on the Legal Regulation of the Relationship between Men and Children', in J. Bridgeman and D. Monk (eds) *Feminist Perspectives on Child Law* (Cavendish Publishing: London, 2000).

Corker, M. *Deaf and Disabled, or Deafness Disabled?* (Buckingham: Open University Press, 1998).

Corker, M. and French, S. (eds) *Disability Discourse* (Buckingham: Open University Press, 1999).

Cornell, D. *The Philosophy of the Limit* (New York: Routledge, 1992).

Crawford, R. 'The Boundaries of the Self and the Unhealthy Other: Reflections on Health Culture and AIDS', *Social Science and Medicine* 38: 10 (1994) 1347–65.

Crossley, N. 'Body Techniques, Agency and Inter-corporality: On Goffman's Relations in Public', *Sociology* 129: 1 (1995a) 133–49.

Crossley, N. 'Merleau-Ponty, the Elusive Body and Carnal Sociology', *Body and Society* 1: 1 (1995b) 43–63.

Crossley, N. 'Body/Subject, Body/Power: Agency, Inscription and Control in Foucault and Merleau-Ponty', *Body and Society* 2: 2 (1996) 99–116.

Crow, L. 'Including All of Our Lives: Renewing the Social Model of Disability', in C. Barnes and G. Mercer (eds) *Exploring the Divide: Illness and Disability* (Leeds: The Disability Press, 1996).

Csordas, T. J. 'Somatic Modes of Attention', *Cultural Anthropology* 8: 2 (1993) 135–56.

Csordas, T. J. (ed.) *Embodiment and Experience: The Existential Ground of Culture and Self* (Cambridge: Cambridge University Press, 1996).

Daniels, C. *At Women's Expense: State Power and the Politics of Fetal Rights* (Cambridge, MA: Harvard University Press, 1993).

Daniels, C. 'Between Fathers and Fetuses: The Social Construction of Male Reproduction and the Politics of Fetal Harm', *Signs: Journal of Women in Culture and Society* 22: 3 (1997) 579–616.

Daniels, C. 'Fathers, Mothers and Fetal Harm', in Lynn M. Morgan and Meredith W. Michaels (eds) *Fetal Subjects: Feminist Positions* (Philadelphia: University of Pennsylvania Press, 1999).

Darwin, C. *The Descent of Man* (London: John Murray, 1871).

Das Gupta, M. 'Selective Discrimination against Female Children in Rural Punjab, India', *Population and Development Review* 13 (1987) 77–100.

Davies, V. *Abortion and Afterwards* (Bath: Ashgrove, 1991).

Davis, F. *Fashion, Culture and Identity* (Chicago: University of Chicago Press, 1994).

Davis, H. and Bourhill, M. '"Crisis": The Demonization of Children and Young People', in P. Scraton (ed.) *'Childhood' in 'Crisis'?* (London, UK and Bristol, Pennsylvania: UCL Press, 1997).

Davis, K. 'Embodying Theory: Beyond Modernist and Postmodernist Readings of the Body', in K. Davis (ed.) *Embodied Practices: Feminist Perspectives on the Body* (London: Sage, 1997).

DelVecchio Good, M., Brodwin, P., Kleinman, A. and Good, B. (eds) *Pain as Human Experience: An Anthropological Perspective* (California: University of California Press, 1992).

Department of Health (DOH). *Protecting Children, Supporting Parents: A Consultation Document on the Physical Punishment of Children* (2000).

Descartes, R. *The Passions of the Soul: Philosophical Writings* (London: Macmillan, 1953).

Diamond, I. and Quinby, L. *Feminism and Foucault: Reflections on Resistance* (Boston: Northeastern University Press, 1988).

Douglas, M. *Natural Symbols, Explorations in Cosmology* (London: Barrie & Rockliff: the Cresset Press, 1973).

Douglas, M. 'Do Dogs Laugh: A Cross-Cultural Approach to Body Symbolism', in M. Douglas, (ed.) *Implicit Meanings: Essays in Anthropology* (London: Routledge, 1979).

Douglas, M. *Purity and Danger: An Analysis of the Concept of Pollution and Taboo* (London: Routledge and Kegan Paul, 1984).

Dowler, E. and Calvert, C. *Nutrition and Diet in Lone Parent Families in London* (London: Family Policy Studies Centre, 1995).

Drake, R. *Understanding Disability Politics* (Basingstoke: Macmillan Press – now Palgrave, 1999).

Eco, U. *Lumbar Thought, Travels in Hyperreality* (Orlando, Fl: Harcourt Brace Jovanovich, 1986).

Elton, D., Stanley, G. and Burrows, G. *Psychological Control of Pain* (Australia: Grune and Stratton, 1983).

Engel, G. 'Psychogenic Pain and the Pain Prone Patient', *American Journal of Medicine* 26 (1959) 899–918.

Entwistle, J. 'Power Dressing and the Fashioning of the Career Woman', in M. Nava, I. MacRury, A. Blake and B. Richards (eds) *Buy this Book: Studies in Advertising and Consumption* (London: Routledge, 1997).

Entwistle, J. *The Fashioned Body* (Cambridge: Polity Press, 2000).

Entwistle, J. 'Fashioning the Career Woman: Power Dressing as a Strategy of Consumption', in M. Talbot and M. Andrews (eds) *All the World and Her Husband: Women and Consumption in the Twentieth Century* (London: Cassell, 2000).

Entwistle, J. and Wilson, E. *The Body Clothed, 100 Years of Art and Fashion* (London: Hayward Gallery, 1998).

Fanon, F. *Black Skin, White Masks* (trans., C. L. Markmann) (London: Pluto Press, 1986).

Featherstone, M. and Wernick, A. (eds) *Images of Ageing: Cultural Representations of Later Life* (London: Routledge, 1995)

Ferguson, M. 'Mary Wollstonecraft and the Problematic of Slavery', *Feminist Review*, 42 (1992) 83–102.

Fordyce, W.E. *Back Pain in the Workplace: Management of Disability in Nonspecific Conditions. A Report of the Task Force on Pain in the Workplace of the International Association for the Study of Pain* (Seattle: IASP Press, 1995).

Foucault, M. *Discipline and Punish* (London: Penguin Books, 1977).

Foucault, M. *The History of Sexuality, Volume 1* (London: Penguin, 1978).

Foucault, M. *Power/Knowledge. Selected Interviews and Other Writings 1972–1977* Gordon, C. (ed.) (Great Britain: The Harvester Press, 1980).

Frank, A. 'For a Sociology of the Body: An Analytical Review', in M. Featherstone, M. Hepworth and B. Turner (eds) *The Body: Social Process and Cultural Theory* (London: Sage, 1991).

Franklin, S. 'Imprints of Time', in S. Franklin, C. Lury and J. Stacey (eds) *Global Nature, Global Culture* (London: Sage, 2000).

Fraser, N. and Nicholson, L. 'Social Criticism without Philosophy: An Encounter between Feminism and Postmodernism', *Theory, Culture and Society* 5: 373–94. Reprinted in Docherty, T. (ed.) *Postmodernism: A Reader* (New York: Harvester Wheatsheaf, 1988).

Fraser, N. 'Foucault's Body Language: A Posthumanist Political Rhetoric?', in N. Fraser (ed.) *Unruly Practices: Power, Discourse and Gender in Contemporary Social Theory* (Minneapolis: University of Minnesota Press, 1989).

Fraser, N. 'False Antithesis: A Response to Seyla Benhabib and Judith Butler', *Praxis International* 11: 2 (1991) 166–77.

Freeman, C. 'Designing Women: Corporate Discipline and Barbados's Offshore Pink Collar Sector.' *Cultural Anthropology* 8: 2 (1993) 164–85.

Freeman, C. *High Heels and High Tech in the Global Economy: Women, Work and Pink-Collar Identities in the Caribbean* (Durham, N.C.: Duke University Press, 2000).

Freeman, J. 'The Disciplinary Function of Rape's Representation: Lessons from the Kennedy Smith and Tyson Trials', *Law and Social Inquiry*, 18: 3 (1993) 517–546.

French, S. 'Disability, Impairment, or Something in between?', in J. Swain, V. Finkelstein, S. French and M. Oliver (eds) *Disabling Barriers – Enabling Environments* (London: Sage, 1993).

Freud, S. 'Fragment of an Analysis of a Case of Hysteria', in *Pelican Freud Library Volume 8* (London: Penguin Books, 1977).

Furedi, A. *Unplanned Pregnancy, Your Choices* (Oxford: Oxford University Press, 1996).

Furedi, F. *The Culture of Fear: Risk Taking and the Morality of Law Expectations* (London: Cassell, 1997).

Furedi, F. *Paranoid Parenting* (London: The Penguin Press, 2001).

Fuss, D. 'Black Bodies, White Bodies: Toward an Iconography of Female Sexuality in Late Nineteenth-Century Art, Medicine and Literature', in H. L. Gates (ed.) *'Race', Writing and Difference* (Chicago: University of Chicago Press, 1986).

Fuss, D. *Essentially Speaking: Feminism, Nature and Difference* (London: Routledge, 1990).

Gallagher, J. 'Collective Bad Faith: "Protecting the Fetus"', in J. Callahan (ed.) *Reproduction, Ethics and the Law: Feminist Responses* (Bloomington and Indianapolis: Indiana University Press, 1995).

Gastaldo, D. 'Health Education and the Concept of Bio-Power', in A. Petersen and R. Bunton (eds) *Foucault: Health and Medicine* (London: Routledge, 1997).

Gatens, M. 'A Critique of the Sex/Gender Distinction', in J. Allen and P. Patten (eds) *Beyond Marxism? Interventions After Marx* (New South Wales: Intervention Collective Publication, 1983).

Gatens, M. *Imaginary Bodies: Ethics, Power and Corporeality* (London and New York: Routledge, 1996).

Gerasimova, T. 'Elderly Women: A Challenge to Russia', in A. Rotkirch and E. Haavio-Mannila (eds) *Women's Voices in Russia Today* (Aldershot: Dartmouth, 1996).

Gilbert, S. and Gubar, S. *Madwoman in the Attic* (New Haven, Conn: Yale University Press, 1970).

Gilman, S. 'Black Bodies, White Bodies: Toward an Iconography of Female Sexuality in Late Nineteenth-Century Art, Medicine and Literature', in H. L. Gates (ed.) *'Race', Writing and Difference* (Chicago: University of Chicago Press, 1986).

Gilroy, P. *The Black Atlantic: Modernity and Double Consciousness* (London: Verso, 1993).

Gittelsohn, J. 'Opening the Box: Intrahousehold Food Allocation in Rural Nepal', *Social Science and Medicine* 33 (1991) 1141–54.

Goffman, E. *The Presentation of Self in Everyday Life* (London: The Penguin Press, 1971).

Goffman, E. *Relations in Public: Microstudies of the Public Order* (New York: Harper and Row, 1972).

Gordon, D. 'Tenacious Assumptions in Western Medicine', in M. Lock and D. Gordon (eds) *Biomedicine Examined* (Dordrecht: Kluwer, 1988).

Graham, H. *Hardship and Health in Women's Lives* (New York: Harvester Wheatsheaf, 1983).

Graham, H. (ed.) *Understanding Health Inequalities* (Buckingham: Open University Press, 2000).

Greco, M. 'Psychosomatic Subjects and the Duty to be Well: Personal Agency within Medical Rationality', *Economy and Society* 22: 3 (1993) 357–72.

Greer, G. *The Whole Woman* (London: Doubleday, 1999).

Grimshaw, J. 'Practices of Freedom', in C. Ramazanoglu (ed.) *Up Against Foucault, Explorations of Some Tensions between Foucault and Feminism* (London and New York: Routledge, 1993).

Grogan, S. *Body Image: Understanding Body Dissatisfaction in Men, Women and Children* (London: Routledge, 1999).

Grosz, E. *Volatile Bodies: Toward a Corporeal Feminism* (Bloomington, IN: Indiana University Press, 1994).

Hall, G. S. *Senescence: The Last Half of Life* (New York: Appleton, 1922).

Haraway, D. *Primate Visions: Gender, Race, and Nature in the World of Modern Science* (New York: Routledge, 1989).

Haraway, D. *Simians, Cyborgs and Women* (London: Free Association Books, 1991).

Harding, S. (ed.) *The 'Racial' Economy of Science* (Bloomington and Indianapolis: Indiana University Press, 1993).

Hareven, T. K. 'Changing Images of Aging and the Social Construction of the Life Course', in M. Featherstone and A. Wernick (eds) *Images of Aging: Cultural Representations of Later Life* (London: Routledge, 1995).

Harris, J. *The Value of Life* (London: Routledge, 1994).

Harriss, B. 'Excess Female Mortality and Health Care in South Asia', *Journal of Social Studies* 44 (1989) 1–123.

Hartouni, V. *Cultural Conceptions: On Reproductive Technologies and the Remaking of Life* (Minneapolis: University of Minnesota Press, 1997).

Haug, F. (ed.) *Female Sexualization* (London: Verso, 1987).

Health Promotion England for the NHS and Department of Health, 'Frequently Asked Questions about Immunisation: You don't hear about most of the diseases we vaccinate against now: so is immunisation really necessary?' (2001) www.immunisation.org.uk

Hebdige, D. *Subculture: The Meaning of Style* (London: Methuen, 1979).

Hepworth, J. *The Social Construction of Anorexia Nervosa* (London: Sage, 1999).

Herlich, C. and Pierret, J. *Illness, Self and Society* (trans., Elborg Forster) (Baltimore and London: Johns Hopkins University Press, 1987).

Holmberg, C. B. *Sexualities and Popular Culture* (London: Sage Publications, 1998).

Home Office. *Supporting Families: A Consultation Document* (1998).

hooks, b. *Black Looks: Race and Representation* (London: Turnaround, 1992).

Hughes, B. and Paterson, K. 'The Social Model of Disability and the Disappearing Body: Towards a Sociology of Impairment', *Disability and Society*, 12: 3 (1997) 325–40.

Human Fertilisation and Embryology Authority. *Ninth Annual Report and Accounts* (London: HFEA, 2000).

Isaacs, S. *Social Development of Children* (London: Routledge, 1933).

Itzin, C. 'Media Images of Women: the Social Construction of Ageism and Sexism', in S. Wilkinson (ed.) *Feminist Social Psychology* (Milton Keynes: Open University Press, 1986).

Jacobus, M. 'Is there a Woman in this Text?', *NLH*, 14 (1982) 117–61.

Jackson, E. 'Abortion, Autonomy and Prenatal Diagnosis', *Social and Legal Studies* 9: 4 (2000) 467–94.

James, A., Jenks, C. and Prout, A. *Theorizing Childhood* (Polity Press with Blackwell Publishers Ltd: Cambridge, 1998).

Jefferson, T. 'The Tyson Rape Trial: The Law, Feminism and Emotional "Truth" ', *Social and Legal Studies* 6: 2 (1997) 281–301.

Jenks, C. *Childhood* (London: Routledge, 1996).

Jiggins, J. *Changing the Boundaries: Women-Centered Perspectives on Population and the Environment* (Washington: Island Press, 1994).

Jones, C. and Porter, R. *Reassessing Foucault, Power, Medicine and the Body* (London and New York: Routledge, 1994).

Kaim-Caudle, P., Keithlry, J., Mullender, A., (eds) *Aspects of Ageing* (London: Whiting & Birch, 1993).

Kennedy, I. *Inquiry into the Management of Care of Children Receiving Complex Heart Surgery at Bristol Royal Infirmary: Interim Report: Removal and Retention of Human Material* (May 2000).

Kimmel, M. *Manhood in America: A Cultural History* (New York: The Free Press, 1996).

Kirmayer, L. J. 'Mind and Body: Hidden Metaphors in Biomedicine', in M. Lock and D. Gordon (eds) *Biomedicine Examined* (Dordrecht: Kluwer, 1988).

Kleinman, A. *The Social Origins of Distress and Disease: Depression, Neurasthenia and Pain in Modern China* (New Haven: Yale University Press, 1986).

Kleinman, A. *The Illness Narratives: Suffering, Healing and the Human Condition* (New York: Basic Books, 1988).

Kolker, A. and Burke, M. *Prenatal Testing: A Sociological Perspective* (London: Bergin and Garvey, 1994).

Kotarba, J. *Chronic Pain: Its Social Dimensions* (Beverley Hills: Sage, 1983).

Lamont, M. 'Symbolic Politics and the Hill-Thomas Affair', *Contemporary Sociology: A Journal of Reviews* 23: 3 (1994) 346–9.

Laplanche, J. and Pontalis, J. B. *The Language of Psychoanalysis* (trans., D. Nicholson-Smith) (London: Karnac Books, 1988).

Laqueur, T. *Making Sex: Body and Gender from the Greeks to Freud* (Cambridge, Mass: Harvard University Press, 1990).

Lattimer, M. 'Dominant Ideas Versus Women's Reality: Hegemonic Discourse in British Abortion Law', in E. Lee (ed.) *Abortion Law and Politics Today* (Basingstoke: Macmillan Press – now Palgrave, 1998).

Law Commission, *Consent and Offences Against the Person*, Consultation Paper No. 134 (1994).

Law Commission, *Consent in the Criminal Law*, Consultation Paper No. 139 (1995).

Lawrence, M. *The Anorexic Experience* (London: Women's Press, 1984).

Lee, C. *Women's Health: Psychological and Social Perspectives* (London: Sage, 1998).

Lee, E. 'Psychologising Abortion: Psychology and the Construction of Post-Abortion Trauma', PhD thesis (unpublished, 2000).

Levens, M. *Eating Disorders and Magical Control of the Body* (London: Routledge, 1995).

Lewis, A. 'Psychogenic': A Word and its Mutations, *Psychological Medicine* 2 (1972) 209–15.

Linton, S. J., and Ryberg, M. (2000) 'The Prevalence and Health-economic Consequences of Neck and Back Pain in the General Population', *European Journal of Pain*, 4 (4): 347–54.

Lobstein, T. *The Nutrition of Women on Low Income* (London: London Food Commission, 1991).

Locker, D. *Disability and Disadvantage: Living with Chronic Illness* (London: Tavistock, 1983).

Lorde, A. *Sister Outsider: Essays and Speeches* (New York: The Crossing Press, 1984).

Lupton, D. 'Foucault and the Medicalisation Critique', in A. Petersen and R. Bunton (eds) *Foucault, Health and Medicine* (London: Routledge, 1997).

Lupton, D. and Barclay, L. *Constructing Fatherhood* (London: Sage, 1997).

Lurie, A. *The Language of Clothes* (New York: Random House, 1981).

Lykke, N. and Braidotti, R. (eds) *Between Monsters, Goddesses and Cyborgs: Feminist Confrontations with Science, Medicine and Cyberspace* (London: Zed Books, 1996).

MacKinnon, C. A. 'Feminism, Marxism, Method, and the State: Towards Feminist Jurisprudence', *Signs: Journal of Women in Culture and Society* 8: 4 (1983) 635–58.

MacSween, M. *Anorexic Bodies* (London: Routledge, 1993).

Marcus, S. 'Fighting Bodies, Fighting Words: A Theory and Politics of Rape Prevention', in J. Butler and J. W. Scott (eds) *Feminists Theorize the Political* (New York: Routledge, 1992).

Marie Stopes International. *General Practitioners: Attitudes to Abortion* (London: Marie Stopes International, 1999).

Martin, E. *The Woman in the Body: A Cultural Analysis of Reproduction* (Boston: Beacon Press, 1987).

Martin, E. 'The Egg and the Sperm: How Science has Constructed a Romance Based on Stereotypical Male-Female Roles', *Signs: Journal of Women in Culture and Society* 16: 1 (1991) 485–501.

Mason, J. V. and McCall Smith, A. *Law and Medical Ethics* (Butterworths: London, 1999).

Mauss, M. 'Techniques of the Body', *Economy and Society* 2: 1 (1973) 70–89.

Mayall, B. 'Children in Action at Home and School', in B. Mayall (ed.) *Children's Childhoods: Observed and Experienced* (London: Falmer Press, 1994).

Mayall, B. and Foster Marie-Claude *Child Health Care: Living with Children, Working for Children* (Oxford: Heinemann Nursing, 1989).

Mayou, R., Bass, C. and Sharpe, M. *Treatment of Functional Somatic Symptoms* (Oxford: Oxford University Press, 1995).

Mayou, R. and Sharpe, M. 'Treating Unexplained Physical Symptoms', *British Medical Journal* 7: 108 (1997) 315.

McClintock, A. *Imperial Leather: Race, Gender and Sexuality in the Colonial Context* (London: Routledge, 1995).

McGuire, J.S. and Popkin, B.M. *Helping Women Improve Nutrition in the Developing World* (Washington: World Bank, 1990).

McLean, S. *Old Law, New Medicine: Medical Ethics and Human Rights* (London: Pandora, 1999).

McLellan, D. *Utopian Pessimist* (New York: Simon & Schuster, 1990).

McNay, L. *Foucault and Feminism: Power, Gender and the Self* (Cambridge: Polity Press, 1992).

McNay, L. 'Gender, Habitus and the Field: Pierre Bourdieu and the Limits of Reflexivity', *Theory, Culture and Society* 16: 1 (1999) 95–117.

Melzack, R. and Wall, P. 'Pain Mechanisms: A New Theory', *Science* 150 (1965) 971–9.

Melzack, R. and Wall, P. *The Challenge of Pain* (London: Penguin Books and Stratton, 1988).

Mennell, S. 'On the Civilizing of Appetite', in M. Featherstone, M. Hepworth and B. S. Turner (eds) *The Body: Social Process and Cultural Theory* (London: Sage, 1991).

Merleau-Ponty, M. *The Visible and the Invisible* (trans., A. Lingis) (Chicago, Illinois: Northwestern University Press, 1968).

Merleau-Ponty, M. *The Primacy of Perception* (Chicago, Illinois: Northwestern University Press, 1976).

Merleau-Ponty, M. *The Phenomenology of Perception* (London: Routledge and Kegan Paul, 1981).

Merritt, M. and Macdonald, V. 'Warning: Shaving Foam can Damage your Manhood', *The Sunday Telegraph*, 19 January 1997.

Millett, K. *Sexual Politics* (London: Hart Davis, 1970).

Minichiello, V., Browne, J. and Kendig, H. 'Perceptions and Consequences of Ageism: Views of Older People', *Ageing and Society* 20: 3 (2000) 253–77.

Mishler, E.G. 'Critical Perspectives on the Biomedical Model', in P. Brown (ed.). *Perspectives in Medical Sociology* (Belmont, California: Wadsworth, 1989).

Mohanram, R. *Black Body: Women, Colonialism, Space* (St Leonards, NSW: Allen and Unwin, 1999).

Morgan, D. 'Psychiatric Cases: An Ethnography of the Referral Process', *Psychological Medicine* 19 (1989) 743–53.

Morris, D. *The Culture of Pain* (Berkley and Los Angeles: University of California Press, 1991).

Morris, D. *Illness and Culture in the Postmodern Age* (Berkley and Los Angeles: University of California Press, 1998).

Morris, J. *Pride Against Prejudice: Transforming Attitudes to Disability* (London: The Women's Press, 1991).

Morris, J. (ed.) *Encounters With Strangers: Feminism and Disability* (London: The Women's Press, 1996).

Morrison, T. 'Introduction: Friday on the Potomac', in T. Morrison (ed.) *Race-ing Justice, En-Gendering Power: Essays on Anita Hill, Clarence Thomas, and the Construction of Social Reality* (London: Chatto and Windus, 1993).

Muehlenhard, P. and Muehlenhard, G. 'Definitions of Rape: Scientific and Political Implications', *Journal of Social Issues* 48: 1 (1992) 23–44.

Mullan, P. *The Imaginary Time Bomb: Why an Ageing Population is not a Social Problem* (London: I.B. Taurus, 2000).

Murcott, A. 'It's a Pleasure to Cook for Him' in A. Murcott (ed.) *The Sociology of Food and Eating* (Aldershot: Gower, 1983).

Naffine, N. 'The Body Bag', in N. Naffine and R. Owens (eds) *Sexing the Subject of Law* (Sydney: LBC Information Services/Sweet & Maxwell, 1997).

Narayan, U. 'The Discriminatory Nature of Industrial Health-Hazard Policies and Some implications for Third World Workers', in J. Callahan (ed.) *Reproduction, Ethics and the Law: Feminist Responses* (Bloomington and Indianapolis: Indiana University Press, 1995).

Nettleton, S. 'Governing the Risky Self: How to Become Healthy, Wealthy and Wise', in Peterson, A. and Bunton, R. *Foucault, Health and Medicine* (London: Routledge, 1997).

Nicholson, L. J. (ed.) *Feminism/Postmodernism* (New York: Routledge, 1990).

Oakley, A. 'Woman and Children First and Last: Parallels and Differences between Children's and Women's Studies', in B. Mayall (ed.) *Children's Childhoods: Observed and Experienced* (London: Falmer Press, 1994).

O'Brian, M. D. 'Medically Unexplained Neurological Symptoms', *British Medical Journal* 316 (1998).

Oliver, M. *The Politics of Disablement* (London: Macmillan Press – now Palgrave, 1990).

Oliver, M. *Understanding Disability* (London: Macmillan Press – now Palgrave, 1996a).

Oliver, M. 'Defining Impairment and Disability: Issues at Stake', in Barnes, C. and Mercer, G. (eds) *Exploring the Divide: Illness and Disability* (Leeds: The Disability Press, 1996b).

Orbach, S. *Fat is a Feminist Issue* (London: Hamlyn, 1984).

Orbach, S. *Hunger Strike* (London: Faber & Faber, 1986).

Ortner, S. 'Is Female to Male as Nature is to Culture?', in Rosaldo, M. and Lamphere, L. (eds) *Women, Culture and Society* (Stanford: Stanford University Press, 1974).

Padgug, Robert A. 'Sexual Matters: On conceptualizing sexuality in history', in Parker, R. and Aggleton A. (eds) *Culture, Society and Sexuality: A Reader* (London: UCL Press, 1999).

Painter, N. I. 'Hill, Thomas, and the Use of Racial Stereotype', in T. Morrison (ed.) *Race-ing Justice, En-Gendering Power: Essays on Anita Hill, Clarence Thomas, and the Construction of Social Reality* (London: Chatto and Windus, 1993).

Paintin, D. 'A Medical View of Abortion in the 1960s', in Lee, E. (ed.) *Abortion Law and Politics Today* (Basingstoke: Macmillan Press – now Palgrave, 1998).

Pearce, S. (ed.) *Museums and the Appropriation of Culture* (London: Althone Press, 1994).

Petersen, A. and Lupton, D. *The New Public Health: Health and Self in the Age of Risk* (London: Sage, 1996).

Pipes, M. *Understanding Abortion* (London: The Women's Press, 1998).

Polhemus, T. *Streetstyle* (London: Thames and Hudson, 1994).

Pomata, G. 'Menstruating Men: Similarity and Difference of the Sexes in Early Modern Medicine (paper presented at the European University Institute, Florence, 31 March 2000, unpublished).

Pratten, B. *Power, Politics and Pregnancy* (London: Health Rights, 1990).

Price, J. 'The Marginal Politics of Our Bodies? Women's Health, the Disability Movement, and Power', in B. Humphries (ed.) *Critical Perspectives on Empowerment* (Birmingham: Venture Press, 1996).

Price, J. and Shildrick, M. 'Uncertain Thoughts on the Dis/abled Body', in M. Shildrick and J. Price (eds) *Vital Signs: Feminist Reconfigurations of the Biological Body* (Edinburgh: Edinburgh University Press, 1998).

Prout, A. 'Childhood Bodies: Construction, Agency and Hybridity', in A. Prout (ed.) *The Body, Childhood and Society* (Basingstoke Macmillan Press – now Palgrave, 2000).

Prout, A. (ed.) *The Body, Childhood and Society* (Basingstoke: Macmillan Press – now Palgrave, 2000).

Prout, A. and James, A. 'A New Paradigm for the Sociology of Childhood? Provenance, Promise and Problems', in A. Prout and A. James (eds) *Constructing and Reconstructing Childhood* (London: Falmer Press, 1997).

Qvortrup, J. 'Childhood Matters: An Introduction', in J. Qvortrup, M. Bardy, G. Sgritta and H. Wintersberger (eds) *Childhood Matters: Social Theory, Practice and Politics* (Aldershot: Avebury, 1994).

Ransom, J. 'Feminism, Difference and Discourse: the Limits of Discursive Analysis for Feminism', in C. Ramazanoglu (ed.) *Up Against Foucault, Explorations of Some Tensions between Foucault and Feminism* (London and New York: Routledge, 1993).

Rayner, C. 'Should Viagra be Free on the NHS?', *BMA News Review* (10 October 1998) 41.

Redfern, M. *The Royal Liverpool Children's Inquiry: Report* (2001).

Rey, R. *The History of Pain* (trans., Wallace, L. E., Cadden, J. A. and Cadden, S. W.) (Cambridge, MA.: Harvard University Press, 1995).

Richards, T. *The Imperial Archive: Knowledge and the Fantasy of Empire* (London: Verso, 1993).

Roberts, D. *The Myth of Aunt Jemima* (London: Routledge, 1994).

Rose, N. *Governing the Soul: The Shaping of the Private Self* (London: Routledge, 1989).

Roth, R. *Making Women Pay: The Hidden Costs of Fetal Rights* (Cornell University Press, 2000).

Rousham, E. 'Gender Bias in South Asia', in T. M. Pollard and S. B. Hyatt (eds) *Sex, Gender and Health* (Cambridge: Cambridge University Press, 1999).

Rowntree, B. S. *Poverty, a Study of Town Life* (London: Thomas Nelson, 1902).

Royal College of Physicians. 'Joint Working Party of the Royal Colleges of Physicians, Psychiatrists and General Practitioners: Chronic Fatigue Syndrome' (London: Royal College of Physicians, 1996).

Royal Liverpool Children's Inquiry, *Report* (London: The Stationery Office, 2001).

Sacks, O. *The Man Who Mistook his Wife for a Hat* (London: Pan Books Ltd., 1986).

Santow, G. 'Social Roles and Physical Health', *Social Science and Medicine* 40 (1995) 147–61.

Saunders, C. M. *The Nature and Management of Terminal Pain in Matters of Life and Death* (London: Darton, Longman and Todd, 1970).

Sawicki, J. *Disciplining Foucault, Feminism, Power and the Body* (New York and London: Routledge, 1991).

Sayers, J. 'Anorexia, Psychoanalysis, and Feminism', *Journal of Adolescence* 11 (1988) 361–71.

Sayers, J. *Kleinians* (Cambridge: Polity Press, 2000).

Scarry, E. *The Body in Pain: The Making and Unmaking of the World* (Oxford: Oxford University Press, 1985).

Shakespeare, T. 'Disability, Identity, Difference', in C. Barnes and G. Mercer (eds) *Exploring the Divide: Illness and Disability* (Leeds: The Disability Press, 1996).

Shakespeare, T. 'Cultural Representation of Disabled People: Dustbins of Disavowal?', in L. Barton and M. Oliver (eds) *Disability Studies: Past, Present and Future* (Leeds: The Disability Press, 1997).

Shakespeare, T. 'Losing the Plot? Discourses of Disability and Genetics', *Sociology of Health and Illness*, 21: 5 (1999) 669–88.

Sheldon, S. *Beyond Control: Medical Power and Abortion Law* (London: Pluto, 1997).

Sheldon, S. '*Re*Conceiving Masculinity: Imagining Men's Reproductive Bodies in Law', *Journal of Law and Society* 26: 2 (1999) 129–49.

Sheldon, S. and Thomson, M. 'Health Care Law and Feminism: A Developing Relationship', in S. Sheldon and M. Thomson (eds) *Feminist Perspectives on Health Care Law*, London: Cavendish, 1998).

Shelley, M. *Frankenstein or The Modern Prometheus* (Oxford: Oxford University Press, 1998).

Shildrick, M. and Price, J. 'Breaking the Boundaries of the Broken Body' *Body and Society* 2: 4 (1996) 93–113.

Shilling, C. *The Body and Social Theory* (London: Sage, 1993).

Simms, M. 'Legal Abortion in Britain', in H. Homans (ed.) *The Sexual Politics of Reproduction* (Aldershot and Vermont: Gower, 1985).

Sketel, W. *Sexual Aberrations: The Phenomenon of Fetishism in Relations* (New York: Liveright Publishing Corporation, 1930).

Smart, C. *Feminism and the Power of Law* (London: Routledge, 1989).

Smart, C. 'Law's Power, the Sexed Body, and Feminist Discourse', *Journal of Law and Society* 17 (1990) 194–210.

Smart, C. *Law Crime and Sexuality: Essays in Feminism* (London: Sage, 1995).

Smart, C. 'A History of Ambivalence and Conflict in the Discursive Construction of the "Child Victim" of Sexual Abuse', *Social and Legal Studies* 8 (1999) 392.

Smith, R. 'A Clinical Approach to the Somatizing Patient', *Journal of Family Practice* 21 (1985) 294–301.

Sommerfelt, A. E. and Arnold, F. 'Sex Differentials in the Nutritional Status of Young Children', in United Nations, *Too Young to Die: Genes or Gender?* (New York: United Nations, 1998).

Sours, J. *Starving to Death in a Sea of Objects* (New York: Aronson, 1980).

Speckens, A., Van Hemert, A., Spinhoven, P., Hawton, K., Bolk, J. and Rooijmans, H. 'Cognitive Behaviour Therapy for Medically Unexplained Physical Symptoms: A Randomized Control Trial', *British Medical Journal* 311 (1995) 1328–32.

Stallybrass, P. and White, A. *The Poetics and Politics of Transgression* (London: Methuen, 1986).

Starobinski, J. 'A Short History of Bodily Sensation', in M. Fehr with R. Naddaff and N. Tazi (eds). *Fragments for a History of the Human Body, Part 2* (Cambridge, MA: MIT Press, 1989).

Steele, V. *Fetish: Fashion, Sex and Power* (Oxford, Oxford University Press, 1996).

Steele, V. *Paris Fashion: A Cultural History* (Oxford: Berg, 1998).

Stephan, N.G. 'Race and Gender: A Scientific Analogy', in S. Harding (ed.) *The 'Racial' Economy of Science* (Bloomington and Indianapolis: Indiana University Press, 1993).

Stotland, N. *Abortion, Facts and Feelings* (Washington DC/London: American Psychiatric Press, 1998).

Strauss, A. *Where Medicine Fails* (New Brunswick, New Jersey: Transaction Books, 1973).

Stychin, C. 'Body Talk: Rethinking Autonomy, Commodification and the Embodied Legal Self', in S. Sheldon and M. Thomson (eds) *Feminist Perspectives on Health Care Law* (London: Cavendish Publishing Ltd, 1998).

Thomas, C. *Female Forms: Experiencing and Understanding Disability* (Buckingham: Open University Press, 1999).

Thomson, M. 'Employing the Body: The Reproductive Body and Employment Exclusion'. *Social and Legal Studies* 5: 2 (1996) 243–67.

Thomson, M. *Reproducing Narrative: Gender, Reproduction and the Law* (Aldershot: Dartmouth, 1998).

Thornton, M. 'Feminism and the Contradictions of Law Reform', *International Journal of the Sociology of Law* 19 (1991) 453–74.

Turner, B. S. *The Body and Society: Explorations in Social Theory* (Oxford: Basil Blackwell, 1984).

Turner, B. S. *Medical Power and Social Knowledge* (London: Sage, 1987).

Turner, B. S. 'The Discourse of Diet', in M. Featherstone, M. Hepworth and B. S. Turner (eds) *The Body: Social Process and Cultural Theory* (London: Sage, 1991).

Turner, B. S. *Regulating Bodies: Essays in Medical Sociology* (London: Routledge, 1992).

Tyrer, S. 'Learned Pain Behaviour', *British Medical Journal* 292 (1986) 1.

UN. *The World's Women: Trends and Statistics* (New York: United Nations, 2000).

United Nations Decade of Disabled Persons 1983–1992, *World Programme of Action Concerning Disabled Persons* (New York: United Nations, 1983).

UNICEF. *The Lesser Child: The Girl in India* (New Delhi: UNICEF, 1998).

Ussher, J. *The Psychology of the Female Body* (London: Routledge, 1993).

Veblen, T. *The Theory of the Leisure Class: An Economic Study of Institutions* (New York: Mentor, 1953/1899).

Vrancken, M. 'Schools of Thought on Pain', *Social Science and Medicine* 29 (1989) 435–44.

Waldby, C. *AIDS and the Body Politic* (London: Routledge, 1996).

Wall, P. *Pain: The Science of Suffering* (London: Weidenfeld and Nicholson, 1999).

Wall, P. and Jones, M. *Defeating Pain* (London: Plenum, 1998).

Ward, T. *Against Ageism* (Newcastle: Search Project, 1983).

Weeks, J. *Sex, Politics and Society: The Regulation of Sexuality since 1800* (2nd edition) (London: Longman, 1989).

Weiss, G. *Body Images: Embodiment as Intercorporeality* (London: Routledge, 1999).

Wendell, S. *The Rejected Body. Feminist Philosophical Reflections on Disability* (London: Routledge, 1996).

Westlake, D. and Pearson, M. 'Child Protection and Health Promotion: Whose Responsibility?', *JSWFL* 19 (1997) 139.

Wilde, O. *The Picture of Dorian Gray with an introduction by Edmund White* (Oxford: Oxford University Press, 1999).

Williams, G. 'Chronic Illness and the Pursuit of Virtue in Everyday Life', in Radley, A. (ed.) *Worlds of Illness* (London: Routledge, 1995).

Williams, S. and Bendelow, G. *The Lived Body: Sociological Themes, Embodied Issues* (London: Routledge, 1998).

Willow, C. and Hyde, T. 'The Myth of the Loving Smack', *Childright* 154 (2000) 18.

Wilson, E. *Adorned in Dreams: Fashion and Modernity* (London: Virago, 1985).

Wilson, E. 'The Postmodern Body', in J. Ash and E. Wilson *Chic Thrills: A Fashion Reader* (London: Pandora. 1992).

Wollstonecraft, M. *Vindication of the Rights of Woman* (London: Penguin, 1975).

Wood, P. *International Classification of Impairments, Disabilities and Handicaps* (Geneva: World Health Organisation, 1980).

Worrall, A. 'Governing Bad Girls: Changing Constructions of Female Juvenile Delinquency', in J. Bridgeman and D. Monk *Feminist Perspectives on Child Law* (Cavendish Publishing: London, 2000).

Young, I. M. *Intersecting Voices: Dilemmas of Gender, Political Philosophy and Policy* (Princeton: Princeton University Press, 1997).

Young, L. *Fear of the Dark: 'Race', Gender and Sexuality in the Cinema* (London: Routledge, 1996).

Young, R. *Colonial Desire: Hybridity in Theory, Culture and Race* (London: Routledge, 1995).

Zarb, G. (ed.) *Removing Disabling Barriers* (London: Policy Studies Institute, 1995).

Index